Cracking the Corporate Code

Cracking the Corporate Code

The Revealing Success Stories of 32 African-American Executives

Price M. Cobbs and Judith L. Turnock

AMACOM

American Management Association

New York • Atlanta • Brussels • Buenos Aires • Chicago • London • Mexico City
San Francisco • Shanghai • Tokyo • Toronto • Washington, D. C.

Special discounts on bulk quantities of AMACOM books are available to corpora-
tions, professional associations, and other organizations. For details, contact
Special Sales Department, AMACOM, a division of American Management
Association, 1601 Broadway, New York, NY 10019.
Tel.: 212-903-8316   Fax: 212-903-8083
Web site: www.amacombooks.org

This publication is designed to provide accurate and authoritative information in
regard to the subject matter covered. It is sold with the understanding that the pub-
lisher is not engaged in rendering legal, accounting, or other professional service. If
legal advice or other expert assistance is required, the services of a competent professional person should be sought.

Library of Congress Cataloging-in-Publication Data

Cobbs, Price M.
Cracking the corporate code : the revealing success stories of 32 African-American
executives / Price M. Cobbs and Judith L. Turnock.
p. cm.
Includes bibliographical references and index.
ISBN 0-8144-0771-4
   1. African American executives--Interviews. 2. African American executives—
   Case studies. 3. Success in business—United States. I. Turnock, Judith L. II. Title.

HD38.25.U6C63 2003
658.4'0089'96073—dc21   2002155253

To future generations:
Work smarter. Travel farther.

Table of Contents

Foreword

Diversity is not a new topic for me. At PepsiCo we believe in diversity and have struggled to understand and to respond, with individual openness and corporate-wide programs, with training from outside consultants and discussions among ourselves. We know things are better and continue to improve. But why does it take so long, and why is it so hard to achieve measurable results? *Cracking the Corporate Code: The Revealing Success Stories of 32 African-American Executives* puts the issue into a complete context.

Cracking the Corporate Code's lessons about thriving in ambiguity, "reading" unwritten rules, building a network of inside support, and acquiring and using power are necessary ones for all young managers. But having to manage the demons of race and gender at the same time makes the path more complex and often more treacherous. Dr. Cobbs and Ms. Turnock make it all seem possible, with insights and analyses that are direct in their simplicity. Illustrating the lessons through the words of thirty-two very senior African-American corporate executives makes understanding literally leap off the page and into our consciousness.

Young women and people of color can learn here how to build their careers in the constantly shifting terrain of corporate America, and they can also appreciate the battles that have already been won for them.

Of particular interest to me, executives and senior managers can finally "get" the subtle issues people of color and women face every day in the workplace. We can see beyond the limited success of early diversity programs to the next generation of diversity strategies and goals, where we will succeed not only in retaining our top talent but also in giving them the enormous satisfaction of seeing their individual contributions valued.

All readers can begin to see how much we all share as Americans—values like loyalty, determination, hard work, ambition, creativity, strength, courage, and passion for our common business purpose.

The business lessons, however, are only part of the gifts this book offers. The thirty-two executives whose experiences are the heart and soul of the book generously invite us behind their current outward polish. By many different paths, they came together in what was essentially a foreign culture—corporate America. Intelligent, resolute, and self-confident, they mastered that culture and became leaders. These are heroes and role models for all Americans.

I have had the privilege of working with PepsiCo's Executive Leadership Council members over the last eighteen years and directly with Dr. Price Cobbs. I have learned from their example, their work, our conversations, and their advocacy, sometimes gentle and sometimes very forceful. PepsiCo, and I, are the better for those experiences.

Cracking the Corporate Code, however, takes that understanding even further. Anyone who reads this book can't help but be inspired to work towards a new, inclusive corporate culture. Now it is possible to communicate in a way that will enable all of us to move together to the next level.

The subtext of black executives' experiences from 1965 to today is the enormous progress corporate America has already made. At the same time, it is obvious how much work remains to be done. *Cracking the Corporate Code* will speed up the forward momentum, because the message is so clear and the logic so compelling. We are on a journey to a very good place, and all America will reap the rewards.

—**Steve Reinemund,** CEO
PepsiCo, Inc.
Purchase, New York
September 2002

Introduction

Setting the Record Straight

IN an era of celebrity worship, we offer here the real stories of thirty-two very successful people who are not household names. Their sterling accomplishments are inspiring, yet, for the most part, they are little known outside the confines of their families and work lives. They are senior corporate executives, at the top of American business, most with long careers at Fortune 500 companies. And they are all African American.

These men and women are in the proud tradition of trailblazers like Jackie Robinson and Muhammad Ali, but without the cheering crowds. They operate below the radar screen of popular culture and without sports' satisfyingly clear standards for measuring excellence. There was no ball to throw, hit, or catch, no knockout punch; they had to learn to excel in a much more subjective environment, which they mastered with determination, intelligence, and above all supreme self-confidence. Invisible to the general population, they soared beyond the limited roles society set for them. While their messages here are directed to young African Americans in corporate America, they in fact resonate for everyone who aspires to leadership in large organizations.

Think of this book as a personal conversation between you and the thirty-two executives. To get the most from this conversation, use it to guide your own process of introspection. In each chapter, ask questions of the executives, and ask yourself questions. Try to find answers. Stretch yourself. This book can be for you the map they did not have. Their collective wisdom can light your career path.

What is the corporate "code" these executives had to crack in order to be successful? Corporate culture is the deeply felt system of shared values and assumptions, conveyed through stories, myths, and legends, that explains how members of the organization think, feel, and act. These shared values operate both consciously and unconsciously to define an organization's view of itself and its environment. This culture, and the level of conformity it imposes, is willingly accepted by the members, and this bargain between the members and the culture gives the organization its stability, predictability, and continuity. One must understand this culture to know how to behave within it.

For those with a feeling of entitlement, a sense of belonging, adapting to that culture is relatively painless. The problems for newcomers, especially outsiders, when they first encounter this new culture begin at the visual level. Minorities and women clearly do not fit the mold. Lacking both the traditional outward appearance and knowledge of the language, imagery, and symbols of the culture, they have to work to make themselves feel they fit in and to make it appear to others that they belong. With so much new data to process, the possibility of thriving there, of receiving and interpreting the culture's messages, initially seems remote.

How were these executives, African Americans who grew up during the two decades before and the first decade after the federal Civil Rights Act, able to take advantage of the new opportunities presented to them? What values and dreams drew them from share-cropper farms in the segregated South, from homes near factories in the Midwest, from families in integrated neighborhoods in the Northeast? How did their view of themselves and their place in the world allow them to attain positions of power and influence within America's top corporations?

These executives' stories take us behind outward polish. We discover how they mastered the demons of race and gender and learned to read their environment objectively and interpret its messages accurately. What they have learned through trial and error, searching the maze without translators and often alone, provides guidance for all outsiders. Their real stories help us understand the insights and information they process on a regular basis, often in nanoseconds, and inspire us to adapt them for our own use.

This group of individuals has an indomitable will to win. They turned the societally imposed burden of racism into an advantage. They used it as a catalyst, a meaningful beacon to inform their intellect and behavior. And very early they developed multiple strategies to transcend the negative aspects of the demon, making the American dilemma of race the problem of others. They choose to ignore words and behavior, to change their circumstances, to look differently at themselves and others, or simply to persevere, using an exquisite sense of time and place.

They have the determination and strength of character to overcome whatever difficult circumstances, disappointments, or frustrations life hands them. You cannot control what other people do or think, and you cannot control all events that touch you, but you can choose to control your emotional and intellectual responses. Our executives recognize and build on the positive and have the fortitude and moral courage to change or eliminate the negative. You can, too. The debate between success or failure, happiness or sadness, satisfaction or disappointment, easy or difficult, risky or safe, winner or loser, is resolved in the head and heart of each individual. How you see the hand you're dealt and how you play it is up to you, and you have a new chance to play it every day.

These executives do not have a formula. They only wish to share their insights and experiences so that your road is clearer and smoother. These corporate players are complex human beings, skilled and eager to test their own influence and effectiveness. They offer no definitive or easy answers. But the words of these executives should motivate you to examine and understand your own environment. The insights you gain can lead to genuine achievement.

Most Americans celebrate their origins here with stories of free choice and brave and adventurous spirits. Almost all African Americans today, including those who came from the islands of the West Indies, are descended from people who did not choose to come here. But despite how they arrived on these shores, the vast majority of them have played the hands they were dealt very well. They have thrown themselves into the development of America: geography, wars, agriculture, industry, transportation, academia, education, economics, business, craft, art, music, literature, science, government, sports, and entertainment. They have loved America and its ideals; they have fought for their own liberty at home and the freedom of others abroad. They own America deeply.

None of their experiences and contributions diminishes those of any other American, of long-standing or recent origin. Their stories of struggle, dreams, and accomplishment are simply part of the American story, added to the stories of struggle, dreams, and accomplishment of every American. They strike a resounding chord in the story of America, the story that inspires the hopes of millions of people around the world. They enrich the history and accomplishment of this dynamic land, where the human spirit has melded and triumphed beyond anything previously known. They are conclusive proof that something special resides here, thrives here, triumphs here. They are not other; they are us.

In 1965 blacks were rare in corporate America except as laborers or assembly-line workers. And most of them were performing the most menial, dangerous, and worst-paid functions. Now, just over thirty-five years later, our executives are joined every day by more than a quarter of a million other African-American corporate managers and executives, and their ranks grow every year. Opportunities for satisfying and financially rewarding careers in business—in corporate America and the exploding entrepreneurial landscape—abound despite any economic downturn. Yet many young African Americans focus their sights only on entertainment and professional sports, where such careers are far fewer by comparison. The stories related here introduce realistic alternatives. Business offers real jobs for millions of real people, and those jobs far outstrip the opportunities for celebrity status.

For more than two generations, there has been an inordinate focus on the pathology of black people and black families, a perception fed by both the media and pop culture. One result of this far-from-accurate focus is the perception that any successful black person is an exception. In fact, the vast majority of black Americans lead satisfying and successful lives, and that critical mass is growing. Telling the stories of our executives is one step in setting the record straight.

In terms of what we as a society have accomplished since the corporate door first opened, 1965 is a very long time ago. But the fast pace of change mirrors the explosion of advances in the twentieth century. The world, but America especially, has absorbed phenomenal change. This change is the twentieth-century legacy, and it sets the stage for a global world, not just a global economy.

Even in the face of horrific events here and abroad, the United States is leading the twenty-first-century charge. American blacks are a part of that gift of leadership. They taught America to challenge the usual way of doing business, and they did it with the time-honored American virtues of hard work, determination, respect for authority, discipline, a positive attitude despite all evidence to the contrary, and a belief in basic justice. Everything they've done, and all America has learned thanks to their insistence, contributes to our understanding of and vision for the future.

Their resilience and their ability to achieve despite being belittled, to seek acceptance despite rejection, to be loyal despite few if any rewards or appreciation, to uncover profound joy despite disappointment, enrich us individually and as a society. In the achievements of these African Americans, we glimpse America's true promise. They challenge all of us to acknowledge their struggle and the depth of their commitment to their heritage and our country. Let their stories move us in what we all know is the right direction—to close the gulf that separates too many Americans.

We invite you to listen, and we hope their words will inspire you to follow in their path. America needs all its best talent.

1.

Ambiguity

Organizations are complicated under any circumstances, and no one achieves success without being extraordinarily creative, especially in the area of human dynamics. For us there are added layers, but what we had to deal with growing up actually prepared us. We did that every day of our lives, at school, at the store, everywhere outside the home.

—**David L. Hinds**, Managing Director (ret.)
Deutsche Bank

I could write a book about all the things I didn't realize would make a difference in my career. They didn't necessarily make a difference at that time, but later in the game they did. If you need instant gratification, forget about it. But there is a cause and effect at work.

—**Bruce G. Gordon**, Group President
Verizon

WHEN black men and women enter the world of corporate America, conflicting feelings are their constant companions. Part of this new world is readily understandable. There is an organizational structure to join, a job to perform, bosses to please, services to deliver, and products to manufacture and market. But other aspects feel like entering a foreign culture with its own language and shifting rules about behavior and expectations. There is uncertainty and confusion much of the time as you try to interpret a setting that seems puzzling, if not alien. At least in the beginning, seamless connections between cause and effect are difficult to make, and it is hard to decipher clear meanings about what is happening, and why. In short, you have encountered ambiguity.

But you can master ambiguity if you acknowledge your confusion, remain open to learning, and accept the reality that the corporate environment is ever-changing and in constant need of re-evaluation. In fact, you already possess a baseline of skills to decode the messages, both verbal and nonverbal, that define this new terrain. Your challenge is to identify these skills and then put them to use in the service of your career.

Ambiguity is a fact of corporate life. At first it seems a bewildering complex of confusing impressions and shifting realities. For those who grow up with the uncertainty and doubt that accompanies being black in America, the corporation presents additional layers to penetrate. The corporate environment was not developed with you in mind. It was created by and for white men. As a result, it guaranteed the success of others like them and excluded everyone else. So to succeed in business terms, to become comfortable in this environment while preserving your own emotional well-being, you must first learn this culture. You must identify patterns in what initially seems like chaos. You must discover how to connect the dots. You must develop a personal strategy for understanding, managing, and influencing this complex reality.

Corporate America has in fact changed significantly from the all-white male enclave whose management doors were opened to African Americans in the mid-1960s. But almost four decades later, newcomers still struggle daily to overcome their outsider status, still shoulder the burden of fighting for acceptance. In fact, you already have a basis for mastering this environment. Living with ambiguity—not being welcomed, understood, or respected, and forever reading and interpreting unspoken messages in order to get what you need or simply to survive—is part of being African American. Far more than you realize, uncovering those survival skills may actually give you something of an advantage, or at least the ability to expand your comfort zone quickly. If you develop the confidence and drive to approach this new environment as a puzzle to be solved, you will be rewarded. The puzzle presents itself in challenging ways, but you can crack its code with intelligence, insight, patience, wit, and most of all, perseverance.

The corporation is a dynamic environment, with constant changes on the surface and subtle shifts beneath, revealing at one moment and hidden behind closed doors at another. Your job of understanding, interpreting, clarifying, and ultimately, mastering the corporation is also a dynamic process. The job is never done. You never close the book, put it back on the shelf and say, "I have finished." And few people will ever say to you, "You have succeeded." Instead, you learn to listen to your inner voice. Analyze every situation, set goals, test yourself, take two steps forward and one step back, re-analyze, adjust your goals, and test yourself yet again. Slowly but surely, you will see patterns. Slowly but surely, you will establish your own footing, and your personal comfort zone will expand. The narrow ledge on which you stand will grow wider.

For African Americans, an additional complexity is merging how your colleagues—subordinates, peers, and managers—view you with how you view yourself. You have years of experience in a world that sees you not as an individual, but as a bundle of stereotypes, most of them negative. Your experience of being viewed through multiple filters causes wariness and makes it difficult to develop trust. Your colleagues have even fewer meaningful experiences across race lines, so there is likely to be as much if not more discomfort and distrust on their side. For African-American women, the complexity is compounded. You are outsiders as both blacks and women. You shoulder the negative stereotypes of race as well as those of gender.

The journey is not easy for anyone. A large and unexplored organization is intimidating for anyone, but adapting the African-American experience to that environment makes cracking its code a daunting task. And you will have no difficulty finding incidents to confirm your initial doubts. You will at times be ignored and at times over-scrutinized. Your intelligence will be questioned. You will have to prove that you belong over and over.

The first task is obvious. You must learn to do your job well. You need to study the business, build alliances, and figure out ways to contribute your ideas so you can add value to the organization. First you must understand the corporate culture.

Blacks in corporate America always have a second job, one that is intensely personal and never completed. You must add depth and breadth to understanding and insight about your personal experiences, so that you can position yourself in this new environment. You must develop a finely tuned sense of how to handle racial slights, when you can and should call attention to them. You must also be able to sift through each incident and determine when race and gender are real factors and when others are operating from different agendas. You must develop strategies to manage your own conscious and unconscious discomfort as well as the discomfort of your colleagues, and you must deal with the stereotypical responses they may have to you. All of this is critical to your success.

These skills are acquired through hard work, determination, focusing your intellect on managing your emotional responses, developing patience, and above all, humor. The difficult reality is that acquiring these skills exacts an enormous physical and emotional toll. But you must acquire and master them to achieve any level of comfort in your work life, let alone to excel there. To do otherwise is to go to work every day full of frustration, despair, and ultimately, rage. You may not work twice as many hours as others, but you will be working psychologically twice as hard.

You must constantly search your own past for strength and greater understanding. The answers are there, if you probe deeply and carefully. As your instinct, energy, and drive deepen, you will be rewarded.

Ambiguity does not have to leave you in confusion and inde-cision. Understanding it can open the door to opportunity and drive you to perform, to engage, to master. It can unleash your cre-ative energy. Success is built by bringing all your strengths to every experience. Once you engage, you can confront or compromise, depending on the circumstances. Then you can revel in the rush that comes from earning influence and effectiveness.

2.

Managing Your Demons

There will always be someone asking, "Why are you here?"
You cannot influence the speculation about you, the conver-
sations behind your back, around the corner. You can only
influence what you've done and how you've contributed.
There will be bumps along the road, and we all, black or white,
have to deal with them in one way or another. The question is,
how do you get yourself beyond the bumps and continue to
excel? Over the years I've seen a number of the people who
question why you are here wind up working for you.
Sometimes they even become your supporters.

—**David L. Hinds**, Managing Director (ret.)
Deutsche Bank

Dealing with racism could wear you down. How do we
change the hearts and minds of managers? I no longer want
to change their hearts and minds. I just want respect. The
rest will follow.

—**Westina Matthews Shatteen**, First Vice President
Merrill Lynch & Co., Inc.

There are men who've had a problem being managed by me.
That's their problem. They had to get over it.

—**Jerri DeVard**, Chief Marketing Officer
Citibank, N.A.

Race

R ACE is surely the most unyielding of the many issues that warrant your time and energy, but it must be addressed if you are to reach your goals. Even though it is not central in every situation, your race is part of who you are, part of how others see you, and a key part of how you see yourself. The discomfort of whites—averted eyes, indifference, the too-jovial laugh, hostility—is there. You must also deal with the discomfort of other blacks, whose response can range from wanting to deal with you exclusively to pretending you don't exist. If you are to succeed in this environment, you cannot lash out in anger, but neither can you ignore it. What can you do?

Strategies vary depending on the individual, and every situation has a life of its own. You are a unique blend of temperament, experiences, and emotional dexterity, and no one can predict when you will encounter these troublesome situations or how you should or will respond. But they are inevitable, and you must be prepared. As you undoubtedly know, there is no formula, but you can develop the mindset to manage them, to analyze your own responses and the responses of others. Race can only deter you if you give it that power.

Here is how **Don Brown** manages discrimination: "You can spend a lot of time and energy just watching for someone who's going to treat you wrong, who's going to try to hold you back. I have spent little or no time thinking about how people perceive my color or my size or any of that stuff. There are very few days I sit around and think, 'What did I do to be black today?' I don't think I have to worry about that. What I do think about is, 'What do I have to do to make sure I do a great job today? How do I help somebody else do a better job?' In the long run, that helps me feel pretty damn good."

Brown does not ignore race. He has settled it in his own mind. That's the way it is, and there is nothing to be gained by discussing it further. He acknowledges that others feel tension because of his race, but he chooses to focus on his work and the work of others, to improve his performance and theirs. This strategy works for him, an operations man, a man of action who sets measurable goals and targets. In the process he achieves job satisfaction for himself and others. By sheer will and focus, he moves others beyond the issue of race. This is not a workable strategy for everybody, but you begin to see how to develop the mindset that will lead you to your own strategy.

Race does not fill the consciousness of most white people all the time. Therefore, you must learn to read the subtleties of their behavior. You must sift through each situation to discover where—or if—race fits and then develop your own strategy for dealing with it, both inside your own head and in your outward behavior. Here is **Sy Green**'s lesson: "Because I have experienced racism all my life, I could easily categorize issues and failures under racism. But many times the problems are more complex than that, and you have to be able to differentiate when an issue is race and when it isn't. That's not always easy. But even if it is racism, you're going to have to deal with it head on. If you don't, it will defeat you."

Frank Fountain has reached a similar conclusion. "There have been times when I thought, 'Maybe this person has a problem because I'm black.' But that doesn't change how you analyze the situation. You simply decide how you're going to get done what you need to get done. The competition within a corporate environment is intense. It is absolutely fierce. And because it's basically a white environment most of the battles are white against white. Most of it doesn't really have anything to do with race per se. You've got to focus on the issues and the problems, and you can't let the race issue stop you."

For Fountain, separating race from his view of himself in the world—not ignoring it but separating it in his analysis—has been an effective strategy all his life. "I've had blacks come and tell me, 'I know people don't like me because I'm black.' And I say, 'Well, tell me how you know this.' Then they start giving me examples. And I invariably say, 'Don't just stop at the first thing.' And often my opinion is, it's because you didn't do this, or you could have taken a different approach and avoided the issue. When I do run across someone with a race problem, I think, 'What business do I need to have with this person? What do I need to get from him or have him do for me, if anything? And how long am I going to be in this environment?' So you sort through all of it, you come up with a strategy, and you keep moving. In most cases somebody with a race problem has other problems and other issues."

Joe Anderson dealt with a difficult boss several years after he joined General Motors. He could have analyzed the difficulty as related to race, and he may well have been correct. But Anderson analyzed it as an organizational issue, and that also may have been accurate. What is indisputable is that his analysis allowed him to master a difficult situation and move on to the next assignment. "When I returned from the Harvard Program, General Motors was going through a restructuring. So I went on a temporary assignment to the reorganization team breaking down the barriers between brand name cars, like Pontiac and Chevrolet, and putting them into large cars, small cars, trucks, and so forth. I went to work for a vice president in that organization. For the first time, I experienced somebody I knew didn't want me there. This was not a race issue. I was a Pontiac guy, and he was from a different division of GM. I was not his guy. There were other guys from other places who were also not his guys. He was old school and traditional and all those things some of us were not about. I had a meaningful job, significant responsibility, but I was never on his team. And so I finally got bailed out and moved to the component group as opposed to the car side of the business."

Green, Fountain, and Anderson have learned to temper their sensitivity and look more deeply into the complex motives of their white colleagues. The ability to manage their reactions when race is used against them is an active part of their comfort zone. Their "weapons" are self-confidence, intelligence, and emotional fortitude, the "scar tissue" built up over years of practice.

They are very different people in very different careers. The analysis plays out according to their individual circumstances. What they share is self-knowledge and the ability to use it effectively in their work environments.

If you can hear and incorporate the message in their experiences, your own journey will be shorter. It is a difficult battle, and, as you well know, easier for some than others, and easier at some times than others. But you can win. You probably have already begun to develop many of the same skills that support their success. Look back through your own experiences. The seeds of those skills are there. Focus your intelligence on uncovering and developing them. Green, Fountain, and Anderson are sharing the collective wisdom of ninety years of corporate effort to master the many facets of the race issue. Don't get discouraged if you haven't put them all to rest in the first few years, let alone months.

Because an intellectual process helps to break down the elements of an emotionally charged situation, you may benefit from this six-step framework:

- step back and slow everything down in your mind
- examine each interaction and reaction
- identify what pushes your "hot buttons" and why
- analyze your behavior
- gather enough data to understand the other person's behavior
- decide on several appropriate responses.

If or when you feel you are confronting bias, for your own emotional health you cannot ignore it. You must engage. Sometimes you have the luxury of taking time with the process of confrontation, and other times events unfold more quickly. But whatever your response, you must arrive at it deliberately and wisely. Our six-step framework is the start of your intellectual process. You may want different steps or more steps. Your experiences will guide your own process. The balance between thinking and responding is unique and exquisite, and you must find it again and again. But with each success you will become more confident and more sure-footed. In time, the process will become second nature, taking place in nanoseconds. That is the mastery you seek.

Focusing on your work is the simplest strategy for bringing the demons of race under control. Not only does it take your mind off matters you can't control, but it also brings important rewards of its own, rewards that play a role in stopping the slights, insults, and condescension that are the more subtle faces of discrimination today. This is a conscious, reality-based strategy; it is not denial.

David Hinds recalls two assignments that drove the lessons home. "I remember at the start, one young fellow said to me, 'I don't know why you are here, and I don't see how you can do this job. Three other vice presidents could not do it.' I just went to work. Six months later he was singing my praises. I even heard him say to his former boss, who was white, 'He's the greatest guy I've ever worked for.' We became friends and have remained friends.

"Another time I got transferred to run a particular business, and I knew before I arrived that someone already there was very upset he had been passed over. This time we did not discuss it, but I knew it was a very difficult management challenge. Halfway through the assignment, he took me aside and said, 'I was upset when you were given this responsibility. But I can honestly tell you there is no way I could have accomplished what you have accomplished. I'm very pleased to be a member of your team.'"

There is much to learn in these two incidents. Hinds is not wearing blinders. He clearly sees the African-American aspect of the two encounters, and he knows who has the problem. But he also sees—and can operate effectively in—a broader context, one which includes his own perspective. He knows he has to neutralize the other person's problems, or he will not achieve the high level of excellence he demands of himself. If he does not, he may even find his own leadership skills devalued.

Hinds has no self-doubt about his ability to accomplish the work. His experience has convinced him that most members of his teams will also focus on excellent work, so he sets his sights there. He has a tough skin, and he operates with an extraordinary degree of finesse. He credits his time as a platoon leader in Vietnam for much of his cool: "Business is important, but it doesn't seem very risky compared to being shot at." But equally significant are his temperament and his determination. While most of us don't have combat experience, we can learn from his cool determination and from his ability to take an extreme challenge and turn it into a positive force in his business life.

More importantly, Hinds does not stop with the gratification of a job well done, and he will not engage in a gleeful "so there" at the expense of the doubters. He immediately steps beyond that tempting boundary and turns former nay-sayers into supporters. That takes both courage and confidence. Whenever you take a risk and survive, whether or not you succeed every time, you prepare yourself for the next step. Hinds's personal comfort zone is indeed expansive.

It took **Marc Belton** some time to conquer his demons. He describes a bumpy process at the beginning of his time at General Mills. "One of my early bosses was a white woman who thought she couldn't understand anything I said. Every time I had a meeting with her, she had another woman from my brand group explain what I was talking about, like an interpreter. Now I knew I was a sharp fellow with the right pedigree, yet in her eyes we could not connect. I don't think she had any real experience working with someone as different as I was. And to be honest, I was so young in the organization and young developmentally, I certainly had not figured out how to meet her needs. It was pretty much a struggle. On my performance evaluations, I was a 'two' performer, two on a scale of five. For a while there didn't seem to be much hope, but I knew I loved the work."

Even with the problems, Belton shows a high degree of self-knowledge. He knew he had much to learn about corporate life that he had not learned in school. He also knew that he was unable to get himself or anyone else past the race issue. What made him hang in there? First, he loved the work. Then a white man from New Jersey, who had grown up in a racially mixed area, became Belton's boss and mentor over three assignments. "He pulled me out of the fire on at least two different occasions and got me assignments that had higher personal freedom and accountability, like Yoplait. I stayed there two years, and then people saw I had some promise. But I still was the last person in my class to be promoted to manager."

The pattern of having to prove himself on one small assignment after another, even though he had won some awards, continued for a few more years. Then there was an abrupt change. Belton's very successful strategy for dealing with corporate stress was his new-found religious faith. "I don't know why I stayed through all of that, but I know when everything changed. I accepted Jesus Christ as my Lord and Savior. He took my gifts and added a level of grace and faith, so I could see beyond the obstacles, persevere, and expect success."

Your own experiences undoubtedly include instances of dealing with race with finesse, or instances where you better understood the intricacies of a white person's response to someone black. Those lessons are not limited to their former time and place. What you learned there can guide your responses today.

Take for example **Bridgette Heller**'s college experience. She grew up in Florida, in what she calls "a very racist environment," and she had been known to resort to fists. That is an unusual strategy for most women, certainly for a woman who would later find success in corporate America. When she went to Northwestern University, however, she allowed her intellectual curiosity to take over, and her attitude changed radically.

"Northwestern was all about intellectual growth. We challenged each other so openly on many levels, and we were all being enlightened. Everyone thought very differently, and it was cool to

14

ask questions. That's how we all grew, through questions and long discussions and arguments. One of my friends was a freckle-faced Jewish woman from Wisconsin who had never met anyone black. She asked me, 'Are you black all over?' If she had asked me that in junior high, I'd have just decked her. If she asked me that in high school, same thing. But by college, it was okay. I'd gotten through a lot of that. She just didn't know. And you know what? The truth was, I'd never met a person with freckles, and I said to her, are there freckles all over you? It wasn't like a white person in Florida. She was just curious. And the truth was, I was curious about those freckles. So that was the environment. It was safe to ask questions."

Heller's level of openness ensures her intellectual curiosity will reign. Her desire to learn, to gather information, took her beyond fear, distrust, and defensiveness. It is a gift to have that kind of openness. For Heller, it just took a fresh—and dynamic—location to unleash it. Look for that openness in yourself and push to have the courage to unleash it. Most people respond favorably to genuine interest and inquiry.

Race as an obstacle didn't hit home for **David Hinds** until he was in the military. Before then, the multiethnic population of Brooklyn protected him from "racism as a negative way of thinking. I was in advanced infantry training in South Carolina, and three of us—two were white—walked into a bar, and the bartender said, 'We don't serve your kind here.' I was past nineteen, but I didn't know what he was talking about. I said, 'Excuse me?' One of my buddies had to pull me to the side and say, 'We'd better leave.' He had to explain to me what was going on.

"Then I began to spend more time observing what was happening around me. I saw signs that said, 'Nigger dishwasher wanted.' Where is that coming from? Now I was out of my own unit, no longer under the protective shell of my family, my church, my chosen community. That was my first real insight into people thinking about me as something other than just a kid who was going to school and doing his thing." By the time this came along in his life,

Hinds could see the statement as the other person's problem and observe the overt incidents around him as not personally threatening. He had enough self-confidence to receive the insult with relative equanimity.

For **Cleve Killingsworth** growing up on the west side of Chicago, however, the lessons were very painful, especially since he believed his natural "orientation" toward science and math protected him. "My sisters talked about the race thing, but I was always kind of ambivalent about it. Frankly, what happened in physics and math was more interesting and more true to me than what happened with societies."

The sad irony is that his love of science is what forced him brutally out of that zone of safety. "When I was a kid, I used to go to the planetarium on the bus from my house. I rode it by myself, all the way to the end, by the Lake. I wandered around in the dark under the stars and looked in the gift shop at the meteor fragments. I just loved it all. So I decided to build my own telescope.

"I ground the lens on an old water-filled drum my father brought home. But there comes a point in the process where you have to do something called 'figuring,' so it's not lopsided. I knew the planetarium had a shop with the machine to do the figuring, because I had looked through the windows and watched them do it. I remember being very nervous about going, I was only eleven or twelve. I wanted to put the lens in a brown bag, and my father wanted me to put it in a briefcase. I felt awkward with the briefcase because I was only a kid, but in his mind, I should present it a different way. So I got there and knocked on the door. I still remember the guy glaring at me. I didn't see a sympathetic eye the whole time. They kind of told me how to do the figuring, and when I didn't get it quite right, they pointed at me and were very mean about it. I don't think I ever got it done properly. I just wanted to get out of there."

All these years later the pain is still intense. The place he loved became a hostile environment, but he completed his telescope and went on to develop more projects, this time with a purpose. He became a Science Fair expert, winning many awards, and later a computer expert. Specific situations don't cause problems; it's how you see them and how you deal with them.

It was not possible for **Frank Fountain** to block out or even exist side by side with racism. He grew up on a sharecropper farm in the segregated South. His temperament never accepted the basic premise on which segregation was based, that he was inferior. He was a rare individual. He was able at a very young age to see the issue clearly, and he did it on his own. "I knew there were people who had more things than our family did. I knew there was the white and black thing; that was very clear. I experienced first hand the water fountains, the colored this and white that. But to me it was almost surreal. It didn't make me feel inferior. I had my own view of myself, and I never felt less of a human being than the white folks. Somehow I never picked that part up. Maybe that's why I majored in history, because I just couldn't understand why they did that."

How many times have you been told—or told yourself—not to let others define you? Fountain is proof of the power of self-definition. Look through your own history for thoughts, drives, and experiences that gave you a clearer definition of yourself. You do not have to let yourself be defined by other people or society in general. Choose your own definition.

Growing up in a small town in segregated Louisiana, **Alana Robinson** found similar confidence, but how she arrived there was different. "I knew a lot about the ills that existed during that time, but I really didn't internalize them. They weren't a part of my life. I ate every day. We did things as a family. I didn't really see the negative things going on outside in the world as affecting my home. You can't miss what you never had. Maybe there were some other things I could have had, but what I had access to was good."

Sy Green knows the obstacles race can pose, but he chooses to see race, or any other obstacle, as a positive driver. He therefore believes African Americans bring an advantage to any table, and certainly to corporate America. "I don't know if I would have been any better off if I had been born with a different skin color, with more riches. I might not value it. I might not try as hard. But one way or another, we all have to deal with the cards we're dealt, in our careers and in our personal lives. You can complain about them for a second, but the key is to move on to solutions. You have to find a way to get over, under, or around whatever your obstacles are, whether it's race or anything else." Successful people don't rest or make excuses. They constantly test their limits and discover more and more effective strategies.

Gender

Race is confusing enough to manage, but African-American women also have to contend with the issue of gender. If mother, daughter, wife, or mistress are the female roles with which men feel most comfortable, how can any woman become a professional colleague? Of course, this question is an exaggeration in order to make a point, but the gender problem is real, and a lot of it is buried beneath the surface, in a place men of all descriptions don't like to go.

Although things are changing, professional women are still out of place in corporate America. However, most of what has been written about the problems of professional women focuses on white women. The complex interplay between race and gender in a corporate setting is just beginning to be recognized and discussed, by blacks as well as whites. It overlaps the prejudice black men face, but not exactly, and it overlaps the discrimination other women face, but again, not exactly. There is a unique character to the discrimination you face, rooted in history, that needs to be appreciated before any of us, men as well as women, can move past it. As black women, you are viewed through many different lenses.

Kim Green arrived for the Chubb training program in 1983 looking forward to the competition she would face as a woman and a black. She was privileged and middle-class, with an excellent education, thanks to her parents, and prestigious business intern-ships under her belt. She was driven to prove to everyone that she could do just about anything as well as, if not better than, anybody else. She was in fact a star in the Chubb program.

"I was pretty well accepted, at least on the outside, with my colleagues, managers, and a few home office dignitaries. They had a certain comfort zone with me because of my answers to the typi-cal questions: 'Where are you from? Where did you go to school? Where have you worked? What do your parents do?' But one thing surprised them. Chubb is the good-old-boy system, and I had no political connection there. It turned out to be an advantage for me, because none of them thought I was any competition.

"I get a major rush when a chauvinistic male colleague prances into my office and demands something, anticipating an emotional reaction. That kind of provocation guarantees I will be calm, direct, and definitive in my response. They usually get red-faced when I don't respond in 'type,' the way they expect me to.

"Moving a male-dominated structure is not an easy task, and traditional conservative, chauvinistic views cross color barriers. Our own men can sometimes be extremely critical and difficult to work with, as managers, subordinates, or customers. Perhaps there is a message here. Is it to put me in my place because in their eyes I 'have it all'? Are my struggles not as intense as theirs?

"Sometimes I think I may even have an advantage over white women, because colleagues often come to me for advice on how to handle strong white women, in personal or business situations. Sometimes I ask them why they don't respect strong white women the way they respect strong white men—'Do I detect a double stan-dard?'—and sometimes I tell them to take care of their own prob-lems. I have a great relationship with my boss, in part because I am evaluated on results."

Green grew up in the decade after the doors were opened, and her expectations of the business world are more in line with her actual abilities. She does not mince words, and she speaks very directly to her white male bosses. While this modus operandi is very effective for her, it may not work for every woman or even every black woman. It helps that she is one of the top salespeople at her current firm, by far the youngest, and one of very few women or minorities.

Maybe Green is right. Maybe black women can speak more openly to white male power than their white female counterparts. But why do white males allow her to challenge them? Is it that she is not such a direct threat to their egos? Do they feel a challenge from a black woman does not diminish their power or make them appear weak, as would a challenge from any man, black or white? Whatever the reason, her observation is a lesson for other black women. She may have defined a critical strength black women bring to the table. If more share her viewpoint, maybe black women can encourage the "male-dominated structure" to adapt a bit more quickly.

Jerri DeVard is working hard to prove that point as well. Another young and confident woman, she has no trouble being heard and is forever pushing the women she manages. "I remember a very frank discussion with one of my subordinates. I said, 'You are one of the brightest women I've been in contact with, and I keep waiting for you to break out. You're too deferential to the other people on the team. You whisper an idea, and then I have to say, why don't you say that? You have to find a way to serve up your ideas to include others. You can't ask me to serve them up to give them credibility. You have to have the confidence to stand up and do that. But if you have the facts and you present them, and, at the end of the day, you can't persuade enough people, then you need to step back and understand why. Because you have the ability.' I tell her that. She and my whole team need to understand how to break out of this mid-rank and become stars.

"Another woman who was close to me always allowed people to take advantage of her. They knew they could always get her to do their work. She never said, 'Wait a minute. You've got to do that on your own.' I like teamwork, but you don't want to be

20

abused. And there are some gender dynamics on my team. The guys get together as a group and put something forward as a recommendation from the team. That isn't a recommendation from the team. I have to find ways to bolster the confidence of the women but at the same time not hold the men back.

"Then there's another woman on my team who's very strong. She's not going to take no for an answer, and I love that about her."

Carolyn Byrd is a decade older than Green and DeVard, and her strategy at The Coca-Cola Company was more indirect. She worked hard and continually requested more responsibilities, always expecting to receive the commensurate pay and position before long. It was a subtle strategy, but as long as there were many positions to be passed around, it worked.

"When I started at Coca Cola, I only expected to do a good job and to be rewarded accordingly. I was very fortunate my undergrad degree in economics and my MBA landed me in the finance office. At this company, finance has always been not just a player but a leader. I have worked closely with many people who have played important roles in this company over the years. I don't think I ever thought about strategic thinking on a very conscious level. I just thought about doing what I needed to do and doing it well. Since I was a child I've always worked. If there is one thing I can do, it is work. I do what I have to do and enjoy it. It's a matter of attitude. I didn't even think it had anything to do with my race or gender. I just thought it had to do with Carolyn. This is who Carolyn is, irrespective of race or gender."

For twenty years, Byrd thought she was on that team. She was working successfully with important players, who willingly accepted her advice and her work on important assignments. And she was excellent at building a broad expertise in finance, operations and international assignments. It appears that as long as she was a supportive cheerleader for their success, the men accepted and valued her and her contributions. But when the pyramid narrowed, the stakes became higher, and the opportunities fewer, she, as is often the case with minorities and women, was not viewed as a serious contender. Clearly, her reading of her environment was off in some critical aspect.

"Most of my career, people placed value on what I believed I needed to do and what I enjoyed doing. But I've come to the conclusion that people really evaluate you based on other criteria, their own personal beliefs." In a corporate power game, subtle messages from women often do not register. When you are a black woman— or a woman of any color, for that matter—and your behavior is not recognizable within the context of the game rules, you are not really in the game.

Sometimes the issues are not so subtle as they were in Byrd's experience. When **Margaret Jordan** was the Dallas regional manager for Kaiser, she attended a quarterly board meeting that included all regional managers. A very senior executive, someone she considered a supporter and a part of her peer group, came up to her in the middle of a conversation with a board member's wife and said, "You know how Margaret is, just bitch, bitch, bitch." This was not twenty or thirty years ago; it was in 1992. The executive's message was explicit: don't pay attention to Jordan, and, at all costs, don't take her seriously.

Linda Keene, on the other hand, started out with a very clear understanding of how women in the business world would be treated. She got her training in a brutal arena, Harvard Business School, in the mid-1970s, and she learned to push back at the men on their terms and succeed. "I'm just such a stubborn person, and I wasn't going to let them defeat me.

"Everybody at Harvard was jockeying for position versus everyone else. At that time only about 10 percent of the students were women, and there were very few minorities as well. Women students often found the points we made in class would be totally ignored by our fellow students and the professor. A man would make the same point one of us had made earlier in the discussion, and it was treated as a completely new idea. It was bizarre! In my section many of the women were discouraged from even trying to participate in the classroom discussions, but four of the ten of us just refused to be ignored. We would call attention to the fact that one of us had previously made that particular point, and then carry on the discussion from there. After a while, they couldn't ignore us, and they even began to include us in the discussion.

"Class participation was such a big part of how you were graded, so if you gave up on class participation, you gave up on being a top student. The biggest opportunity you had to demonstrate your smarts was opening a case discussion. Professors wouldn't call on women to open. This was very frustrating to us because we could never dazzle the class with our brilliance. The Women's Student Association leaders finally had a meeting with the faculty to discuss the problem. Their patriarchal attitude was unbelievable. They saw themselves as protecting us by not putting us in the 'hot seat.' We told them they were really handicapping us by not allowing us to compete on equal terms with our male classmates. Things improved after those discussions, but there were still a number of professors who just didn't get it.

"I remember the day I finally had the chance to open a case discussion. It was during the second semester, when some of the students had started to slack off a bit. The professor called on the guy sitting next to me to open, but he wasn't prepared. He called on all the men around me, and they were all unprepared. He finally asked me if I had anything to say. I was so pumped up, I must have talked for 35 minutes. After recovering from his surprise, the professor complimented me on the thoroughness of my analysis and stated that he felt there was little to add. That was a very gratifying moment.

"Women had to be so persistent. We constantly urged each other on, and we were constantly beating on the door to achieve recognition. The blatant sexism in cases, in everything, was terrible. It was a hostile environment, even down to the bathrooms. There were men's rooms on every floor of the classroom building, but only one women's room. And even then it was just a converted men's room, with all the urinals still on the wall.

"People also voiced racist assumptions that went unchallenged. I remember several classmates saying that blacks were only there because of affirmative action. But most of the women and minorities there had to have strong records of achievement just to be admitted in the first place. We knew a lot of our white male classmates had lesser records. The skills I learned through dealing with these challenges at Harvard prepared me well for the issues I later encountered in the business world."

Since then, Keene carefully selected her business environments to make certain she would have the opportunity to be valued. As an expert in marketing, a relatively transportable skill, she had more choices than many.

Discrimination against professional women is no longer so blatant and easy to recognize. One may not encounter the hostile work environment Jordan encountered at the board meeting or Keene encountered in business school, where she was assaulted daily by overt gender and racial discrimination. Today's discrimination is the deeply submerged, subtle and unarticulated attitudes that allow men to accept women's work contributions, even value them, while dismissing or ignoring the women as real partners. For example, in Byrd's case, the men were surprised she considered herself a serious contender.

In today's world, these gender-related issues can often be more difficult to address than those of race. They add an additional layer of elusiveness. To begin with, many men—and women—across every race, class, and age line do not perceive the problem. If a woman wants to participate in an environment where the rules of behavior and expectations were written by and for men, the women have to learn those rules and figure out a way to be effective within them.

Behavior that has historically served women well in their private lives may actually be a hindrance in the corporate world. If

24

women interact differently with others, seek to influence others in a different way and go about accomplishing their work differently—often described in shorthand as "nurturing," "consensus seeking," and "inclusive"—they may not be understood or respected in the work environment. When women try to act like men, they frequently find the metaphors of competitive sports and warfare, which so aptly describe the behavior of successful men, do not fit them very well. How do you identify those gender-based attributes, language, and behavior patterns that allow men to discount you? What do you do about them? How do you adapt? How do you deal with insults like Jordan had to face? How do you get the men who make the decisions to take you seriously, to see you as a professional? The first step toward overcoming barriers is to recognize them, not an easy task.

If you receive a single-sex education, or choose a career that has traditionally been considered suitable for a woman, such as teaching or nursing, it may take longer to recognize the boundaries that limit your behavior and ambitions. When you push those traditional boundaries, even inadvertently, you feel them quite clearly. For example, it was a shock to **Kim Green** to realize her father applauded her achievements as long as she did not become independent of him. In college, when she was chosen for the Procter & Gamble summer internship and managed all the travel, shipping, and living arrangements on her own before calling home to ask 'permission,' her parents had trouble adjusting. "I think I caught them off guard. I said to my father, 'I was expecting you to say, you made the right choice, you handled everything, and I'm so proud. Instead you tried to convince me to do something else, and I don't think you would have treated my brother that way.' We had a long discussion about men and women then, but I don't think he really got it. That was a major turning point for me."

Bridgette Heller's realization about the boundaries came in high school. She was one of two blacks in advanced placement classes, and she had researched colleges and potential careers on her

25

own. Her very high board scores led to numerous offers for college scholarships. Many colleges were calling her guidance counselor trying to obtain inside information on what additional aid they should include to influence her choice of college. Her guidance counselor, however, didn't even know her. "I'd never even met him, so when he called me to his office one day, I was nervous. I knew I didn't trust him, but I couldn't figure out why he was asking me to tell him which school I was going to accept. He finally said, 'I think you should hurry up and decide so the other African-American student in the honors program (a male) can start looking at your other offers.' It was as if the offers had nothing to do with me or my ability. He didn't even congratulate me or say, 'Good work.' He just wanted to talk about the guy. He continued to call me into his office to tell me to decide quickly and turn the other offers over. I just couldn't believe it." Heller was already accustomed to race discrimination, but in high school she learned about gender discrimination, a double whammy.

Because of the added layer of discrimination, as women you must work more diligently and creatively to define your critical strengths and then to make them known and valued in the work context. You must be extraordinarily persistent, aggressive, and tough-skinned, even though those qualities might be held against you. That is the only way you will ever be taken seriously. It is an exquisite balance you must learn to maintain. Your ability to speak openly to powerful men is an asset you can develop, so eventually you can convince everyone to take you seriously and view you as a real player. You do not need to leave behind all your personal attributes as a woman and become "mannish." You must simply realize which behaviors are not effective in the business environment and then adapt them to assist you in achieving your goals there. This is not selling out; it is developing the ability to read your environment accurately and objectively, and then to speak and behave in a way that allows you to be heard.

Trusting Yourself

Confidence in your ability is the bedrock of success for anyone. Blacks, however, struggle daily just to turn down the background noise of "You are inferior," however muted, in order to function effectively. Even though experience and time have moved the bias to a different level of consciousness, the barely veiled negative assumptions—you're not as well trained, you're not as smart, you're replacing a better-qualified white man—continue to attach themselves despite what your resume shows and your work proves. You are asked, or worse, not asked, questions about your ability that others don't face. You are excluded from meetings, activities, and memos that are important to your particular project. However these events may be rationalized, you recognize the message. Your white male colleagues enjoy an atmosphere of positive assumptions about their abilities, unless or until they perform very poorly. You, on the other hand, must prove your ability in an endless cycle of "guilty until proven innocent." The process is exhausting. The emotional rather than physical stress of "working twice as hard" will eat away at your ability to perform if you're not vigilant.

Lloyd Trotter handled the constant testing this way: "Once working with other folks, I started realizing, 'I could do my boss's job. I know I could do this.' When you can evaluate your skills realistically—and I emphasize realistically—against the skills of others, you start formulating different strategies for what you want to do. And as my experiences and self-confidence about what I could accomplish grew, my view of where I wanted to go expanded. You set your sights higher, trying to achieve. For instance, my goal was to become a plant manager, and then when I did that, my goal became to manage multiple plants.

"You play to your experiences, the things you see around you. I'd never heard of a CEO when I started. If I had, I would have just thought it was alphabet letters out of order. To say to your first manager, I want to replace the CEO, has no meaning. There are so many steps between here and there. You must first talk about what you want to do over the next two years, maybe even five years. It's not that you won't get there. It's that there are so many career experiences you need first." Trotter's words show how he built his confidence. Apply his lessons to your own experiences. Each success builds your confidence and conditions you to accomplish more.

Bob Johnson's second boss was a major factor in building his confidence. That boss pushed him to take on tasks he thought were beyond his ability. "My supervisor in the shoe department had confidence in me and gave me so many opportunities. He would say, 'I'm not sure anybody can do this. Will you do this for me?' It wasn't long before I realized he said that because he knew I could do it. His confidence helped me try, and most times he was right. I found I could do a lot more than I originally thought I could.

"For example, I really questioned whether I could be a national sales manager because it's a schmoozing job. You're leading the company in its effort to position itself in the market to sell a particular product. I think because of the shyness in my nature, I don't like to get out on the stage and run the program. Plus, it's indefinite; success and failure is hard to measure in dollars and cents. Did the program fail because it was a bad program? Because they didn't implement it? Because the market shifted? It's got a lot of ifs to it, and accountability is diverse. And he just told me, 'I want you to do it. I know you can do it. End of discussion.' So I said, okay. Actually I did very well, and it built my confidence."

For **Chuck Chaplin**, self-confidence grew over a period of time as a result of thrusting himself into new assignments, testing his limits over and over. "My personal psychological make up is one where I never seem to get adequate joy and pleasure from my successes. I've always been the type of person who looks at a report card full of A's and B's and worries about the B's. I won't get any psychic value out of being congratulated for the A's. I'm constantly trying to eliminate the 'low scores,' so my self-confidence requires continuous renewal.

"I came to realize what I call my lack of self-confidence, or never being satisfied with what I achieve, actually drives me to do more. Fear of failure is an enormous, powerful motivator. Every time I went into something new, I sat there the first day saying, 'You really bought it this time. Now you're going to be exposed as the fool you are, and you have no one but yourself to blame.' I can't tell you how many times a year I go through that experience. I'm constantly being thrust into new situations I have no particular training for. But now, I get to that phase, and I'm able to convince myself intellectually, 'Well, there's no reason for me to be afraid of this situation. I was able to do X, Y, and Z, and, while this is different, it's no harder than X, Y, and Z.'

"I used to think I was foolhardy, but that's not the right analysis. If I hadn't thrust myself into some of those places, tried something new and done well, I never would have gotten the self-confidence boost associated with success. Improving that aspect of my psyche has allowed me to reap professional success along the way. It's happened that way over and over again. I still consider myself a nervous and high-strung individual, but I am confident about my ability to find my way through a new situation, whatever it is. So in the end, I think it's a good thing, at least for me." In reality he has a great deal of confidence, built up over years of succeeding in new situations. He craves the next new challenge and the rush of adrenaline it brings.

Gerald Adolph has gone through a similar process. As he approached age forty, he suffered a bit of a midlife crisis. He began to doubt his future career options and even his own ability. At the same time and purely by coincidence, key supporters left the firm. "I was really very close to being out of here. Everything that you would not want to happen, happened all at once. My senior mentors and sponsors all left and went in different directions. I had to begin finding and nurturing large clients on my own, without more senior people. It all coincided with that just-past-forty anxiety."

Adolph began a rigorous process of self-analysis and reasoned his way out of his crisis. "One of the things that keeps me going is the belief that I'm actually not quite as good as everyone would have me believe. I mean, if you believe your own press clippings, you can get in trouble. So I just try to stay ahead of that. On the other hand, I think a number of us suffer from what I heard a psychologist call 'the great imposter theory,' where you worry you're really not anywhere near as good as you've been made out to be, and you live in constant fear you'll be exposed.

"I'm willing to go out there and give it a shot, to see what happens. I say to myself, 'Even if I fail, it won't hurt that much.' All through my career I've always said to myself, 'Well, if this doesn't work out, I'll just put it down as a long summer job.' Certainly I can go get a job somewhere else, as opposed to getting all wrapped up in, 'Oh, my, I'm a failure.' And the only time I actually got into trouble was when I got out of that mood and started worrying about risk and managing it, being a little bit too careful, too cautious. 'What's everyone going to think?' With the opportunities and the background I've had, I have to be willing to take chances and go for the upside rather than worry about keeping a job.

"For me, rightly or wrongly, when I turned forty I believed I was at a vulnerable period. I was getting to be too old and too highly paid to transition easily into some of the jobs people transition into when they leave consulting. But I wasn't yet senior enough for someone to make me president of something, so it's sort of a career no-man's-land. That's when I, in my own head, attached more risk to what I was doing, and it actually worked against me. I tensed up. I was no longer doing something because I enjoyed it.

"But the same mentality that says, 'Even though I don't feel well, I've got to get up and go to school today,' applies at work. Even though you may not feel your best, you may feel anxious, there may be all sorts of things going on in your work life or your personal life, none of that changes the fact that you've got to be on your game today. You somehow compartmentalize the two things. You do what you have to do over here, and you keep all of that other stuff over there."

Adolph has devised a workable strategy for building and maintaining self-confidence. He uses the analytical approach. He identifies risk and barriers, both external and self-imposed, and uses this internal conversation to talk himself through the difficult stretches. The struggle is never really over, but it does become easier.

Fortunately, thanks in large measure to desegregation of schools and the military, the message of inferiority has lost much of its power to defeat. But the transition was far from easy, especially for those who entered first. Here is how **Mannie Jackson** remembers fifth grade in small-town Illinois in 1950, when he and five other blacks were hand-picked to go to the white school. "I went with my best friend. The teacher stood there in front of the class, and she said, 'You colored kids, we don't expect you to be able to keep up. You just do the best you can, but I can't penalize the rest of my students for you.' We sat there, just the two of us, and she talked right around us. I thought to myself, 'What are they going to do here that's supposed to be so magical? I can't wait to see it.' When I looked at the first test, it was easy. I said to myself, 'When is the hard part going to start?' We did well, and the first thing she said was, 'Did you cheat?'"

Historically, the competition of sports has been a building block for the confidence of many men. In sports, there are clear winners and losers, clear measuring sticks for ability, and athletic ability is universally admired in men. If you can translate love of competition, devotion to discipline, skill under pressure, grace in success or failure into accomplishments in academics and in influencing people with your ideas, you are ahead of the game.

Lawrence Jackson very literally made that transfer. When he entered a top military high school in Washington, D.C., doubts about his own ability caused him to perform very poorly. It was his first time in a racially mixed environment, and this one was barely mixed: 3 percent of the 1500 students were black. He was in the low-performing classes and scoring in the low 80s instead of his usual high 90s. "I started to think a lot of people were smarter than me, and I let that whole self-doubt thing start." The second semester he played intramural football, and things turned around. "My sports achievement rolled over to my academics. 'I play better than you,' and I took that attitude right into the classroom. In tenth grade I insisted on being put in a special math class they told me was too much for me. I argued and argued, because that was just the challenge I needed. I did fine, and by my junior year I was a top student and a football star."

His achievements, however, did not solve all the issues. "There were games where I made plays that won the game, and Monday morning I'd find out there had been a party Saturday night to celebrate, and I wasn't invited. I tried to find other explanations for those things, but eventually I couldn't. I'm glad I had an all-black school experience for so many years, to build my academic confidence."

Sports prowess can have a negative side, as it can be very difficult to move from the role of 'jock' to intelligent human being. For black men, making the transition can be difficult if not impossible, not in their own minds but in the minds of whites they encounter. **Ron Parker** chooses not to talk about his football career, and **Mannie Jackson** paid his own way to take parallel courses at a second college where he did not play basketball, because he wanted to have serious academic challenges.

Thanks to his refusal to accept the "jock" label, Mannie Jackson made a very successful transition from sports to business. He took a "quick look" at the Knicks—"it wasn't much money, and it was all basketball"—and then went to New Rochelle to visit a small company that manufactured pressure-sensitive tape, a competitor of giant 3M in Minnesota. The company owner was almost as serious about his industrial league basketball team as he was about his pressure-sensitive tape. Both recognized a winning combination. "My analysis was that pro basketball was for jocks who didn't have any other direction in life. I also had a pretty good idea that as the company's team star, I would have a competitive advantage within the company. I had a chance to play more ball and get good business experience. It turned out I analyzed it right. I had a great year, played a lot of basketball, and got the best job assignments. I also gained business confidence."

Although there are now more opportunities for women to compete in sports, the benefits are not as clear cut. Female athletes are by no means universally admired, and the adjectives that describe male athletes can turn very sour and even sneering when applied to women. Another confidence builder, academic competition, however, is open to both men and women. **Carolyn Byrd**'s godmother sent her to Fisk University so she could meet a good husband among "a better class of blacks." But instead Byrd found her business calling. "The head of the department in economics at Fisk University taught the class, and he was very famous for giving bad grades, but I got three A's. So I said, 'Well now, this is not so bad. Let me try it again.' I found economics easy, since I was a logical thinker and could draw a graph and explain it intelligently. It was a breeze; it was wonderful.

"That professor retired right after that, but there were lots of others. We had some very wonderful young professors from Harvard and Yale. They taught and conducted economic development studies. They brought a lot of new and young ideas, and many of us became very excited about economics and business. We started something called the Fisk Student Enterprises where we ran businesses. We had an African-American bookstore, we had a baby-sitter service, we rented portable refrigerators in the dorms, and we made some money. I thought I was going to stay in economics—I had been accepted to Harvard's PhD program—until I found out about MBAs during a break in Chicago. The rest is history."

For women, however, even academic excellence may not be

enough. But as usual there are solutions if you pay close attention to your environment and read the signals correctly. **Alana Robinson** earned one of the first degrees in computer science at Grambling State University, and she was certainly the first woman. "IBM wanted all twelve of us. They came in and did a clean sweep." It was not a slam dunk for her, however. Discouraged from summer internships by her father—he believed it was inappropriate for girls to work outside the home—and wearing her engagement ring for each campus interview during her senior year, she got no interest from any recruiters. "All of my friends were going on trips everywhere to interview. I wasn't. I couldn't understand why, especially because IBM had been so interested in me before. One of my friends finally told me, 'You need to take that engagement ring off.' So I did, I put on my class ring, and I got an interview every time after that. All I had to do was take my ring off, and things starting clicking."

As much as we would like or hope or wish, we have not yet reached the point where the background noise is silent enough for confidence to be easily gained and maintained. **Sy Green**'s advice to young African Americans tells the whole story: "You've just got to hang in there. You can never lose confidence in yourself. You just have to revisit your strengths and stick with them. Then you have to look at all the things you need to improve, and take care of those. That's life."

Confidence can come from many sources in addition to the obvious ones like school and sports. It all depends on how you look at your own situation and what you do with it. **Bob Johnson** learned about self-confidence by analyzing his parents' political position against racial prejudice in the context of his segregated Chicago community during and just after World War II. "I had to kind of live in two worlds, surviving in both that community and at home, each with a whole different set of values. I used to think a lot about the conflict. What impact would it have on a kid growing up? I think it provokes thought. If there is no reliable truth and you have to figure it out for yourself, you're probably not going to accept authority either. Once you start figuring things out for yourself, you're not going to stop. But that just means that you're going to find your own way, you're going to find your own truth, and you're not going to be easily dissuaded. And so I learned not to be dominated." Johnson's ability to find strength in a situation which might simply confuse others was a key factor in his later success.

Bridgette Heller got used to standing up for herself in arguments with a fiercely independent father. Although he died when she was eleven, his fighting spirit lives on within her and has served her well. Heller worked hard to win a scholarship to Northwestern's Medill School of Journalism, but in her senior year she decided she didn't want to be a journalist. She had learned most journalists don't get paid very much, and, even worse, many never get to voice their own opinions. She simply picked up the telephone and asked Northwestern to switch her to the college of arts and sciences and to transfer her full scholarship there as well. They agreed! "You start out and you really don't think about it, you just do it. You don't stop to think, 'Oh, I can't do that.' The worst anyone can say is no."

Indulging a passion for science and math, on his own, proved **Cleve Killingsworth**'s savior. Since there was very little science and math in his school curriculum on the segregated west side of Chicago, he developed his own. When he was only twelve, he read about physics until he was stopped by a symbol no one could explain to him. A chance suggestion that the symbol had "something to do with calculus" sent him to the library. There was only one book on calculus—not enough to be intimidating. So Killingsworth taught himself calculus, slowly deciphering the meanings of function symbols by studying the results of their use in different equations.

His favorite job, however, was cleaning and organizing the science room. "For me, the science room was nirvana, and I got it all to myself. Just imagine, I'm surrounded by all this equipment: test tubes, magnets, dry cells, photoelectric cells, wires. I was in there alone, and I could work with it all. They'd forget I was in there. I remember asking my parents for a science table for one of my birthdays. They didn't know what I was talking about. One of those gray, metallic tables with the sink and the big mirror so that the class could see. I didn't ultimately get it, but that was OK, because I had it at school." With very few alternatives at his disposal, Killingsworth found ways to indulge his passion and develop his skills. In this context cleaning the science room was as important to his development as teaching himself calculus.

These stories show that your particular circumstances do not have to be confining. What is important is how you look at them and what you do with them. If you look at your circumstances along one dimension, you could decide to give up, to close up shop mentally and shut down emotionally. But you have choices, and if you listen to the voices we have recorded, those choices are many. The only limit is your ability to imagine them. You can choose to concentrate on the negative, or you can find your true strength in the challenges. This is hardly a suggestion for you to wear rose-colored glasses. Quite the contrary. It assumes a difficult, rigorous, reality-based analytical process that continues throughout your life. Your choices, and the actions that result, will determine your path. With persistence you can push through the negative and the risks to the personal rewards, toward a life of significant achievement and valued contribution.

3.

Fitting In

*I've had numerous conversations with people who say, why
should I have to compromise my individuality just to get
along with those people? That attitude means you're going
to have trouble wherever you go. If you're going to be successful, you are going to have to learn how to be culturally
flexible, and cultural flexibility is something blacks are very
good at.*

—**C. Edward "Chuck" Chaplin**, Senior Vice President and Treasurer
Prudential Financial, Inc.

*As I got more experience and moved into leadership roles, I
expressed more of who I am, not less.*

—**Linda Baker Keene**, Vice President (ret.)
American Express

Overcoming Isolation

IN every relationship throughout the organization, being a black American is a salient feature. There are times you feel uncomfortably visible, as if in a fishbowl. At other times you feel you are not seen at all. Not very long ago—not even two generations—each black in corporate America was in fact isolated as "the first" and "the only." We can learn much from how they dealt with their isolation. **Lloyd Trotter** eventually became president and chief executive officer of one of GE's largest operating divisions, but in 1963 he literally had to push open the corporate door. He arrived at Cleveland Twist Drill as an applicant for its new journeyman program. He was armed with high expectations after meeting the program director at his high school. The guard at the door, however, did not know about the new program.

"I saw the waiting room and the personnel office, and I thought, boy, anybody could walk in and pick up an application and talk to someone. But then a guard stopped me with, 'Can I help you?' And I said, 'I have an appointment. I'm here to fill out an application.' And he said, 'We don't have any jobs.' That was the answer. I gave him my explanation, and he said, 'Wait here.' I still didn't get into the waiting room. This company was making a conscious effort to do something about past discrimination, but I think they started doing it without a lot of planning or communication. So right away I was reminded of what I was getting ready to face."

Trotter was eventually shown in and received an apology from the president, and certainly the indignity of standing and waiting outside that door has faded into the background with his enormous success. But what was in his mind and heart then? He had entered totally new territory with optimism and enthusiasm, and he hit a brick wall almost before he processed his first impression. What prompted him to remain? Where did he find the fortitude? One factor was the long arguments he'd had with his father about pursuing this program instead of going straight to college. He was not about to suffer the additional indignity of admitting he had abandoned his hard-won independent decision so easily, an incentive with which every young person can identify. But he also took, under the circumstances, a great leap of faith in his willingness to trust himself, the program director, and the organization. He forced himself to stay despite his doubts and discomfort.

Walking to meet the supervisor for his first assignment, he was painfully aware of complete isolation. "When I walked through the door, you could hear a pin drop. The only thing I could hear was my brand new shoes squeaking as I walked. I don't think any of the skilled trades guys knew about me until I got there."

He did not ignore the pain. Decades later he can still hear his shoes squeaking as he walked across the floor. But even then the pain did not stop him from continuing the walk, getting the assignment, and, we must assume, performing well. Trotter is a man of action. He did not analyze or intellectualize the experience. With dogged determination he kept his eye on the prize: his own goal of making good. He found a place within himself and within the work where he could function effectively.

By most measurements that walk across the floor was a small step, but viewed from the perspective of those times, it embodied significant risk. His willingness to take that small step, to withstand the isolation and then build out from it, was in fact an early indication of his eventual corporate success. These acts of will, simple but strong, are available to everyone.

Sy Green, too, felt the profound isolation of being "the first" and "the only" when he began a training program at Chubb's New York City headquarters about the same time. Chubb was viewed as the "Tiffany" of the insurance industry and had a very conservative reputation even within a conservative industry. All of the leaders were Ivy League, particularly Harvard, Princeton, and Yale. So this move was a great leap for Green, who came from a small college in Ohio not far from his home town, with his high school sweetheart.

His starting place in the corporation was above Trotter's—he was a management trainee—and his strategy for dealing with his isolation was appropriately different. In his mind, he turned it into a list of advantages.

"I had advantages kids today don't have. First of all it was just me, so who am I a threat to? No one. Mr. Chubb made the decision to hire me, and I'm sure he made sure his leaders were committed to supporting me. My wife and I were even included in socializing with my peers. I got a lot of exposure that helped my early development. I also think I might have been better off being as naive as I was, because things were happening that I didn't know about. You can't care or worry about things you don't know about or have no control over. Kids today come in knowing so much, and they worry about it all."

Green was well aware of the downside of being the first. "It's terrible to be the center of so much attention, with so much riding on your every move." But he added a critical skill to that perception: He could look at the full picture, decide where he fit in and where he did not, and then identify areas of advantage, even in isolation.

Back then, Green's isolation did not stop at the Chubb doors. He and his wife had a struggle he kept to himself. "Once I received my Chubb job offer, I read *The New York Times* in the college library and saw there was ample affordable housing in the metro area. However, when my wife and I arrived and began our search, what was available to us was quite interesting. I'd complete my application. Let's say it was a new building, hadn't even opened yet, rental sign out front for studios, one bedrooms, right on up to four or five bedrooms. Well, invariably, the only thing that would be available would be the five bedroom, which they well knew I could not afford and didn't need or want. We got to the point where we would call on the phone and say we were black, because we were wasting so much time going and being turned away. We finally found an apartment, but it took a long time. We did it completely on our own, and I'd still do it that way."

Finding a first apartment is an important step toward independence for all young people, as it was for Green and his wife. But what the Greens needed to accomplish that simple task was critically different. They had the fortitude to face rejection again and again. Green could have fallen back into his comfort zone and returned to teaching in small-town Ohio, especially given his isolation at Chubb. He knew nothing about property and casualty insurance. He'd never worked in a large organization. The New York metropolitan area was a big adjustment. Where others might have been deterred by pain, exhaustion, and bitterness, he remembers simple pride in his ability to solve the problem on his own. He pushed on until he prevailed.

If you examine your own experiences, you will undoubtedly find similar examples to draw from. You have emotional and intellectual reserves to fuel the drive to reach your goals, even in the midst of confusion and pain. New experiences can be impossibly painful or accepted as necessary steps toward long-term goals that are more important. You make the choice. In choosing to continue, you prepare yourself for the next step, and the next, sustained throughout by your focus on long-term goals. This focus will not necessarily filter out the short-term stress, but it can hinder and even stop the chipping away at your self-confidence. Therefore, doubts and fears will not be able to sidetrack you.

As a young adult, **Ed Howard** also turned feelings of isolation into a competitive edge. He attended predominantly white Marshall University in Huntington, West Virginia, in the early 1960s. "You weren't greeted with open arms by any means. They didn't even want you on campus. Every weekend I visited the two black colleges nearby, because there was absolutely no social life for blacks at Marshall. None. I received academic training, but I can't say I really enjoyed the school. I was there for one reason, to get an education, and I was ready to leave the very minute I completed that education."

He had no pretense about the isolation. It was raw. Yet pain did not deter him. He had calculated that getting a Marshall degree would open up 50 percent more job opportunities. He even devised a stress-relief strategy for those college days. He spent weekends at the nearby black colleges. This survival strategy allowed him to tolerate the terrible indignity of pariah status. Howard's experience highlights a truth for all of us. You need a high threshold for emotional pain if you are to succeed.

Bruce Gordon eventually became a group president at Verizon, but he was unprepared for his intense isolation at Gettysburg College. He was five years younger than Howard and grew up in an integrated neighborhood in Camden, New Jersey. Unlike Howard, a serious student, Gordon had the added struggle of reversing his school priorities: he had been a football jock who was a casual student.

"I was one of three blacks on the campus, and the only one in my class. I said to myself, 'I should have thought about this more. Gettysburg was not a good move. Not only am I a minority in the most extreme sense of the word, I am also in the middle of nowhere.' I was trapped on an all-white campus in the middle of central Pennsylvania. And it was very tough academically. I had never liked being a student, so I didn't have the day-in-day-out, do-your-work-on-time, don't-procrastinate kind of study habits. It was very hard for me to figure out how to study. I often tell people I majored in diploma, because my sole objective was to get out of there. I envy my friends who went to black schools, because they have great memories and lifetime friendships from their college years. I don't."

Gordon's deep sadness about his college years could be just another commentary on how difficult it is to close the racial divide in this country. Instead he chose to find a personal benefit in a painful experience, and his ability to make that choice foreshadowed his corporate success. "I got a complete education on how to survive in a white environment, and that learning experience transferred straight to my corporate environment. From that standpoint, it was all pretty good. Back then I didn't know I needed that lesson, but it has served me well." Blacks pay a high price to achieve in America, and they pay it every day.

Cleve Killingsworth, five years younger than Gordon, went to MIT. He was not alone, but he was not much better off. He was part of a small group but still separate from campus life. "Being at MIT was like being invited to a cocktail party where they don't really expect you to come. There just was no place, no gathering you could walk into at MIT with the feeling you were supposed to be there. It never happened. And when you're not embraced, most tend to withdraw. The saddest part is you're a student in a place of immense resources, and you're withdrawing. What we had at our feet, if only we could have connected to it. There were so many things black students didn't do at MIT. We simply gathered together as this little cadre of people apart from the broader institution. It takes a long time to get comfortable with that other world. First you have to get to the point in your life where you understand what it means to be who you are, but that takes a long time. Unfortunately, you don't get to go to MIT twice."

Milt Irvin had done well academically and athletically at a predominantly white Catholic high school in New Jersey and then at the Merchant Marine Academy. But he was totally ignorant about business, and he still doubted his ability when he arrived at Wharton in 1972 to start work on his MBA. "I thought, if there were 500 people accepted at Wharton, I was number 500." Rather than grit his teeth and bear racial and academic isolation, he pushed back. Irvin demanded and received the clarity he needed.

"One day, everyone was running into the auditorium, and I asked a guy, 'What's going on?' He said, 'Gus Levy from Goldman Sachs is making a presentation.' So I said, 'Who's Gus Levy and what's Goldman Sachs?' And the guy looked at me and said, 'If you have to ask that question, you shouldn't be here.' And I said, 'Oh my goodness.' I felt so bad."

Feeling bad did not make Irvin withdraw, however. He opted

for personal growth. His love of competition and the self-confidence he nurtured with past successes in sports and academics were his jumping-off points. Rejection did not stop him, nor did he succumb to self-doubt. Befitting Irvin's style, he aggressively sought comfort in his new environment. This style has brought more than a few setbacks to his work life, but it has also given him the capacity to bounce back and the creativity to find different paths.

At Wharton that style was effective. "The next day I went to the placement director. I said, 'I'll be honest with you. The only reason I'm at Wharton is somebody told me it was a good school. I don't know what I'm studying for, I don't know anything about business, I don't know what to do once I graduate. I just have no idea. I was embarrassed yesterday because I didn't know who Gus Levy was, I didn't know what Goldman Sachs was, and I was told I shouldn't be here.'"

His honest approach was risky but more directed than a stab in the dark. The insult from the fellow student wounded him because it was in fact true, so he selected the person most closely associated in his mind with the business world, the placement director. Since he did not know that particular individual, he might have faced more rejection and insult. But he took the chance and minimized the downside by soliciting the placement officer's expertise. It paid off. "He took me under his wing, maybe because he'd never seen someone with such brutal honesty. He set me up at General Motors, Bankers Trust, and Goldman Sachs, just for informational meetings, to learn context, to ask questions, just to talk to them."

The placement officer had seen hundreds, maybe thousands of business students. He knew the world. Perhaps he responded to Irvin's openness, intellectual curiosity, drive, and self-confidence, traits that fuel his determination and will to succeed. Irvin, who saw himself as simply ignorant and lost, was a good bet in the eyes of the placement officer.

The meetings Irvin attended could have been simply informational as billed, but he recognized them as opportunities. He knew the talk with the placement officer was not any kind of permanent solution to his lack of knowledge but rather the beginning of another process, and he wrapped his arms around the challenge. He approached the meetings with the representatives of three different companies as tests, and he passed with flying colors. "I ended up getting summer job offers from all three. I took the one at Goldman Sachs, because I thought it was the hardest one to get."

Since payback every now and then is part of the game in the business world, especially on the rough and tumble Wall Street trading floor, Irvin sought out the student who had started the ball rolling. "It was a recession year, 1973, and jobs were hard to come by. I said to him, 'So, what are you doing this summer?' He said, 'Aw, job market's tough, I'm just going to summer school. What are you doing?' 'I'm working at Goldman Sachs.' His jaw fell open." This can be a dangerous game, but Irvin pulled it off. Here it is an indication of Irvin's self-confidence, his belief that he will follow up this particular battle with more achievements.

Linda Keene went to the Boston Consulting Group for some business experience before going on to graduate school in the mid-1970s. This environment, which she described as full of "intellectual arrogance and entitlement," made her feel like "a fish out of water. Being around people so hung up on power and prestige was very different from anything I had ever encountered before." Her questions were right on the surface, but in a very real sense, many of the rules of behavior and measurements of value were secret. "Personnel matters were handled in a clandestine way. Periodically the partners and senior managers went into a room and talked about your performance, but they never told you what was said. You never got a performance appraisal. You had to try to find out what was said about your work by asking somebody who had been there to tell you. It was very Machiavellian."

Like many successful people, she began looking for a way to get a handle on this new environment, to make sense out of it in order to develop an operating strategy. As a black woman (and one of only two black professionals) she was able to find support from a unique inside source—an administrative assistant who had been at the firm since it started. "She looked out for the other black consultant and myself, and we needed that. She was always giving us information and telling us what was being said about our work." Here was a person who, because she was black, female, and not part of the professional staff, was invisible to many. But she was observant and knew a great deal about the inner workings of the organization. To Keene she was not invisible. She was an obvious comrade and a source of valuable knowledge. Their friendship gave the administrative assistant an opportunity to use her knowledge and gave Keene an important touchstone in an unfamiliar and stressful work environment.

The knowledge she would be there for only two years, to gain business experience for her business school application, made it unlikely Keene would be dragged down by the pressure-cooker environment. Because she was not planning a career in consulting, she was able to concentrate simply on the intellectual challenge. "The people were very smart and fun, and I enjoyed working on the kinds of problems we worked on. But I learned a lot about the kind of environment I didn't want to be in." She took her life lessons and moved on. There was also a bonus: "Other things were easy after that."

Sometimes memories of safety and security from childhood blunt the pain of isolation. **Don Brown**'s memories of belonging to his rural Arkansas community have always helped sustain him, even through the most grueling conditions. "Friday night boxing matches were a huge social event in my little community, because that's when all the men came in from their jobs to see how the fights were going. Dad and all that gang—and my dad was never young, you know, he was always dad, this old guy—all the old guys would come over, and they'd have the radio on. If it went static, they'd go out to the car and try to find the station on the car radio. It was always everybody from Joe Louis and Jersey Joe Walcott and Ezzard Charles and Sugar Ray Robinson. So they'd all get around and then they'd have a domino game and of course as long as you could stand you could stay. But of course Mom would drag us kids off to bed because she didn't want us to see the drinking, cursing, smoking cigarettes, and all that stuff, but it was great. It was wonderful."

Sometimes that security of a strong and resourceful family fosters the optimism to make mature decisions. As an eight-year-old, **Paula Banks** was diagnosed with a bone disorder associated with rapid growth. She had to decide between spending several years on crutches or in a wheelchair. While crutches would allow a more normal childhood, her recovery would probably not have been as complete. At an early age she had the capacity to understand delayed gratification and chose the wheelchair with its promise of a better recovery. "I remember that time like it was yesterday. My parents built ramps down the back porch, down into the yard, and rearranged everything in the house. My dad went out and bought a station wagon so it would be easier to transport the wheelchair. They made a game out of it and made it fun. Our life, as far as I was concerned, didn't change. I don't remember anything about those years being negative." Like most successful people, she converted what could have been a long-lasting trauma into positive inspiration. Terrible pain and a debilitating social experience—she was out of school for most of those years, in and out of hospitals and involved in extensive physical therapy—became for her an adventure. Her discipline and determination are predictors of corporate success.

Finding Your Place

How do African Americans, individually and collectively, fit in to corporate America? How do their values align with the values of the organization? What are values? They are one's personal system of beliefs about integrity, loyalty, honesty, subordination. They are the result of a complex interplay of knowledge and perceptions brought from one's life experiences. They shape and influence your behavior as well as the way you perceive and evaluate the behavior of other individuals and other groups. They set the limits of what you call ethical behavior.

Are your values out of sync with those of your organization? In order to answer this question, you must slow down, step back mentally and emotionally, and make a meticulous examination of all those values. You must really stretch your own thinking in examining your values as well as the values that drive your organization. This does not mean changing your values. It means understanding them—and those of the organization—more precisely. What are the gaps? Can you identify specific things the organization does that conflict with your values? For example, what issues do you perceive are connected with race and gender? With integrity? Loyalty? Honesty? Subordination? Do you find organizational dishonesty where others see standard business practices? If you are objective in your analysis, can you find ways to close these gaps?

If you are truthful with yourself, do your "values conflicts" in fact mask a fear you will not be able to win in the organization? Is it a feeling that too many things are beyond your control? Does a perception that the organization's values are "white" make you feel a victim? Are you uncomfortable being evaluated on more than measurable business results? For example, do you believe your manager is unable to be objective about your leadership abilities? Do you think he sees you through a lens that downgrades your performance as well as your potential? Do you fear you have a limited ability to network, socialize, and find internal sponsorship? How can you communicate your genuine concerns about those limitations, without being labeled "Johnny One Note," always playing the race card? These questions require rigorous emotional and cognitive analysis. They call for a continuous application of confidence, courage, and new insights.

You may indeed find gaps that are difficult to close. But it is just as likely some roadblocks of your own making are preventing you from finding your place. If you are ever to move forward in any large organization, you must examine these issues and resolve each one yourself. While there are no prescriptions for what to do on any issue, experience shows that unexamined gaps will adversely affect your performance. You may lose interest, disengage, become apathetic, perhaps even leave, and all for the wrong reasons.

"I have had numerous conversations with people who say, 'Why should I have to compromise my individuality just to get along with those people?'" said **Chuck Chaplin**. "That attitude means you're going to have trouble wherever you go. If you're going to be successful, you are going to have to learn how to be culturally flexible. When American businessmen go to meetings in Bermuda, they wear shorts, because all the men there wear shorts.

"The rules are fairly simple, and you just need to be aware of the cultural mores. This is something you would think blacks are very good at doing. You may reject those cultural mores, and that's perfectly all right. But it will be very difficult to be successful in business if you do. There are other perfectly honorable lines of work in which your individuality is celebrated, and you can and should go there. All I say is, you need to understand the difference between the two and make your own choice.

"To live your life every day against your values, you'd have to be a lot smarter than I am. It takes enormous skill to engage successfully in that kind of duplicity, especially in the ambiguous environment we operate in. I've seen people do it, but I've not seen them do it successfully for very long. You compromise your value as a leader every time you compromise your personal values."

People who succeed have examined these issues and resolved them to their personal satisfaction. Often they discover their values are largely consistent with those of their organization. Where their values conflict, however, they don't allow the conflicts to hinder their performance. Some even find value conflicts diminish as they move higher. They find more freedom to express themselves, not less.

Linda Keene has reached a similar personal comfort zone. "What has happened as I've gotten more experience and moved into leadership roles is I express more of who I am, not less. This is particularly true for the caring, nurturing side of who I am. And there hasn't been any negative impact. That's good for me, because I don't think I could live with the dichotomy. I think sometimes people are afraid to show themselves, because they think it won't be accepted. I've found when I try it, it is accepted. I'm probably more outspoken than many of my peers, but I feel comfortable with that." That is a powerful reward for managing your demons and finding your place, for transcending fear and distrust.

Ed Howard found in his corporate environment that he never had to compromise his values. "Once you find out what makes your clock tick, you can then develop ways to accomplish what you want to accomplish. But you have to start by knowing yourself. You can surely make adjustments to fit the culture, to fit the corporation, but you cannot compromise yourself. You have to know where to draw the line, where to say, 'This is it, I'm not going any further.' I can truthfully say I never compromised anything that was important to me. I have to be able to sleep at night, and I've never had any trouble doing that."

Pushing Back

Self-confidence and self-knowledge will eventually compel you to begin speaking up for yourself. Make no mistake, it feels risky, especially the first time, but it is probably not as risky as it seems. When you begin to have successes within the organization, you will feel the confidence to push again and to push harder. And if, over time, you are not satisfied with the responses, you will find the pride, dignity, and ability to locate places where your contribution will be valued.

Some people arrive at an organization with the confidence to push back. Because Bob Johnson was already thirty years old in 1965 when he applied for the Sears Roebuck management training program, he had already had a number of disappointing work experiences. Even though this opportunity could potentially open a whole new world to him, one he felt he'd been wrongfully denied earlier, he did not come with his hat in his hand. He refused the first offer and then argued for six months over salary, the difference only $500. But in that process he developed a respectful working relationship with the recruiter. What was it that made him argue? Self-confidence? Arrogance? Fear? Being just plain ornery? Whatever inspired him in this situation, it worked. The person he challenged obviously liked his persistence, and Johnson's many visits allowed them to build a real relationship. "Finally he said to me, 'I'm going to give you what you want, but don't tell anybody.' So I took it. That's where it started. There was no strategy."

Mannie Jackson also pushed back as soon as he arrived at Honeywell. By that time he had been around the world with the Harlem Globetrotters, owned his own business, and then excelled for three years at General Motors. He was no beginner. It also helped that Honeywell's chairman had recruited him. "When Honeywell recruited me from General Motors, the chairman told me I would be on his management team, that I'd eventually be a general manager. That made sense to me, because I'd run successful businesses at GM. When I arrived, I found myself the equal employment opportunity officer. I was in the aerospace defense business, the training ground for Honeywell top executives, but it was my teenage bartender job all over again—well paid but dead end. I said to the chairman, 'With my background and all I've been through, why am I working as an equal employment opportunity officer? Am I loony? I'm leaving in two weeks.' He said, 'Stay two months; I'll get you out of there.'" In one month Jackson was placed on an important five-member acquisitions and management committee that reported to the chairman of the company's computer business in Boston.

Kim Green took advantage of her first evaluation to speak up for herself. "I didn't know any rules for handling an evaluation, but I sensed my boss wasn't comfortable with me. I filled out my self-evaluation, wondering, 'Have I done this the way it's supposed to be done?' She started by telling me, 'You did pretty well, and your self-evaluation was accurate.'

"Then the real dialogue began. She said, 'Well, obviously I can't give you all "outstanding" marks because you're still a trainee.' I let her go through her whole spiel, but I was thinking inside, 'This is not right. This makes no sense.' I'm steaming on the inside, but I'm trying to be the cool trainee while I figure out what to do.

"At the end she said, 'Now, do you have any questions?' Very calmly I said, 'I have a lot of questions.' I went through each evaluation category very analytically and requested examples of where I was not up to par, and by that I mean 'good' as opposed to 'outstanding.' Is it servicing? Interpersonal skills? Working with others? Risk assessment? Financial analysis? Presentation skills? Her evaluation stated, 'People like Kim very much, but sometimes she seems too professional.' I asked her to define 'too professional' for me. The only example she gave was, 'When we all met after work at a bar, you ordered a Diet Coke. You wouldn't drink a beer.' I said, 'To the best of my knowledge, that get-together was about networking, not about what beverage you drink, and I was networking.' She said she would take my feedback into consideration. To make a long story short, she changed everything and gave me the scores I deserved—'outstanding.' The embarrassing part of this scenario was that the home office had a very high opinion of her, so now I had to deal with that issue."

Green stood up for herself and her reputation and won. She was prepared. She carefully and deliberately picked the time, place, and topic. She thought about the process, took the self-evaluation seriously, and paid careful attention to what her manager said, even taking notes. Her questions were not designed to cover up performance deficiencies, because she and her boss both knew her work record was excellent. But if she had a deficiency, she wanted to work on it. Her critical mindset was one of entitlement. She would allow no one else to define her, and she demanded—and got—fair treatment.

In standing up for herself, she was unable to neutralize her boss's discomfort. In this situation there was probably no way to do both. Fortunately, something unanticipated rescued her from the situation. "Somebody I knew in the New York office got promoted to run the New Haven office, and she asked to have me come up there as her full-fledged underwriter. I had beat some odds, but not all of them."

Virgis Colbert pushed back at an early boss in the late 1960s, when he, too, was not satisfied with an evaluation. "I was the general manufacturing superintendent in one of Chrysler's parts plants when a new CEO took over. He wanted an assessment of the plant's managers, and the plant manager did mine. He wrote that I was a 'good' black manager who could someday run a small plant. I said, 'Why do you have to categorize me as a good black manager who could only run a small plant? It's obvious I'm black. And I could run any size plant.' Of course he said he didn't mean anything by it, and he would take it out. He took it out. At least he told me he took it out.

"To me that evaluation was an indication that I was pigeonholed at Chrysler, that I wasn't going to be able to go very far. He had me in a different category. So the call from a headhunter recruiting for Miller Brewing came at the right time. At that time I wanted to be a plant manager, and at the end of the day I thought I could do that quicker at Miller than I could at Chrysler."

Pushing back at his boss and starting over at a new company were both risky strategies. But Colbert assessed his competition enough to know he was a more valuable commodity than most. That knowledge and his sense that his boss "didn't get it"—that even if he took the offending and irrelevant sentence out of the evaluation, his chances were limited—gave him the self-confidence to take the next step. Since Colbert rose to executive vice president at Miller, it was obviously an excellent decision.

4.

"Reading" Unwritten Rules

*You learn the rules of corporate culture, and most of them
are unwritten; you can't go to a manual and pull them out.
You keep the antenna up for what's happening and try to
work your way through that maze.*

—**Virgis W. Colbert**, Executive Vice President
Miller Brewing Co.

*You need a sixth sense to succeed in the corporate environ-
ment. If you wait until something has happened, it's too
late. You need your instincts to see a situation developing if
you are going to operate well.*

—**W. Frank Fountain**, Vice President
DaimlerChrysler Corp.

*White men don't realize that people of color have a sixth
sense, the ability to reach the point of compromise without
giving away the store and then to bring everybody together.*

—**Ronald C. Parker**, Senior Vice President
Frito-Lay North America

Realizing

NOTHING makes your outsider status so crystal clear as the realization that the organization operates according to a set of rules you know nothing about. The rules are not written in a manual, and you do not learn about them in any training program. Many tributaries lead to an awareness of those rules. For some, the realization comes quickly, perhaps by a fortuitous circumstance—a casual word of description or something obvious that grabs your attention and sticks in your mind—but most often it dawns slowly. The realization can come by watching other people's masterful performances as well as their mistakes. It can come during your own performance. For example, you are making a presentation and get that sinking feeling in your stomach, when you say something you immediately realize you should not have said. It can arise from a question you were unable to answer, or a dead silence when you finish. You know something is off, but you don't know what. You may be operating with a vague awareness that something else is going on you can't quite put your finger on. Some greater understanding may fall into place, or you may continue to struggle with something known but not yet fully understood.

Each organization indeed has its own set of unwritten rules that guides the behavior, action, and evaluation of everyone there. Certainly everyone successful understands these rules at some level and knows how to operate within them. How did they learn them? Some required years of effort, others had an immediate instinctual understanding, and for still others the silent cues of the organization so paralleled their own they did not notice any difference. One thing is certain: The more ambivalent you feel about the organization and your place in it, the harder it is to receive the correct signals. Sometimes you may feel others know but are withholding necessary information. At times this is true, but most often those who have learned the rules probably assume you have reached the same point. Keep in mind that, more often than you realize, others near your level are struggling to understand as well.

Whatever your learning process, you must see and hear what is happening all around you. To do so you must keep all your instincts on alert. You are the constant observer, trying to see through the eyes of the other person, looking at behavior from different angles, running over every incident and interaction again and again in your mind. And the rules themselves change. A large organization is by its very nature organic. Profits go up and down. People come and go. Priorities change. New rules are constantly being "written." You must watch for new signals and be prepared to decode them.

Frank Fountain reaches back to his mother's words when he was growing up on a sharecropper farm in rural Alabama. "My mother always warned me not to trust people, that the way things look are not necessarily the way they are. For example, if someone gives you something, you should find out why. She was always suspicious, always cautious. Her lessons also taught me to watch the other person's movements in every conversation, to try to understand what's happening underneath the surface. There can be other things going on. You need a sixth sense to succeed in the corporate environment. Now, you can't go around feeling afraid and nervous about what may or may not happen, but you do have to pay attention. If you wait until something has happened, it's too late. You need your instincts to see a situation developing if you are going to operate well. You've got to look at the elements in the environment and be able to put them together and position yourself accordingly, offensively or defensively. These instincts have served me very well as I've moved through my career."

Cleve Killingsworth started learning the unwritten rules the hard way. His first job after graduate school was as an administrator at the University of Pennsylvania Hospital. He got several promotions very quickly, after his boss left. "Opportunities arise when someone moves, and you're there. That's when I learned about being in the right place at the right time." But just as quickly the tables turned. "They brought in a guy and put him between me and my boss, even after they had me participate in the interview process. When I had to give my office to the new guy, I knew it was time to start looking elsewhere. Later I realized he wanted to build his own team, and I might not be a part of it. But I didn't know that's how it worked, and I didn't know they wouldn't just say, 'Cleve, you're not going to work for me anymore, you're going to work for that guy.' They just kind of let it evolve.

"I began to understand that the rule was: You've got to keep improving your title and raising your salary. Your responsibilities have to keep increasing and moving into different areas. So all of a sudden I had a plan for my career. I wouldn't take jobs that were a step back, only ones that were a step forward. The money was not so important, but the job needed to be better, with more responsibility, different types of responsibility. I knew I wanted to demonstrate my ability to manage people, and ultimately I wanted to see how far I could go."

Milt Irvin also learned the unwritten rules the hard way, but he fought back. When he was going through the interview process at Salomon Brothers, they asked him how flexible he was willing to be about geographic location. He voiced a lot of conditions and didn't get an offer. "So I thought, what is going on? Someone told me the guy didn't like the fact that I wasn't flexible, that I wasn't willing to relocate. I couldn't believe it, and I said, 'C'mon!' So I got them to let me back in. I told them I really wanted to work for Salomon. I got an offer, went to the training program and did very well.

"Now my wife and I were living in the city and talking about buying a condo in New Jersey. I didn't want to make the same mistake twice, so I went to the head of the department and said, 'My wife and I are thinking about buying a condo. Since I want to be flexible and I want to stay in the program, I'd like to know, should I go ahead and buy, or should I hold off?' I was told, 'No, no, go ahead and purchase it.' So we did.

"Two months later, I was one of the first in the program to get an assignment. The Boston office. I was really pissed off. I said, 'I don't want to move to Boston. I lived in Boston for a year, and I don't want to live there again. And furthermore, you told me I was going to be in New York.' 'Well, things change. You have to learn to be flexible.' Immediately I was *persona non grata*, I fell to the bottom of the barrel. I got no assignment. I asked, 'What is going on? What am I going to do?' 'Well, you don't want to go to Boston.'"

What had Irvin done wrong? He thought he had protected himself against a repeat of his first mistake. Had he made too great a demand too soon? Was it a personality conflict with the head of the training program? Did he want to "put Irvin in his place"? We may never know. But the real question is, what would Irvin do about his situation? He could walk away and try to start at another bank. He could agree to move to Boston. Or he could try to find a compromise position. The latter course is what Irvin chose, and with great difficulty he succeeded.

"I had to find a place to put myself and then talk my way into being there. I lodged myself in the New York International Sales Department, and I just decided, 'This is where I am going to stay.' I worked my butt off. If somebody went on vacation, I would cover those accounts like I'd been covering them my whole life. I just got myself involved. People on the trading desks thought I was assigned to that department, so finally I went to the manager and said, 'Hey, look, I've been here for months now, everybody else in my class is assigned, why won't you just assign me?' He said, 'Well, you need to check with the head of the training program.' He knew what had happened there, so I had to find another way to convince him. I said, 'I don't think he cares, and it's your business. If you think I can do a good job, just give me a shot.' So we went back and forth until he finally gave me the shot. So I officially started out in New York International Sales."

He was indeed *persona non grata*. He had no specific assignment, and nobody wanted anything to do with him. But he refused to read the writing on the wall. Was it pride, not wanting anyone to know he was out? Was it determination to prove them wrong? Talk about ambiguous status! But he didn't quit, and Salomon didn't specifically tell him to leave. He was determined to find a niche for himself. His confidence—and his strategy—came slowly, but he certainly succeeded. It was his hard work and an unshakable focus and determination that eventually molded others to his view of himself and his ability to add value. This kind of maneuverability, where he had no formal status but was not specifically put out the door, may only be possible in certain parts of investment banks, where performance is mostly measured by simple return. The point is that Irvin read his environment accurately. He found a strategy that gave him the opportunity he wanted within the circumstances of his particular organization, and he pushed until he made it happen.

Because Irvin frequently goes with his gut, he has found himself more than once in a career hole he has had to climb out of. Not many people willingly put themselves in such unstable positions, with no allies, no markers for clarity, not even a job assignment. This is not a strategy that works for everyone. You may want to go with the flow a little longer, build up a reservoir of results and good will before you make heavy demands. This is certainly a more dependable strategy, and no one will think less of you for it.

In some situations encoded messages bring opportunity. It is up to you to receive and understand the signals and act on them. **Chuck Chaplin** was performing happily and very well as the head of the New York City office of Prudential's mortgage company when the company president approached him regarding development plans for high-potential employees. Chaplin was not surprised to be included, but it took him a while to figure out what was really being offered and then to accept the challenge. He took the following steps to decode their messages and analyze the offer: "The president and his boss said to me, 'We think you have a lot of potential to be a leader around here, and we need to think about what is the appropriate way to broaden your experience.' So I went back and thought about it as best I could on my own. At our next meeting, I said, 'I've been doing real estate debt for going on 10 years now. How about real estate equity?'

"They said, 'Your thinking is too narrow. We think you have potential to go well beyond the real estate environment. Are you willing to view yourself as a finance generalist?' They didn't say it in exactly those terms, but after I did some more soul searching around what they'd suggested, that was what I came up with. As I caught up to them, they became more specific. They said, 'Here is an opportunity for you to get positioned for the role of Prudential treasurer, and, frankly, we think you could do it. It's rotational in nature, because we use it as a way to groom senior executives. You would have to move laterally and work as an assistant treasurer for a couple of years. You can see how you like it and demonstrate you can do the job. If you do, you will be on the very short list for treasurer.'

"I was completely taken aback and didn't know what to say. Their offer was mind boggling in its import. I discussed it with my wife, but I didn't really know anyone else who could help. This was such a unique set of circumstances, well above anything I'd thought about. I tried to organize my thinking so I could make a decision.

"I knew there was a minority angle here; I wasn't completely naive. One of the motivators was trying to bootstrap us into getting a black senior executive soon, and they knew they had to do some extraordinary things if they wanted to make that happen. So being black was one of my assets in this situation. But as a minority I was going to be in a fishbowl, and the penalty for failure would go far beyond just me and my career. Whether anybody else black got a chance was on my shoulders. In addition, I knew absolutely nothing about treasury or what anybody did there. And I would have to chuck real estate, where I really did know almost everything, and start all over again proving myself. All of those things were negatives.

"On the other hand, there were positives. It was an awesome opportunity, if I could make it work, to have real influence and juice around this place. Also, it would benefit the company to have a black face in the annual report, and I could make that happen. Finally, and perhaps most importantly, the president and his boss, whom I had decided to trust, thought I could do it. I didn't know why they were so confident, but the fact that they were meant a lot to me. I'd had a very successful run with them at Prudential, and they knew what treasury did.

"Then there was something between positive and negative. I didn't want anyone to say I wasn't a risk taker. If you work in the same job in an environment like this for a long time, people view that as a negative. I saw my decision just fraught with enormous risk. But for reasons only my mother could explain, it was very important for me to become a managing director. I realized going with their idea was the best way to do that. So I decided to move.

"By the time they came to me with this offer, I realized I was no longer the naive person I had been. I figured out what they were really saying, although not right away. I think I learned to do that through many experiences, such as where I hadn't really understood people's motivations and where things I didn't anticipate happened. Experience is a great teacher. There's a process by which scales fall from one's eyes."

Chaplin read his situation on many levels. Far more than most, he looked straight at his own motivations. He took the time to assess all angles of his managers' motivations and then saw how all of that linked to the interests of the corporation itself. He read between the lines, heard what was unspoken, and applied it honestly to his own personal drives and ambitions. With extraordinary focus, he brought all his insights to bear on his decision-making process. He considered the positives and knew they squared with his own ambitions. After years of testing himself and his abilities, he knew he could work his way through these challenges. He studied the negatives and realized they were not really burdens; he could handle them.

The process of decoding unwritten rules does not always herald such an advancement. Sometimes small signals deliver a different message. When **David Hinds** became a senior vice president and managing director, it was a significant promotion, but at first he did not realize how significant. "When my boss delivered my first bonus check, he came in, put his arms around me, and said, 'Welcome to the club.' His words were interesting in that there was a performance dimension associated with it, but there was also something else I couldn't quite figure out. The check itself was a further shock. It was vastly larger than any I had received in the past. It was one-third of my annual salary. When I opened it, I said, 'Excuse me?' This was real big money.

"At that moment I began to be consciously aware that there were other things in the mix here. I was entering into a different realm within the company that I was completely and totally unaware of. No one was coming in to say, 'Oh, by the way, here is the set of opportunities in front of you.' People were not going to be as straightforward as that. If you figured it out, you figured it out. It was almost like a secret. That is probably the best way to describe it."

Hinds took a long time to pick up the message, just as he was slow to recognize hatred defined by skin color. Once he decoded the message—or was hit over the head with it—he pushed back with strength and great confidence. He concentrated on work and built a strong reputation for excellent results. "I happened to be sitting at a meeting, and my boss said something about the partners meeting. I said to myself, 'partner's meeting? Here is something else new.' After the meeting I asked him to explain. There was another realm of compensation, a higher echelon. It was very quiet, and few people really knew about this structure. I told myself, 'This is crazy. Here I am trying to do the best I can, and there is another level of recognition that is a secret.' I got as much information as I could and then had a conversation with the president. Soon I became a partner."

Kim Green, on the other hand, loved the challenge of searching for the unwritten rules. She made a discovery while a summer intern at Procter & Gamble during college. "Each intern had to do a presentation in this multipurpose room with maybe fifty or sixty seats. It was on a schedule, and anybody could come. My project was to present to our department why we should have Pampers in Japan. A week before my presentation, just to kind of figure out what to expect, I sat in on another intern's presentation. I realized the most important part was the Q&A and your thought process in responding. I would never have thought of that, and none of my mentors had mentioned it. Somebody had obviously talked to this intern, and he had people strategically placed in the audience with questions he had prepared, in case nobody asked any. So when I prepared my presentation, I also anticipated questions and answers. Then I did a dry run with one of my mentors over dinner. That was great experience."

Sometimes the unwritten messages are not about opportunities but about limitations. Here is how **Mannie Jackson** realized he would never become the Honeywell CEO. "You're raised in a company with a peer group, so I knew what my seven or eight peer guys had done, and I knew what I had done. I knew their strengths and weaknesses, and I knew how fast I could run, how high I could jump. I knew I was better than half of them, a toss up as to a couple, and then there were one or two I knew were better than me. I knew that. I was one of seven people on the executive committee, the chairman's right-hand person. And I knew I could do his job at least as well as he did. But I realized the culture—the corporate culture—has to make the decision that it wants you to be successful. It has to intervene to start preparing you to succeed, or it will be very difficult for that ever to happen. I knew there was no way they were going to make me CEO, and I knew they were eventually going to pay me off. I just knew it, could feel it intuitively, and so I no longer set being Honeywell CEO as an objective. Race was partially an issue, but I wasn't just window dressing. I earned every penny I made, and I made a lot of pennies from the company.

"I think the culture—not an individual—had a grand plan for

me, but the plan wasn't that I'd be one of the two or three contenders for the top. Their idea of success for me would be number two or number three guy, get the title of president, make a lot of money, and be respected in the community and go to all those functions and be the breakthrough. They probably thought I should have been very happy and they probably think I am very happy with my final position. But I wanted the culture to prepare me to be the number one guy. There were opportunities that I didn't get, and I said to myself, 'Why wouldn't they send me to do that assignment? That's the assignment you need before you do this, before you do that.' Then I knew it wasn't going to happen.

"Merit, whatever that is, is something, but there are many intangible qualities, qualities that have nothing to do with anything measurable, that go into the decision of who is chosen CEO. A nontraditional package, like race, is one of those. It's tangible but not exactly measurable. A lot of people work hard, do great work, and are rewarded well. The company has invested ten to twenty years in all those people, and most of them aren't going to become CEO. You are not a bad person if you don't make it, and the company should not be labeled racist if you don't get it. Those stars have to line up just right. It's as simple as that. But if enough of us are in the pipeline, eventually the stars will line up for a few of us." And they have.

Jackson's analysis is highly refined. He wanted to be CEO and believed he would be an excellent one. He could see himself and his competition objectively. He knew his strengths and weaknesses, and theirs. This insight helped him to understand the broader context in which these organizational decisions are made, in general and in his specific corporation. "I was a drum major; I wanted to be the leader. I wanted to be number one, at the top of what I was doing. So I knew I would eventually have to leave." He has never allowed himself to be dragged down with bitterness or confusion, about race or any other issue. Instead, he inventoried his advantages and leveraged them to build the knowledge, credibility, and

65

access to capital that positioned him to do well as owner and CEO of his own company.

Gerald Adolph reached the same conclusion about how CEOs are selected, but his vantage point was as an outside observer, a senior partner at Booz, Allen, Hamilton, an international management consulting firm. "If you see someone black lose the CEO spot, there are two things you can take from it. You can say, 'Oh, no, if he's not safe, none of us black folks is safe.' Or you can say, 'It's certainly no criticism of the person, just not the best fit at this time.' It's not like he was tossed out for being a bad performer. He wanted to be CEO, but he didn't win the horse race, so he decided he'd rather enter another race than stay. There have been a lot of white executives who've gone through that. There just aren't very many of us who've played that lofty game."

Jim Kaiser describes how he realized he would never become CEO of Corning: "No one comes out and says, 'Well, I don't like him because he challenged me too much.' They say, 'Well, you know, we're not as comfortable with him as with others.' At that point in my career I was a senior vice president and setting the standards for other division managers to follow. We had the best diversity record. We had the best quality record. We had the best innovation record. We met or exceeded the operating targets. We had the strongest people ratings. And then I got passed over. My boss said, 'No, you haven't done anything wrong. Yes, you've done everything I wanted you to do. But you already have a good job. What more do you want?' I said, 'I've got a great job, but I've been in it eight years. How long do you want me to do it? Another eight years?' And there was silence. And he walked to the window, looked out and said, 'I wish it could be different.' And that was it. I think he meant what he said, because we were fairly close. I mean, he had always shown a liking to me. So I said, 'Okay, I understand. Either play me or trade me.' That's what I told him. I went away, didn't ask any more questions.

"The next year was one of the most successful of my career. I went back to my former boss and said, 'Well, we had a conversation a year ago. I've done what you asked, just as always.' They made me CEO of a subsidiary."

Decoding unspoken messages comes from trial and error, from the courage to risk being wrong, and from years of observation and building relationships. If you re-examine your past you will find that as an African American you already have had many such experiences. **Don Brown**, growing up in rural Arkansas, describes an idyllic childhood. Paralleling that was another reality that was quite different.

"I always reflect back on this as a unique community. I never, ever remember not playing with white kids or with Native American kids. All my life, whenever there was a game, whenever there was something going on, there were always kids of different colors. We were all poor. We made our own toys, and we played together. But when it was time for school, we went to this little one room schoolhouse in our community and the other kids went to their school in their community. After school, on weekends, and over the summer, you'd work together, you'd play together. Come school time, you went back to your communities. Come to think of it, the Native Americans went to the white school. There weren't a lot of them, and I kind of feel that was key. That's just the way it was."

Mannie Jackson's parents didn't talk about racism per se, but their message about achievement was confusing when he compared it to his reality. "They talked in terms of achievement, and that still amazes me. They were people who had never seen their kind rewarded, yet they set high standards and talked to their kids about achievement. They had to know how improbable it was for their kids to break through in a society that was so completely divided, and they didn't define success as having the best barber shop in the black community. They said, 'You can own the bank one day, you'll be mayor of this town, and when you get your own company, you'll be able to do that steel mill different.' I'm thinking, 'What are you talking about?' I was always amazed. I look back and say, 'With their circumstances, how can they dream, how can they even think about this?'"

He got a part of an answer when he was finishing high school. He realized one close relative did not completely believe even the ambiguous message his parents delivered. Because Jackson was a basketball star, many colleges rolled out the red carpet for him. By this time he had worked his way up to bartender at the country club, making $200 a week in salary and all the tips on top of that. That was big money in the 1950s. "My parents wanted me to go to college, but that relative said, 'Why go to college? All you're going to do after college is teach or preach. You make more than teachers make already.' I know now he said that because of his own experience, but I was confused then. The college thing wasn't quite in his success formula yet. He knew it worked for those white boys, but he didn't have a lot of hope for my chances, given what he'd seen happen to some of the blacks who'd finished college. You listen to people around you, sometimes you get mixed signals, and you just kind of make it through." While sifting through the well-intentioned but conflicting messages, he found his own clarity. He chose to go to college.

For **Frank Fountain** in rural Alabama, the daily high school struggle was around social and economic class status. He came to "town" to attend Monroe County Training School, one of only two black high schools in the county, where the children of the teachers were the elite. He was a poor country boy from a "feeder" school. "I could see grades weren't necessarily based on just performance. I remember one of the teachers spending a lot of time trying to explain a problem to one of the elite students, and when I got up there to get the same treatment, he threw the eraser at me. I guess it was during that period I learned the world wasn't quite fair. You didn't always get a good hand of cards, but so what? Find another way." Fountain heard the nonverbal but very clear message: You are second class. The important lesson is what Fountain did with the message. He rejected it.

Trial and error is another way to pin down the rules. At West Point during the height of the civil rights movement, **Joe Anderson** felt he was missing out on an important part of history. Therefore between his junior and senior years he chose to participate in Operation Crossroads Africa in Uganda instead of serving on the senior training cadre for incoming plebes, as he had the prior two summers. After having served as a battalion or regimental commander, he was passed over for significant leadership positions in his senior year. "I don't think I appreciated the consequences. In my opinion I gave them the excuse they needed for a black kid not to have that prominence and leadership in the Academy. They certainly couldn't understand my need to go to Africa at that time, my need to have a broader perspective on the world, and they were not willing or prepared to make an exception. I made a choice, and it was the right choice, but I was never going to make that mistake again. They would never have another excuse not to appoint me."

Was the leadership of West Point looking for an excuse to exclude Anderson? They may have been oblivious to the conflicting emotions Anderson felt or they may have admired and understood his choice. Whatever their thinking, they gave the honor to someone who had completed the leadership training. They did not make an exception for Anderson under these circumstances. No one told him he would lose the position by choosing Africa, and he did not consider that possibility in making the decision. Perhaps more information or understanding about how West Point worked would have led him to a different decision or perhaps not, but he certainly would think differently about every career choice he made in the future.

Playing the Game

"African Americans bring an unusual level of determination regarding performance and doing the right thing," said **David Hinds**. "You also bring what I see as a cultural dimension that really helps in working with others to accomplish the tasks at hand. Whether you grew up in a predominantly black or multicultural or white neighborhood, the fact is that you had to find a way to acquire the skill to make things happen, in schools or the workplace. You had to go through a great deal in order to achieve any level of success. The way in which you manage your emotions and relationships is also very different. None of this stuff is easy.

"When you think about a world that is very complicated, very competitive and very dynamic, and a business world where you have to negotiate on multiple fronts, you need people who have developed a variety of skills and the determination to achieve excellence. Organizations are complicated under any circumstances, and no one achieves success without being extraordinarily creative, especially in the area of human dynamics. For us there are added layers, and what we had to deal with growing up actually prepared us. We did that every day of our lives, at school, at the store, everywhere outside the home. We had to figure out multiple ways to communicate." Hinds knows the African-American cultural experience brings a valuable dimension to managing new and complex situations in a competitive environment. He's right.

Frank Fountain faced a tough decision when he got close to the top of Chrysler, where there are only a handful of "corporate officers." He had spent twenty years in finance and was implicitly on the short list for three of its top jobs, all corporate officer positions. Then an unexpected offer came and forced him to rethink his entire finance career.

"On an early performance appraisal, where we had to list jobs we wanted, I put down heading the Washington office, a corporate officer job, along with all the finance jobs. My former boss, who was now the new VP of personnel, remembered what I had written. The head of the Washington office had recently retired, and they had a young person groomed to replace him. That person grew up in Washington and on the Hill, so they decided his number two ought to be a Detroit person, from the car business side. That person was me.

"So now the big decision for me was whether or not to leave finance, where I was implicitly on the short list for the three top jobs. The tension of the downturn cycle was diminishing, but it was still not the most enjoyable place to be. And of course all the other assistant controllers were aiming for the same top finance jobs and also aiming at me from time to time, just for good measure. I never liked number crunching per se and never even thought I was that good at it. My interests are broader, so I had some feel for the macro analysis, the big picture. That's what I enjoyed the most. I would have taken the treasurer's job and the finance company's top job. But they were still occupied by the same people, so they were long shots, and there was nothing else in finance I wanted to do. I'd had the toughest job through the downturn, so I'd already run the gauntlet and survived. And I also knew I wasn't likely to replace the head of the Washington office, because he was young. On the other hand I would be in a whole different arena and would enjoy learning a new business. I had been assured if I took the Washington job I would remain in the queue, but I knew if I left Detroit it would be difficult to maintain that position. I decided to go to Washington, even though it was a lateral move and probably out of the queue.

"My title was executive director of Washington, government affairs, and I had most of the people in the Washington office reporting to me. So it sounded almost as if I was running the Washington office, even though I could barely find my way to the White House. But I was able to make a contribution early from an administrative and management standpoint, because I understood Detroit, understood headquarters, and the years in finance had taught me how to analyze and make a presentation. The Washington office did not know how to do any of that well.

"Then, in less than a year, everything in Detroit changed again. The CFO left, and my old boss, then the VP of personnel, became CFO. If that had occurred before I went to Washington, I would have stayed to support him. There was some talk of my reneging on my Washington commitment, but that would have upset another EVP, an important person. So I decided to stay in Washington. But shortly, it got confusing again. I had dinner with the new CFO, and he said, 'I want you to run Chrysler Financial.' That was evidence I was still in the queue. However, when the finance company head retired, right after I had that dinner, the job went to the VP of quality, who was an ex-finance person as well. Quality is a hazardous spot, one with a lot of casualties over the years. People there often get into serious trouble with the operating people.

"I was now out of the finance queue, but because I had gotten that close to becoming a corporate officer, the powers-that-be felt I deserved it. They were looking for opportunities. When the person who had responsibility for state and local government affairs, a corporate officer position based in Detroit, took mandatory retirement at 65, I was viewed as the natural replacement. But even then it did not go smoothly. When all of the appointments were announced, including the finance company's job, the CFO and the VP of personnel both called me in Washington to tell me, 'Don't worry, you're going to be taken care of.'

"Leaving finance and taking government and then state and local affairs was a tough decision for me. I considered them and community affairs soft stuff. If I had wanted to take the career path to VP there, I could have done that in half the time it took me to plow my way up the ladder in finance. I also wanted to become a VP in finance, because not many blacks do. They often ended up in those soft jobs, and I had earned the finance job. I even toyed with taking finance jobs outside the company. Headhunters were still pursuing me, but the Chrysler compensation was more than many other Fortune 500 companies. Those stock options add up over time, so I had done quite well financially even before becoming an officer and certainly had choices. But even my boss in

Washington told me, there's no way you can say no to an officer's job. So I took the job of VP of government affairs. It should be VP of state and local government affairs so it's not confused with the Washington office, but we just let this confusion continue."

Even at the top, the game is never won. You must constantly interpret ever more refined messages and decide how to use them to your advantage. You still have to prove yourself every day, and the terrain is always in flux. But you understand it. It's no longer intimidating. You have allies. You have gained self-confidence from your experiences, and you are used to the challenges. You know you are a valuable commodity, and not just to your own company. Ambiguity is no longer an enemy; it becomes your friend.

Before you decide the price of attaining senior status is too high, listen to how **Bruce Gordon** describes the process and its rewards. "When you're a senior executive, it doesn't matter what your discipline, you've got a serious job. You get a seat at the table, and you get to set policy. It's a very different environment, a very different responsibility, and a very different transition from any other job transition. I don't like to use the term politics, because I think it's negative. I use the game metaphor. You have to know the rules of your game. Michael Jordan is a normal human being in his house and driving his car to the stadium. Then he puts on his uniform, goes on the court, and plays the game of basketball. He knows the rules, he knows the subtleties. He is a master of that game. But at the end of the game he goes to the locker room, takes a shower, puts his suit back on, and goes home.

"Look at Muhammad Ali at a press conference. When he went home, he was not running around his house like a madman. He knew who he was, and he knew his value system. He was so masterful at playing his game, he ended up changing the entire game.

"If you play the corporate game, you don't have to be a sellout or even lose the person you are. You can know who you are and continue to be who you want to be. You simply bring that person to the corporate game, and you play that game to win. Whatever you chose to do, you will end up playing in one game or another. You may play a corporate game, you may play an education game, you may play a health care game. You can play any game, but if you want to be successful, you need to understand the rules and the subtleties of that game. Take it seriously. It's a serious game."

5.

Making Your Mark

You need to be identified with something valuable. Very early I became identified with handling mergers and acquisitions. It was like Lee Iaccoca with the Mustang. M&A became my Mustang.

—**Mannie L. Jackson**, Senior Vice President (ret.)
Honeywell International, Inc.
Owner, Chair, and CEO, Harlem Globetrotters

I've learned to accept that as an African American, you're somewhat vulnerable. Knowing that, I use it to push myself to higher levels of excellence. You could say I thrive on beating the odds.

—**Alfred Little, Jr.**, Vice President (ret.)
Newport News Shipbuilding

I did not want to leave any question. My record would be the best record of anybody who'd ever worked there.

—**Ira D. Hall**, Treasurer (ret.)
Texaco, Inc.

FOR many black Americans the compulsion to work twice as hard and to be twice as good, no matter how physically and emotionally exhausting, is how they make their mark. They use this as a powerful motivation to succeed. Some even enjoy it; they're built that way. Make no mistake, if your ambition is to climb the corporate ladder, hard work never stops for anyone. It may change in character, to what **Sy Green** calls "more *agita*," but it will never stop. So steel yourself.

For **Al Little**, making his mark is tied to a work ethic which he has reduced to a three-point philosophy. "First, I am eager to do whatever it takes. I get great satisfaction from doing things right and producing an outstanding finished product. Second, I try not to leave my flank exposed. Observing others' careers and talking to people I respect, I've learned to accept that as an African American, you're somewhat vulnerable. Knowing that, I use it to push myself to higher levels of excellence. You could say I thrive on beating the odds. Third, I recognized long ago that you have to get noticed if you're going to succeed. Great work the key decision makers don't see won't help much in advancing your career. I was fortunate enough to conclude successful negotiations in some very visible and difficult labor strikes. That put me on the map."

Little's analysis is matter-of-fact. He takes charge, gets the job done—and enjoys it. For him, personal satisfaction, proving his ability, and having fun are a powerful combination. These are all skills he has developed over many years of observation and determination, skills he still enjoys honing.

Ira Hall has a similar philosophy but a very different temperament. His first corporate experience, a summer job at Western Electric when he was an electrical engineering student at Stanford, uncovered the personal incentive that has guided him throughout his career. "There were two older African Americans there, both electrical engineers, and it was a while before I realized they were only assigned drafting projects. They would turn out neat drawings, but they were not allowed to design. That angered me greatly. I decided to make sure that people knew at the end of summer the caliber of work that people were capable of, whether they were black or not. I made a point of being off the charts in terms of excellence in what I did. I did not want to leave any question. My record would be the best record of anybody who'd ever worked there in the summer period."

This pursuit of excellence drives his determination, and he learned early how to make it work for him. Here is how he demonstrated his excellence that same summer in the early 1960s. "We had a new IBM computer installed recently, but it wasn't being used because it required a then-new programming language, COBOL. Nobody was even scheduled to learn how to use the computer before the end of the summer, when the in-house programmer was going to IBM-sponsored training to learn COBOL. So I took the manual, learned COBOL on my own, and wrote the program before my colleague ever went to class. When IBM arrived to do more diagnostic tests, they were quite frankly amazed we had a COBOL program written, let alone one which allowed them to perform better diagnostics under production circumstances. They asked, 'Who wrote this?' When I said, 'I did,' they asked, 'How did you learn COBOL?' I told them my 'self-teaching' process, using the manual they had provided. Better still, the program worked, and enabled substantial cost savings in the manufacturing process. During the rest of the summer, I enhanced the program to make it a lot more universal. They could use it at other manufacturing locations and generate even more substantial savings. These worked as well. The management was so pleased, they offered me part-time employment during the school year at the Systems Equipment Engineering Lab near Stanford, and summer employment for each successive summer."

Hall used a powerful "I'll show you" drive to demonstrate his own technical mastery and went one step further. He made sure others knew about and valued his accomplishment, and he timed it to have the maximum impact. The critical question—"Who did this?"—was asked in front of the IBM experts and a good number of Western Electric managers responsible for the new computer. The answer drew all eyes to Hall and cemented his own reputation as well as knowledge of his contribution to the company.

Not all lasting impressions are made as quickly or are as remarkable as Hall's, and you don't always have a ready-made audience to recognize your accomplishments. But other strategies and motivations are equally effective. Early in his career, **Lloyd Trotter** turned a passion for making things into a unique opportunity. Once he had completed journeyman training, he set his sights higher. He was attending college at night and had been promoted to product design and application engineering, even without a degree. While working in tandem with people in sales, he realized he would be good in that role as well. The idea of working with customers appealed to him, as did the amount of freedom that came with the job. With perseverance, he got that assignment.

"I was working for about a year or so with a distributor who sold cutting tools to the General Electric equipment division at Menlo Park. I went to GE with the application engineer to see how the tools were working out. I could see right away it wasn't going well, so I started talking. 'Number one, the tools are not right for the application. We'll fix that. No problem.' But I also said, 'There are a lot of other things wrong with this prototype. Is this your first cutting tool application?' The guy looked at me and said, 'How did you know?' I said, 'Well, it seems to me the way it holds the part is all wrong.'

"So they asked me if I would help them. I said, 'I don't live far from here. Why don't I come in every Monday? I'll give it my best shot. I'll tell you what I think, and you can decide what you want to do.' Well, that went on for about six months, and then we scheduled another qualifying run on the machine. I noticed there were a lot of people standing around, and this run was really successful. My contact there introduced me to his boss, who said, 'I want to get right to the point. Would it be a problem for you to come and work for us?' I told him I really had to think about it. Compared to Cleveland Twist Drill, that part of GE was really home-grown then. I said, 'I still have about two years of night school left, and I'm not planning on starting anyplace in a nonprofessional category.' They offered me a service engineering job, so I joined GE in 1970."

How did the apprentice journeyman transform himself so quickly into an expert with the confidence to sell himself? It was a combination of many things, but believing in his expertise was key. He had something to sell, and he knew it. "I worked with guys who were engineers, and I found I added value to their thought processes. Knowing I could do that kept me going. And people appreciated my ideas. I ran across individuals who didn't want me there, no question about that. But mostly I found if I could help them be successful, they were more than willing to let me do that.

"But the main thing for me has always been loving my work. I knew as a kid I wanted to be associated with making things. I didn't understand exactly what that meant as far as a career, but that has never changed. So while a lot of people take many twists and turns, I didn't. I hit the right one in the very beginning. I had that one right."

Simple fear drove **Chuck Chaplin** to make his mark when he finally landed a job with a real future, at Prudential Mortgage Company. "When I started the job I had all this passion, but I was also worried and scared. It was a big step up, a brave new world, and I was nervous about whether I could really be successful." But something else drove him as well. He feared he had overstated his knowledge. "I was especially worried I might be exposed as a charlatan. In my interviews I was completely unfettered in what I could say about my last job in the government agency, because they didn't have a clue about municipal bonds. But the truth was most of the underwriting work was done by the bankers who sold the bonds. I was a glorified order taker; I went out to find the deals, and then managed them through the reporting. I didn't lie. I just allowed them to form their own conclusions about my experience. So when I got there, I just threw my whole self into learning the business. I worked really hard, studied everything I could find. At that time in my life I didn't do anything else."

What Chaplin is articulating here is another example of someone relating the imposter theory to a career. Believing that other people think you know more than you do and fearing the rug can be pulled out from under you at any moment is certainly stressful, but it can also drive you to excel, as it did Chaplin. It gave him an edge and kept him intensely focused on working harder than anybody else.

Chances are, his bosses were not focusing on his technical skill, about municipal bonds or anything else. Was there a rug to be pulled out? His initial fears were probably exaggerated. He was undoubtedly too hard on himself. He had in fact done what every ambitious and capable person does. He put himself and his experience in the best light and, in the process, displayed confidence. He may have had many doubts, but he was able to project a positive image. To his boss, he truly was an attractive and promising candidate. The point is that fear did not paralyze him or even slow him down. It drove him to make a mark.

Management training programs provide an early opportunity to shine, and it is best to know in advance they are tests. Poor or mediocre performance can sometimes be overcome later, but excellent performance can undoubtedly establish your reputation as a star in the making. **Sy Green** made the best use of his training program in the early 1960s. The pressure of living in the fishbowl was intense, and he had no one to turn to for advice or even to vent. He was already beyond the experience of his family and friends; he had to find the emotional and intellectual reserves completely within himself.

"I had a tremendous learning curve; I knew very little about business, let alone insurance. I tried to learn as quickly as I could. I really worked at it. I was determined not to be like the first black CIA agent in *The Spook Who Sat by the Door*. Just thinking about that book gave me fortitude. I wanted to be the very best trainee and bring real value to the organization. I thought back to my college track coach saying, 'They put their pants on the same way you do, but you've got to be better.' Mount Union College was only a small school, but he had a way of instilling such a high level of confidence that we over-achieved. He added that little bit of arrogance about what you think you can do. Now I said it to myself, 'Look, I've been successful all my life, I can do this.'

"I made copies of the different manuals, took them home with me and just read them and re-read them. It was tedious reading, but I would try to apply it to a particular risk analysis, a particular fact pattern, so I could remember them. Then I started sitting myself down at someone's desk and saying, 'Well, tell me what you do and what is required to become successful in your job.' I think it was difficult for them to say, 'Go away,' when it was their program, and after a while I think they got used to me. I showed a great deal of enthusiasm, and I guess I was hard to dislike. I read everything in sight and talked to everyone. I really became a student of the insurance business. I knew the manuals, I knew the classifications, I knew the terms, I knew the coverages and pricing. Later, when I started dealing with brokers and sharing my knowledge with them, they began to use me as a reference point. My knowledge became of value in terms of satisfying the customer, and no one could take that away from me."

Through enthusiasm and common sense, Green developed "Brand Green." After he had studied everything on his own, he turned to the in-house experts for their knowledge. Talking to them was also an excellent strategy for establishing relationships with company leaders. Reaching out gave him the opportunity to learn more, and, at the same time, he let people know, in a confident but nonboastful manner, the success of his own studies. Later, when he began working on his own, taking calls from brokers in the field, he had all the answers they needed. The news spread that Green could be counted on to help them look better to their customers, and he started to get referrals. He was gaining respect within the organization's operating network, and he was bringing in new business.

Twenty years later, when **Kim Green** arrived for the Chubb training program, she "expected to conquer their world, to rock their socks," to be the top trainee in her class of thirty.

"I was one of only three women, one other black and an older French-Canadian woman who had been in a different industry. They asked the other African-American woman to leave even before the training was over, so I felt additional pressure. The training class had a strong Northeast presence—Harvard, Yale, Princeton, etc.—and at least half of them had a Chubb connection. And then there was me. Hampton. 'Hampton? What's that?' I knew they thought they had nothing to worry about with me. So I smiled to myself, 'Watch out, bucko.' P. S., I worked my tail off.

"I knew from my summer at P&G that these training programs were serious tests. The senior people watched you twenty-four/seven, and not just the managers. Even the chairman, the president, and the department heads sat in. They knew who you had lunch with, what position you played in the softball game, what you ate for dinner, and they made it very clear they were watching everything. During class, they sat in the back of the room taking notes. So it was a very competitive environment, and presentation of case study material and class participation were very important. I felt some of the eyes were focused on me, and I know I raised a few eyebrows because of my firm handshake and eye contact. But I wanted them to know I was ready and serious. Fortunately, I was one of the top trainees in the class, by all criteria, and I was assigned to the flagship office, New York City."

Circumstances had changed in the twenty years since the 1960s. Green had an excellent education and the benefit of corporate internships. She was not alone in the class or, more significantly, at the company. But some things had not changed, for example, the attitudes of many of her colleagues: "You are separate; you are different; you don't know very much; and we don't need to worry about you as any real competition." A critical difference for Green, however, was that she was not even annoyed by other people's low expectations of her. They simply spurred her competitive spirit. In fact, she still revels in the surprise she knows she will spring.

Green also has a finely tuned ability to read her environment. No one had to tell her the training program was more than a chance to learn the business. It was a very important test. When she saw the senior people sitting in, and her male counterparts outdoing each other, she jumped right in. How many women, minority or not, would have had the confidence to respond with the same gusto? And another question: How many women, or minority men, for that matter, would have felt comfortable or been accepted displaying such aggressive behavior? In positioning herself for top honors, Green clearly read her environment and herself. She made quite a favorable mark from day one.

Frank Fountain beame a master at the corporate game. Although he did not start that way, he was able from the beginning to put his personal stamp on every assignment. When he started in finance at Chrysler, by his own account, he "created his own program." Even early in his career he had a keen sense of what was important to learn. "I was part of a high-potential group of five people, and we were supposed to have three rotating assignments in the first year. I wasn't around more than three months when they said, 'Well, now we'd like you to take a permanent assignment someplace.' So I said, 'I accepted this job because of three rotations. That made sense to me, and I'm not changing.' I didn't know it then, but they were just trying to get the whole group off the personnel budget and onto different department budgets, and they could only do that if we each took a permanent assignment. But for some reason they left me alone."

While Fountain's decisions at that time were the product of a limited field of vision, his mind was always picking up new information. As soon as he saw limitations in a plan, he changed it. "I decided later on my own I wanted to slow the rotation down, because I didn't want to leave the budget department until we finished the capital budget. It didn't make sense to me to leave in the middle. I only wanted to do that budget once, so I stayed five months on that assignment."

Soon he changed his plan again. "When one of the budget people I was working for became controller of one of the major assembly plants, he asked to have me assigned to him. I wanted the plant experience, and I'd completed the budget cycle. After a few months he wanted me to stay there permanently, which meant I wouldn't continue to rotate. By now I was ready to settle. First of all, I had figured out that when you go to a department for only a few months, you don't get the serious assignments, and I wanted serious assignments. Also I had experience in the budget department of the controller's office, and now I wanted the same experience in a plant. And I wanted to stay there long enough to learn what was going on, so I didn't have to come back later. I basically created my own program."

Fountain began to get a feel for how the organization operated and where he might fit in. No one explained it to him; he kept all his senses on alert, watched how other people operated, observed reactions to his behavior and how things worked together. He drew from his lifetime of figuring things out on his own, and he was comfortable doing that. As we have seen, it didn't always lead him to the right conclusion the first time, but he kept moving, picking up more data, refining his skills, consciously making a mark.

Before long he found an opportunity to make a more lasting and very unusual impact. "One of my first Thanksgivings there I got a telegram saying, 'There's no need to show up to work. We'll call you when we want you to come back.' I had been laid off. And I remember thinking, 'Well, I really screwed this one up. It wasn't that long ago I had an office in Washington with an antique desk and lamp, and now, after Wharton and an MBA, I am in an unemployment line in Detroit.' But everyone told me this was temporary, because of the cycles in the industry. So I went to work every day as if nothing had happened. I figured the work would still need to be done when we got back, so there was no point in losing the time. After all, this was the year-end closing at the plant, and we had to do the books and the records. I needed that experience, and I only wanted to do it once." Some called his desire to work for no pay "wacky," but others at Chrysler say it made him "legendary." He was

84

eventually asked to stop, and he agreed to "go along with everybody else." Fountain makes his own reality, but he also knows when he has to bend. It's a matter of reading your specific environment.

Working hard at a job she loved was how **Brenda Lauderback** got noticed at Gimbel's. Since high school she had dreamed of a career in retail and wasted no time once she began. She did well in the training program and landed a plum assignment in ready-to-wear on the main floor. "My career took off because I loved what I was doing. I supervised all the salespeople on the main floor, and I kept them moving. No leaning on the counters, and no standing around. And I'd work along with them. 'Let's straighten the racks if we're not waiting on customers.' We always had things to do.

"The executives regularly came down and walked the selling floor. When you're in retail you spend a lot of time there, because that's the first thing your customers see. Of course you can know what's selling from computer sheets, but it's not the same as being on the selling floor. One man—I later found out he was the general merchandise manager for all the commodities on that floor—always wanted to talk to me about the people on the floor, their quotas, the sales. I was always up-to-date on everything. In time our conversations went beyond that selling floor, and eventually I was telling him my dream was to become a buyer. Before long, he said to me, 'You should come into the buying office.' I think I caught his eye because of my discipline."

As with many of our executives, Lauderback was passionate about her business. She didn't just supervise her employees, she worked along with them. It may well have been the discipline that caught the GMM's eye, but it must have been her grasp of everything going on that showed she was ready for the next step. She communicated her goal clearly to the right person.

Many ambitious managers make their mark by learning how their job fits into the larger picture. **Don Brown**'s intellectual curiosity led him to begin to explore beyond his immediate assignment. He did realize soon, though, that others were beginning to be impressed by what he considered just doing his job.

"I wanted to learn as much as I could about not only my particular job, but also all the work around it. For example, I found a guy in finance, took him aside and said, 'I need to learn our accounting system.' No problem. So he taught me that and also how it affected my department, what I was supposed to look for. I thought, 'If I am going to be in business, knowing something about finance is a high priority.' I did the same thing with human resources.

"At each job you get to the point where you feel you've learned so much that you're a master at what you're doing. Then you say, 'Hey, it's time to do something else.' I never rested on my laurels. So every time I'd get about where I wanted to be, I'd get another job, as regular as clockwork.

"Once when we got a new plant manager, I began to see how others saw me. He was looking for someone to be his assistant manager, and I sized up the competition. I thought I was number three on the list, so I said, 'Okay, let him have the job. I'll get the next chance.' I'd already learned how to handle not getting a promotion. When I got offered the job, I said, 'Excuse me?' The plant manager started into a litany of my qualifications, which I had evidently underestimated. 'You're the one person who understands the system, and what you don't know, I'll teach you. But you also have the confidence and respect of the workforce. People in this organization come to you when they have an issue to resolve. And you have a reputation of not trying to step on people as you build your career. I need someone I can depend on, so when I have to be out of this plant doing other things, I don't have to worry or lose sleep at night. I think that's you.'"

Lloyd Trotter's intellectual curiosity also drove him. He speaks from years of management and executive experience. His words point out some pitfalls for those without his perspective, those not yet aware of how every small step is related to the whole. "As I came up, I realized the common denominator among the top people was broad-based experiences, jobs that led to demonstrating broad-based skills and the ability to increase your sphere of influence. That was the key in building a career, expanding your learning and adding value along the way. Every job that looks like a promotion may not be a good job for you. I've seen people derail their careers with what I call 'chimney careers.' You go up very fast, but you're very narrow. Without intending to, you become a specialist. You are blocked, and there's no way to connect the dots to get back. I was lucky in this way. What was fun for me was to find a new job that was a new experience. If a job offered that, even though it was not up, I went for it. I did a lot of different things just because I thought they would be fun to do, and those turned out to be building blocks for broader skills and greater influence.

"I didn't recognize what I was doing then as strategic thinking. It wasn't until I started talking about it with some folks who became mentors that I saw a pattern and put a name to it. But I wouldn't put it into the lucky-guess category either. I have a lot of intellectual curiosity, so I always sought out people and asked them, 'How did you get there?' And when you ask somebody to talk about themselves, they will talk. I don't care how they feel about you, they will talk. I had the right instincts, and I was inquisitive, very aggressive in wanting to know more. I assimilated all the data, and then I was able to do something with it. When I wanted to run a manufacturing plant, it wasn't until I'd been a front line supervisor, a manufacturing and engineering manager, a materials manager. Then I was ready for the plant. I had most of the elements down cold before I went there."

Trotter's moves were not hit or miss. He was relentlessly working to understand his environment, asking questions, showing interest, slowly and deliberately building a resume of experience, and looking for places where he could add value. "I'm not saying there aren't many, many real problems that we all need to work on, but the trick is truly looking at what you can accomplish and giving it that shot. You have to believe you can improve. Giving up is a definite no."

To make your mark in an organization, at some point you have to market yourself. This requires careful reading of other people, the ones you are talking to as well as the ones who are watching you.

Sometimes these opportunities are ready-made, like an annual evaluation. Others you have to spot on your own. **Virgis Colbert** recognized such an opportunity at a retirement party for a colleague.

"I was saying, 'Boy, we'll miss him; he really does a good job.' The plant manager said to me, 'Virgis, you're doing a hell of a job. You're doing a better job than the guy that's retiring.' Then I started looking around and realized, most of the people here are doing less than what's expected of them. I always tried to do the best job I could, no matter what I was doing. Like my father, hauling trash, sweeping the darn garage over and over, telling me, 'Always do your best.' That's what I did when I started as a supervisor, the only black one. I did more than what I thought I was supposed to do. I kept a clean department, had the guys pick up their stuff. I made the numbers, kept the repairs and defects down, and I worked well with the union. I handled the labor situations that came up. I did what I thought I was getting paid to do.

"But some supervisors were missing their blocks and tackles, not really getting the job done. And I said, 'Heck, blocking and tackling isn't too hard. I've been doing that all my life.' If I got rejected for jobs, I just kept going. I'm driven to achieve results. It's performance; it's discipline; it's cleaning your own garage. That conversation at the retirement party showed me that most people's level of expectation wasn't very high. Most people are just do-what-they-can-to-get-by-with types. I'm oversimplifying, but the point is, if you do more than what's expected, other people look at it as something above and beyond. Then you've got all the opportunities in the world. And that made me start thinking. It put everything in a totally different context for me."

Soon he was looking for opportunities. "If you're interacting with other divisions and you notice something missing, you can go in and do it. It doesn't necessarily have to be in your area of responsibility. You just do it. It can be dangerous, so you have to be selective. You have to know the politics of it. The politics could be that you do it and don't let anybody know about it, or that you let the right one or two people know about it. You don't write a letter or send an e-mail and copy a list of people." As Colbert realized, there are no rules, except that you must do it. Every situation is different, and you must figure out what is the right tactic at that moment for your specific circumstances in order to make your mark.

While recognizing the dangers Colbert describes, **Lloyd Trotter** also stressed the importance of getting credit where credit is due. He attributes his tact in this delicate process to some of his childhood experiences. "The trick is to make sure you get credit for your part in what's being accomplished. And that's a fine line we all walk, not just African Americans or females, it's true for everyone. I think for me it was some luck and just my own ability to persuade people. It wasn't something I read a book about or that someone coached me on. Being under the microscope at my father's church helped, because I learned how to make people see me favorably. Being involved in sports helped, because I learned how to motivate people to work together."

Trotter has figured out how to get noticed in the right way. Given this skill and his excellent performance, promotions were inevitable. The opposite is also true. When you do not get yourself noticed, even the best performance does not lead to promotions. Trotter has a saying to describe this too-narrow performance strategy: "Show me an individual who does a good job and nothing else, and I'll show you an individual who will do the same good job almost forever."

He is constantly looking for opportunities. Here is one example of how he acts: "I have something I call the 'elevator drill.' If you were on the elevator with the CEO for eight seconds, that's the time it takes to get from the second floor to the third floor, how are you going to get him to notice you? Or are you going to miss the opportunity? That's what you've got to work on."

Seizing these opportunities requires constant preparedness. **Sy Green** learned that lesson not at work but from his minister. "One thing I always remember, and I use this a great deal, was you need to have a prayer in one back pocket and a sermon in the other. And my minister meant that literally, because you never knew when you would be asked to get up and either talk about something or to deliver an opening or a closing prayer. You learned to do that, because you knew you were going to be called upon. That helped a great deal in platform skills."

As a beginner in international sales at Salomon Brothers, **Milt Irvin** made his mark partly thanks to his clients. "I started learning from my clients. At that point in time, people believed that some banks had all the information, and everybody thought Salomon walked on water. So, the clients were always trying to let you know how smart they were, bragging about how much they knew. I'd write notes. Then when I spoke to the next customer, I'd tell him what the last guy just told me, and then he'd tell me more. Over time, I developed a pretty good rap, and these guys never knew that I was parlaying what they were saying. With that I began to gain some confidence, and I started making some decent sales. I was selling a lot of products for a guy in London, so he and I became pretty close. I was making him look good."

When Irvin landed his first big trade, he achieved maximum impact for the announcement through perfect timing and orchestration, exactly the right strategy for the Wall Street environment. "The best trade I did was a real epic. I don't know what made me announce it that way, but it was an epic. We were doing an underwriting for Banco de la Nacion in Argentina, a floating rate bond. This was around 1980, and nobody wanted to buy Argentina or anywhere in Latin America, for that matter. We were about to lose a lot of money, even though it was only a $50 million deal.

"I had been working to develop a relationship with a Japanese bank for the longest time. I had figured out that most salespeople covering Japanese clients left early, so I would start having in-depth conversations with my Japanese clients between six and seven in the evening. That's six or seven in the morning, Tokyo time. I said, 'I figure you are always busy during the day, so this might be a good time to talk to you.' I knew they weren't very busy then. They just had to be there when their bosses came in, so it was a great time to get them. I could explain all about deals, I could tee everybody up. Then one night, one of them said, 'I will take nine million of those Argentinas.' I said, 'What?' He said, 'I'll take nine million.' I said, 'Whoa. Great. Done deal.' And I confirmed everything to him.

"When I got in the next morning, it must have been seven or so, I told the guy next to me, I got nine million of these Argentinas done. The guy was shocked, and he said, 'Why don't you go tell everybody?' I said, 'I'm waiting until 10:00.' By 10:00 everything is abuzz, everybody is back from breakfast meetings, the whole floor is filled, and everybody's there in London. So 10:00 in the morning, which is about 4:00 in the afternoon in London, I called my London guy on his desk and told him, 'I got nine million of those Argentinas done.' It spread like wildfire. Next thing I know, the CEO is coming by my desk to congratulate me, the guy who worked on that deal, the guy in charge of all investment banking with Salomon. They all came down and shook my hand. That was a defining moment."

There is no formula, just a mindset that allows you to read your environment accurately, to find the crack in the wall for you to slip through. To the people on the telephone, Irvin was just any American, so his ability was judged purely on the merits—his knowledge and determination. And Wall Street rewards anybody who gets the deal done.

Bridgette Heller's concentration was marketing, and she began calculating her own marketability before she began her first job after business school in 1984. "I remember the recruiter at Johnson & Johnson talking about the first-rate team of people he'd hired from Kraft and P&G, and it started to click for me. Those were the people that were desirable. So I said to him, 'Why wouldn't I want to be one of those people? Why wouldn't I go to Kraft instead of to Johnson & Johnson? Because three years from now, nobody's going to be saying, 'Gee, I want the person from Johnson & Johnson.' They're going to be saying, 'I want the person from Kraft,' just like you are. He really didn't have a comeback for that. It seemed to me J&J, with its unsophisticated, male-dominated marketing culture, needed me more than I needed them."

Heller viewed her first job as an additional credential, a post-MBA degree. It turned out to be pretty smart reasoning. "Basically, by talking to other people I got the idea that I needed to have the strongest resume of credentials possible. So I saw my first job as another degree. Going to Kraft Foods meant making sure I mastered the solid core of marketing. They would teach me raw skills, and saying I went through that training would give me credibility."

Heller had an awareness of what would allow her to have the greatest impact down the road. She knew the best credentials are more important for minorities, where any weakness can be marched out to exclude or eliminate you from the competition. Heller was on the right track. She took her own advice and went to Kraft, where she indeed made a mark.

Any strategy for making your mark carries risk. How do you talk yourself into taking what may be a major risk? Although everyone says no one achieves greatness without mistakes, what does that mean for African Americans? The consequences of making mistakes are undoubtedly more severe. Your colleagues, managers, and even the people who work for you are likely to focus more on your mistakes. Unfortunately, the stereotypes of "not good enough," "not smart enough," and "too cautious" rear their heads quickly. Are you fearful you are less well prepared, or have you somehow bought into the myths yourself? You will never get beyond these concerns unless you try.

Keep an eye out for assignments that have the potential to bring career-making visibility. **Chuck Chaplin** used the time-honored strategy of volunteering for such an assignment. He worked on the Macy's leveraged buyout. It was a leap into the abyss for him, but he acted with confidence, worked extraordinarily hard, and took everything one step at a time. This assignment brought the exposure that catapulted him into a senior position.

"About a week before Christmas the president of the mortgage company called looking for a volunteer to work with Prudential corporate. None of the people senior to me, the more logical choices, were either available or interested. I was. I knew squat about LBOs and I knew squat about working with corporate. I did know it was something important because the president of the company was asking, but that was all I knew. Some of this stuff is luck, right? You've got to take your motivation where you can get it. You're not always all-seeing, all-knowing. There are many waves on the ocean of life. All you've got to do is find one and surf it.

"I told my boss, 'Man, please let me go. I mean, let's rock and roll!' He told me, 'Chuck this is b.s. This is never going anywhere. You're going to end up sitting here over the holidays, and it's going to be a waste of time. But if you want to do it, I'm not going to stand in your way.' So he called corporate and said, 'One of the guys here is interested in doing it.' 'Who?' 'Chuck Chaplin.' 'Who the hell is that?' I didn't even know how many levels were between me and that guy on the phone.

"So I went over to corporate—it's right across the street from my field office—and met with the president, other senior henchmen, and some bankers from Goldman Sachs. 'Here's what we need to do, this and this and this and this.' The guy from Goldman Sachs handed me a disk and said, 'We need to appraise all the properties Macy's owns, and it's all on the disk.' I said, 'Sure, no problem, I got it. When do you need it?' 'A week from tomorrow.' 'I can handle that. If I have any problems, I'll get back to you.'

"Sounded great, but I felt terrible. I had no idea how to do any of the things that they said needed to be done. I didn't even know how to open the file, let alone analyze the data on the spreadsheet. This was 1985, and we had just received our first PC in the office, one, and we all shared it. So I got the Lotus manual, broke down the PC, put it in my car, took it home and started trying to figure it all out.

"Then I got a little lucky. A woman who'd just graduated from

Columbia Business School popped into the office one day. She was supposed to be home in the Philippines, but she hadn't left yet. I said, 'Terry, you know PCs. Please help me.' She gave me a quick primer on Lotus and some ideas on how to approach the data, because she'd had a similar case study at Columbia. So I went home, sat down, went through the stuff again, and came up with a theoretical framework for the appraisal. I didn't know if it was right. I didn't know if it was consistent with accepted professional practice or anything like that. I didn't have time to go and research exactly how people value stores. But over the course of the week I'd convinced myself that the approach I came up with made sense.

"The president, unbeknownst to me, had asked a couple of other people to look at the same data, just to think about it. So when we went back into the meeting, those people talked first. They said basically, 'We can't do it. It's not like anything we do. We can't come close to the dollars. It doesn't make any sense because of this, this, and this.' I said, 'If you look at the value in layers—there's a layer that's really safe, then a layer that's less safe, and so on—if you can be comfortable about getting paid for those different layers, you can do it. You look at the components, and you figure out how to price the risk associated with lending more against these assets than you ordinarily would.'

"I sort of knew my analysis was part of the way people were doing the new real estate securities at that time. But I probably didn't understand as much of what I was saying as they were receiving, you know what I mean? And I'm sure there were other people at Prudential then, probably more senior and smarter than me, who could have done the analysis also. They just weren't around. So I presented it.

"After what seemed to me a very long pause, the president said, 'You know, this does make some sense. You need to refine it here and there. I don't like the way you looked at this. You've got to firm this up. You've got to meet with the people at Goldman Sachs.' So I did. I'd never met an investment banker before, and I'd certainly never been inside an investment bank. It was like going to the Vatican. I was kind of starstruck, but I tried not to let on. So we worked, and it went back and forth with the seniors. Finally we made a proposal to Goldman, Goldman made a proposal to Macy's, and Macy's said, 'Let's do it.' I didn't know it then, but there had never been a leveraged buyout done this way.

"Goldman had the deal broken up into four pieces. We could buy any one of them, and then we'd get other insurance companies to come in on the other three. I'll never forget this meeting. We're sitting around the coffee table in the vice chairman's office, someone I'd never met before, and he said, 'We'll have more leverage over the company if we do the whole thing, right?' The answer is, 'Of course. When you're leveraged like that, you're really a partner.' And so he said, 'Let's buy the whole thing.' Wow. This was the cowboy 80s, remember? I didn't know then we'd never made a loan this large, and I think it's still the largest loan ever made from one lender to one borrower. Macy's was going to have debt up the wazoo, and we were going to be on the hook for it.

"This back and forth process went on for eight months, and slowly everybody else went back to other work. One of the senior VPs of the mortgage company was sort of supervising me, and I was the helper, but it ended up I was the one left working with Goldman and the lawyers. I went to a meeting, then reported to the senior VP on the phone, and he'd tell me what to do next. So I'd be up all night doing whatever it was he said to do. Then the next morning I sat in the meeting all day, called him and told him what happened, and he told me what to do again. I stayed up all night and went back to the meeting. This went on for a couple of weeks before he told the president what had been going on. 'Chuck is in the meetings by himself?' 'He's doing all right. But now he needs to work with you, because I'm going to be stuck out in California.' So now I was calling the president directly. I'm sure he was talking to plenty of other people trying to keep tabs on what I was doing, and I'm sure somebody else would have stepped in if I was making decisions outside of my authority. But it never happened, and ultimately I got to take on more and more responsibility. I never filled out a time sheet, I never filled out an expense report, nothing. Nothing but Macy's, Macy's, Macy's. I had Macy's coming out of my ears.

"We ended up signing the loan agreement with Macy's on March 8 of 1986. And Macy's handed me a check for our $8 million fee. Whoa, what do I do with this? So I got on the subway and took it back to Newark. Four months later we closed the loan. I got a nice picture of me giving the president and general counsel of Macy's a check for $800 million. It was one of those great moments, certainly the highlight of my career to that day. I ended up getting a couple of great promotions right away, but the notoriety has carried me on and on and on and on."

Chaplin took an incredible gamble, and he knew it, even if at the time he didn't realize the full extent. Driven by his fear of failure, he took it one step at a time and learned as he went along. The particulars of this assignment are long, but they illuminate the step-by-step growth process that will help you acquire skills and build your confidence. Although the project was uncertain at first, its eventual success meant Chaplin had extensive exposure to the most senior people in the company. Taking the risk really paid off. He made his mark, and they did not forget him.

Mannie Jackson had a similar career-making assignment at Honeywell, but he didn't have to volunteer. The chairman dropped it in his lap. "Only a few months after I started at Honeywell, the chairman put me on a five-member team to handle the transition of General Electric Computer, a business we had just acquired in what he called 'a market breakthrough for Honeywell.' At first I didn't get it. I asked him, 'What will I be doing?' He said, 'Any and everything you're asked to do. This team will report directly to me, and I'll meet with you once a month.' The first time I met with the other four guys, I thought, 'I've arrived.' I went back and told the chairman, 'I don't believe you gave me that job.' He said, 'What do you mean, you don't like it?' I said, 'It's a hell of a job,' and I never looked back.

"What a phenomenal opportunity. I was humbled by it. I just

could not believe he gave me that gift. I'm sure there are a number of reasons he did it, and one was probably he thought he could win some points with the government, having a black guy on that high visibility blue-ribbon panel. But I also think he liked me and knew enough about me to know it wasn't going to hurt him. There's a lot on the upside and probably not much on the downside. He rolled the dice, and I got an unbelievable opportunity.

"When you get a chance to have that kind of leverage and you don't blow it, it can carry you through your career. You need to be identified with something valuable. Very early I became identified with handling mergers and acquisitions. It's like Lee Iaccoca with the Mustang. M&As became my Mustang."

Few of you will soon be on a committee of five reporting to the chairman. It's much more likely your breaks will come in smaller increments. Your job is to build each opportunity into something meaningful. **Bob Johnson** remembers his first big assignment. Although it turned out to be a terrible problem, his ability to solve it impressed his boss, the company—and himself.

"I inherited a problem, a real hot potato, but I had to make something out of it. At the time I got it, my boss had no idea it was such a mess. Sears ended up with a huge excess inventory of shoes, most of them off the books. We were stuck with them, and I had to figure out a way to get rid of them. When I realized the extent of the problem, I tried to tell my boss, but he didn't want to listen. 'Get it fixed,' he said. So I collected one sample of each shoe style, set it up in a huge sample room and took him through it. Row after row of shoes. Then he got it. So he assigned the controller to work with me to inventory and cost everything. Then we developed a nationwide program to sell them all. We went out to each market and presented them with a complete program—ad, display, training materials, purchase orders, everything they needed. All the market had to do was sign up. We did it in a year, half the time I had originally projected, and at about 60 percent of my original estimate. We actually made money getting rid of them, because we had such big sales. My boss was very impressed.

"My next move was a big reward: a development job. For one year I got to do anything I wanted, to learn everything about the company I thought would prepare me to be an executive. It was a clear signal I had been tapped for success. This just shows what a company can do for someone it wants to support, in this case an African American."

Jerri DeVard, a young female marketing executive, arrived in corporate America with the ability to handle just about anything. Her business expertise, marketing, is transportable, and she actually enjoys frequent changes, whether from corporation to corporation or from state to state, or both. She made her mark when Travelers acquired Citibank just a few months after she started working at the bank.

"I got a call at home on Sunday from my new boss. 'We're having a meeting on Monday morning at seven. I'd like you to come.' I said, 'Okay, I'll be there.' No questions. I hadn't been there long enough to think the call was weird. Everybody else was like, 'What's up?' To me it was just a regular call. First thing, he says, 'Welcome to your new company. Now we're Citigroup.' I wasn't worried at all, not at all. After my first job, in the commodities world, a bank doesn't seem very risky. I didn't even think about it. Hey, who knows? I asked my boss, 'What does this mean for you, because I signed up for your vision and your view of the world.' He said, 'I don't know what's going to happen to me.' Then two weeks later he was assigned to Latin America.

"A week later I'm sitting in front of my new boss from Travelers. He said, 'Tell me what it is you do? Why are you here?' He listened and said, 'We need to get you a real job, where you can make some money for this organization. I don't think we've harnessed your talent yet. So let's start to work on that.' I saw the handwriting on the wall. The job I'm in won't be here, so I'd better find something else. Unfortunately, I'd only been here for three months by this time, so I hadn't built a lot of relationships.

"I walked into two opportunities very quickly. One was keeping the same job I had, but working for someone else in the retail bank. The other was working on the start-up internet banking division and setting up online banking. Everyone said, 'Do not go there. It's not going to work, they'll never launch it, and it's spending money like water. We're counting paper clips, while they're building technology. There are only a few people over there, and it hasn't gotten senior management endorsement,' and on and on and on. I thought, 'Well, let's see, I could go with the traditional bank and figure out how to eke out another percentage point of market share or how to increase fees. Or I could go to this new division that's potentially a great new business. I thought, 'E-commerce, internet, areas I haven't tried. I'll take the risk.' I went over there, and I liked everybody I met. I mean, they rolled up their sleeves, 'Let's just get this thing done. We're not going to be bogged down with bureaucracy, rules of engagement, long lead times, approvals, meetings. We're just going to do this.' And you know what? We were making it up as we went along. It's like a book we wrote. Chapter One, how to start this. I like that."

You could say DeVard has a high tolerance for risk, or you could say very little seems risky to her. She was attracted by the challenge of a business few expected would ever launch. It proved just the place for her to make her mark.

As you search for a way to make your mark, you may have to live with a few surprises. You may even get thrown in before you are ready. As **Kim Green** learned, you can still win respect. "My third day in the New York office, my first week after the three-week training program, was the day of the managers meeting, and my manager was out of the office. I got volunteered to represent our division. They threw a spreadsheet to me—the IBNR (incurred but not recorded) for our department—and said, 'Here, Kim, I'm sure you'll do fine.' Was this some kind of test to see if they could get me to fail? This meeting was for all the managers of each department to report on their results. You had to explain both positive and negative results, and the numbers meant nothing to me. The training class was designed to prepare you to underwrite—to do financial analysis, case studies, policy language. There was nothing about management reports. I had literally three minutes to figure out what I was going to do in this stressful situation. To say I was extremely nervous is too mild.

"I walked into a room of senior managers. At the head of the table was clearly somebody with a lot of power, because everybody was trying to get his attention. He was the branch manager of the New York office, the largest in the Chubb system. I'm a new trainee. What am I doing here? The branch manager opened the meeting by introducing the visitor—me—and suggested they begin with me. I was sweating, and my stomach was tied up in knots. But I knew I had to rise to the occasion, and I did.

"Thank goodness my father's dry sense of humor was with me. I smiled and opened with a joke: 'I've been with Chubb for twenty-two days, and eighteen of them were in New Jersey. This is my fourth day in New York.' Fortunately they all laughed, so I had a few more seconds to think about my real response. But the most I could do was make fun of what I didn't know. 'Well, I have a spreadsheet in front of me, and this was not included in our training session, so bear with me. I see a negative number in this column, where every other department has a positive number, so our department probably needs to work on bringing that to a positive number.'"

Putting Green in the spotlight at this early point was a signal that the management had identified her as a comer, whether she knew it or not. Her reputation as a star of the training program had undoubtedly reached the head of the New York office. Although her excellent work there was important, she now knew more was required. In this case, she had to demonstrate she could perform with grace under pressure. Some kind of signal that you have been singled out comes to every successful executive, but most people get more than three weeks to prepare.

6.

Managing Relationships

None of us has gotten here on our own. We may have busted our butts, worked extremely hard, made lots of personal sacrifices, and brought some talent and ability to the table. I believe all that is true, but we didn't do it alone. We've all had people who have been there either directly or indirectly and made a difference.

—**Bruce G. Gordon**, Group President
Verizon

BRUCE GORDON expresses a simple but important truth. You must cultivate relationships at your corporation with those who will give you honest feedback on your performance and behavior as well as critical information on company priorities and trends. You need to find people who value you, your work, and your future in the corporation.

Lloyd Trotter reached the same conclusion but expresses it differently. "The network matters the most. A career is about doing a good job plus something else, and the something else is the network. You've got to force yourself to network, especially if you are a minority. You've got to decide to participate, even the going-away parties, at lunch, and on weekends. You can't socialize only with those you feel most comfortable with. You've got to go out and network." Trotter learned what **Cleve Killingsworth** learned at MIT: There is little to be gained when a small group keeps itself separate and apart from the larger organization.

Those most likely to succeed in an organization engage daily in the process Gordon and Trotter describe. Networking can be difficult, but you cannot allow the belief you are an outsider to hold you back. A formal mentoring program can break the ice for you and provide early opportunities to begin learning how the organization really works, but it is still up to you to cultivate those relationships that can exert a positive impact on your career. Potential allies appear in as many different relationships as human beings can conceive: long term, short term, sporadic, constant, easy, difficult, intense, distant—and they can be found at any level and at any time in the organization.

How do you go about cultivating those relationships, finding support, and building a network? Steps can be as simple as a phone call or e-mail to a key person with a question after a meeting. Or knowing someone's interest and copying her on a report or memo, or sending someone information he needs, even though he didn't ask you for it. Sometimes it is introducing yourself to someone at an event and striking up a conversation, **Lloyd Trotter**'s elevator drill in another venue. When Walter Wriston of Citibank gave a talk at Harvard Law School, **Lawrence Jackson,** an undergraduate, was the only student who stayed to talk with him afterwards. Wriston and Jackson remained in contact because of Jackson's efforts. You will connect with some in small groups around a work issue, but you must be the one to follow up. Become a sponge for information that expands your database and refines your observations about people and the organization. Be on the alert for circumstances where you can interact with the right people, for topics on which you can connect. You must extend yourself across race, class, gender, and age barriers.

A key aspect of managing relationships is learning to trust the organization and the individuals within it. Trust only develops over time. In relationships with white colleagues, trust can be even more difficult to come by. Past experiences may have caused you to look through a lens of distrust. You should not abandon that lens because there are times when it will serve you well in the corporate environment, but you also need to add many filters to that lens. You need to learn when to trust if you are to be successful.

When **Lloyd Trotter**'s manager sent him to Iowa to run a large plant, he learned how important a supportive relationship can be. It was his first real opportunity to lead, to run a business segment, so it was an important move. To his great surprise, it turned out to be one of his most rewarding assignments. "I was in the middle of the corn fields, where the black population was 1 percent. I was a little bit nervous, but my manager, who was from the Midwest, said, 'You don't have to worry about a thing. It's going to be a great assignment for you. Here in the East, people say yes when they mean no. They tell you they want the whole truth, but they're not willing to deal with it. The Iowa farmers mean what they say. If they say they're not going to do something, they're not going to do it. But if they say they are, they're going to try like nobody you've ever seen in your life.'

"And he was right. They accepted me. They knew my manager and had a lot of affection for him, so they started by saying, 'If he sent you, we believe you have talent and skill.' They had a different work ethic and in some ways a totally different mindset about diversity than I had ever encountered in my life or my career. These people were willing to apply their value system without regard to my color. All I had to do was be worthy of their work ethic. People are full of surprises, and we're always learning. That's what I encountered, and we were able to accomplish an awful lot together."

Trotter must have felt at least a twinge of regret that his first real opportunity was in Iowa, but he took the leap. Fortunately he was open enough, partially because he had decided to trust his boss, to work at seeing Iowans as individuals. He was able to capitalize on the Midwestern work ethic.

Don Brown's wary response to a compliment early in his career may be typical for many of you, even though you probably have a good deal more knowledge than he had in 1970. "In one of my first few performance reviews, my supervisor said, 'You're going to go far in this company.' I had no idea what he was talking about. What does that mean? Quite honestly, I thought he was giving me a line. I didn't even know what a vice president was at that time, let alone what it meant to be someone who could lead some significant piece of the organization. I was a naive kid. I had a job I liked, and I just wanted to do it better than anyone else who'd ever done it before. That was all. I really didn't even think about trying to influence someone's opinion."

One of the most straightforward situations in which to establish trust is a work assignment, yet even there Brown was wary. If a manager urges you to take on further responsibilities, it is generally a sign that the person in the best position to evaluate your work has seen beyond the stereotype. If you succeed in those new assignments, you have probably found a valuable supporter.

Brown eventually believed that his managers respected his work and that there were indeed white people who were capable of evaluating him as an individual. "The ironic thing about my career is that my breaks all came from white people I would never have expected to help me. The first big break I had was given to me by a Welshman, the second by a guy who grew up in Mississippi. And the biggest break I ever had was given to me by a guy who grew up in South Africa. That's why I maintain the belief that most people are really good. There are people out there who are going to have an opinion about you. There may even be people who treat you nice but still have some problems with race. But in corporate America, most people need good people working with them. They are not fools. They look around and say, 'Hey, who's doing the best job? Who's going to make me look good?' They didn't let the fact of where I come from stand in the way."

Marc Belton didn't realize it was possible for whites to regard him as an individual until he went to France. During a semester abroad in college he lived with a French family and had a French girlfriend. "I began to understand the box I was in was self-imposed. It was very much like the response of the expatriate blacks who left the U.S. for Paris in the 1950s. I went places, and folks treated me like a regular person. The experience allowed me to grow culturally. I got a worldview instead of a view-of-the-world." These experiences allowed him to cultivate supportive relationships when he got to corporate America. **Bridgette Heller** turned her wariness of whites into an advantage: "I always think growing up black in the South prepared me well for corporate America. I knew how to read between the lines. I knew who to trust and who not to trust."

Evaluate white colleagues' mistakes within the context of the full relationship. **Milt Irvin** remembers problems he had with the high school track coach, someone he not only admired but also valued for his personal support. "We were preparing for a winter track meet, and he said, 'Now, colored people (he still used the word colored) really don't like the cold, but you guys are special because you go to Essex Catholic.' What he meant was, you can beat these other all-black schools. On the one hand it inspired us. But after the meet, when I thought about it, I was really distraught. I didn't feel he did it in a malicious manner, but here was somebody who was close to me, a supporter trying to help me get through school, but he just didn't really see the picture.

"I didn't confront him then, but I told him that story last year, when he was finally being inducted into our school's Hall of Fame. He did remember saying something like that, 'Jeez, in retrospect, it wasn't so good.' I said, 'In retrospect, the school made a mistake when you weren't the first coach inducted into the Hall of Fame.' And now he's in and we play golf together." Learning to trust against the backdrop of insensitive comments is frustrating for everyone, but every aspiring African-American manager must find ways to keep such comments from derailing a career. Allow the relationships to be human, and work to maintain them. Find those who value your contribution and want you to succeed. As difficult as it can seem initially, you must seek common ground with your white colleagues, to identify potential allies.

These stories emphasize your personal responsibility in cultivating and managing key relationships. This is the best way to make yourself a part of the company's collective pool of information, where you can sift the real, and therefore useful, information from unfounded gossip, and unobjective observations or experiences of others. In any organization, you are deluged with information, so you need to be sure your conclusions are based on fact rather than presumed "facts."

Understand that senior managers and executives want and need to know junior managers. They are constantly on the lookout for new talent. That's their job. Help them perform it. If you have done your homework and picked the right time, you are not likely to be rejected. Everyone ambitious is trying to be recognized. This is not "ass-kissing." It is an essential skill.

Start with Your Boss

The most logical place to begin a career-building relationship is with the person to whom you report. Whether or not this manager becomes or remains one of your supporters, that relationship is an excellent laboratory for you.

As a first step in understanding this most basic relationship, look at your boss as a person. What is her managerial style? How does he resolve conflicts? Is she conflict averse, asking others to resolve her conflicts? Does he seek consensus, making certain all sides understand? How does she arrive at the ingredients for decisions? Does he trust himself, or does he pass decisions on to his boss? Is she willing to make hard choices, even though they may be unpopular? How does he communicate his decisions? What are her performance strengths and weaknesses?

How does your boss define successful performance? Does your work match that criteria? What are his thoughts, feelings, and perceptions on issues critical to you, such as race and gender? What are her priorities? Are they in line with company priorities? Have you asked enough questions to know? Does he work for a difficult person? What do you know about her personal lifestyle and outside interests? Does she share any of that? These questions help you see ways to connect or issues to avoid. Finally, if your boss is non-white and/or female, as is increasingly possible at lower levels, how does that affect your analysis? Do you find yourself making certain assumptions about that person and your relationship?

There are no right or wrong answers to any of these questions, and no single answer will be definitive. Keeping these issues in mind as you observe and interact will improve your ability to analyze objectively and to communicate, with your current boss and with the many others you will have in your career. This process never ends, and your job is to stay on the case.

Now move to another perspective. Observe the way your boss interacts with you. Does he check your work closely or leave you on your own? How are expectations about work assignments communicated to you? What is your impression of her regard for you, separate and apart from your performance? Is it adversarial, trusting, supportive? What is the quality of the relationship?

Receiving honest feedback on your performance is critical, but many managers are uncomfortable giving it. One of **Bridgette Heller**'s reports once said to her at the end of an evaluation, "No one's ever done that for me before." What kind of feedback does your boss give you, and in what context? Does she just wait for formal performance reviews? Some bosses make this easy. For example, **Jerri DeVard** never waits till the end of the yeár. "What good does that do me?" she asks. If your boss is not so inclined, can you find ways to engage with him, so you have opportunities to get feedback regularly, when you need it? Can you find ways to make the evaluations interactive, so you can get answers to the questions you consider critical? Are there things you can or should do to influence your performance appraisal? Think back to how **Kim Green** handled her first evaluation. Because these evaluations are so important in your career, you must constantly be on the alert for ways to bring more control and clarity to the process.

At her first corporate performance evaluation after graduate school, **Elynor Williams** had a tough time. But she assessed the situation, developed a strategy, and succeeded in turning the tables a year later. "At my first review, my boss told me I couldn't speak, write, or communicate effectively in any way. These were all the basic skills necessary for me to do my job, so I was really stunned. Although I didn't believe him—after all, I had a master's degree in communication arts from Cornell—I spent the next year writing for the company newspaper and working with one of the best editors in the business. My feature stories were so good the editor gave me a byline, which was unheard of for a stringer, especially a woman, in those days. I started accepting speaking engagements anywhere; you name it, I was there. I wrote speeches for other people. I did my homework. So at the next annual review, when my boss started the same nonsense, I called his hand. I showed him the newspapers with my byline, because I knew my boss felt the editor was excellent. I showed him letters praising my speeches from other people my boss knew and respected. I was ready. My boss turned beet red and started stuttering. I walked right out of his office and went across the hall to the human resources EEO manager. Although I only went over there to ask if she wanted to go to lunch, sometimes a veiled threat of authority is enough. I got a better performance rating that year."

Equally important is being open to honest feedback, even when it's negative. Make certain you are not defensive. If constructive criticism makes you angry at the messenger, your boss, you may lose important information and miss out on an early chance to improve your performance.

Now look at the relationship from yet another angle. What are your boss's promotional opportunities within the company, as far as you can tell? What is her support base? Who are his mentors, sponsors, or supporters? How does she interact with her boss? What is your assessment of his career history and future in the organization? Can you link your own career interests to hers? What are your promotional opportunities if he values your work? Can you find ways to make her look good, as a strategy for cementing the relationship?

Also, analyze your boss's place in the overall business environment. What is his organizational intelligence? Is she politically savvy? Does he share his observations and insights with you? Where is she in relation to the power and influence in your department? In the total organization? What has been his contribution, and is it known and valued? Is she senior executive potential? Is his work vital to the company, but he's not likely to move up? Even in this case, you have much to learn from him. **Cleve Killingsworth** learned how to analyze issues and present the most cogent argument from a boss he knew would always remain the head of research. **Chuck Chaplin** is eternally grateful to the person who gave him his start but would never move up because he could not accept the importance of developing good people skills.

Relationships with managers cannot all be good, and if there are initial problems, do not assume they cannot be fixed. **Bruce Gordon** remembers finding a boss impossible for quite a while, only to learn later that the problem stemmed from the very difficult manager his boss reported to. Other times you may learn your boss has made a misstep and is working to recover lost ground. He may have been a valuable team player who is now marking time until retirement. Even if you do not click, it is still on your shoulders to make the relationship neutral or keep it from turning sour. People will turn to your former managers for opinions about you and your work for years to come. Others will notice how you handle relationships, good and bad. Your ability to neutralize a bad situation speaks volumes about your maturity, character and flexibility. Many managers have received promotions based on handling someone known by the organization to be difficult.

As you assess your managers, make sure you develop your own balanced view, where the picture is painted with information from many sources over time. Never rely on just one impression, only a few interactions, or even several stories. Striving for a balanced view is a continual process, one that allows you to recognize positives and negatives in the style and performance of both you and your managers. You do not want to fall into the trap you abhor others setting for you: stereotyping your boss and not seeing him or her as an individual. The following stories illustrate how three executives handled difficult situations with bosses early in their careers.

Alana Robinson butted heads with her first boss, but not immediately. The experience was particularly painful for her, because he knew her when she was a student and recruited her directly from Grambling. He also praised her highly when she ranked third in IBM's nationwide special training course and promoted her as a reward. But then she began to notice a change. "One of my early Dallas assignments was to teach customers about our telecommunications products. At that time there were hardly any women on the technical side, and I was probably the only black woman. I taught everything from concepts and facilities through programming and problem solving. There was no question I was adding value, because the customers had to rate us every week, and I was always the top. It wasn't subjective, it wasn't my opinion, there was something very concrete to point to. It was really clear.

"At first I felt safe with my boss, but then I started noticing that every conversation I had with him, he emphasized the fact I was a black female, different from the norm. With him, everything in its minutest form broke down to the fact that I was a black female. I couldn't do the things the white guys did. He said, 'I can't promote you now because the other guys will think I'm doing special favors for you.' But I had a great relationship with the eleven white males. My issue was not with them, it was only with our boss. That's when I realized, 'Gosh, I'm dealing with a dishonest person.'

"I wanted to resolve this with my boss, because he had given me my great start. Also I was a Christian, so how could I be a good Christian and have such conflict with him? It was just that literal. I even told him one day, 'Gosh, I'm not the same little green-eyed girl you tapped out of Grambling. I've grown up a little bit. I have a family. I have a baby. I have bills.' But I wasn't getting anywhere with him.

"Then I turned to one of my mentors for advice. She was a white woman who had been my manager in Louisiana before she moved to headquarters in New York. She had always taken a personal interest in me and my career, and I continued to talk with her. With her help I realized that I, in an honest, proactive way, had to put my reality on the table and hope that the right thing would happen. I kept a diary of every encounter with my boss. Later my mentor was the little birdie that told one of her managers at headquarters that he should talk with me, that I was somebody with value. She even counseled me on how to have the conversation with this big muckety-muck from headquarters and how to organize my thoughts and be honest. But I didn't know when or if he was coming.

"One night I was in Houston teaching my regular class, and I got a call at about 11 P.M. in my hotel room. I had already talked to my husband, so I was, like, 'Who's calling me here?' It was my secretary in the Dallas office, a Jewish woman. She was just a wonderful person, and she knew I was having difficulty with the boss. She said, 'I can't sleep. The boss is about to pull a fast one on you tomorrow.' I said, 'What do you mean?' As usual, I was too naive to have a clue. She said, 'He's going to call you tomorrow to verify you're still on vacation next week. But what he's not going to tell you is the IBM executive from New York is coming and has asked to have a one-on-one with you.'

"Sure enough, he called the next day. 'Oh, hi, Alana, how are you?' I said, 'Just wonderful.' And he said, 'I'm doing some vacation plans, I just wanted to verify that you're not going to be here next week.' I said, 'Oh, I had to change my plans. My husband had a conflict, so I'll be there. You can count on me.' There was a lot of silence on the other end of the phone. Finally he said, 'Well, then, I've got a great opportunity for you. Someone from headquarters is coming to town, and I thought it would be nice for you to sit down and have some quiet time with him.' I said, 'I'm so grateful. I really do appreciate that. I'm really looking forward to it.'

"Of course I was very nervous, because I had never done anything like this before and because I was probably going to face some retaliation. But my one-on-one went very well. I used my diary to go logically through my encounters with my boss. By the time I finished, the New York executive was shocked that I had all these problems and, lo and behold, that I had kept a record. Of course my boss thought I had betrayed him. Maybe he sincerely believed he was doing the right thing for me, just in his way. It was almost like: You say you love me, but you're not loving me the way I need to be loved. As of the next pay period, I got a 17.5 percent increase and a promotion. I said, 'Well, thank you. I appreciate that. I can check that one off on my list now.' He said, 'Aren't you excited? That's probably the biggest raise you'll ever get.' I said, 'Of course I'm always glad to earn more money, but I'd be more excited if it were retroactive. I'd rather get my 2 percent or 3 percent every year the way I ought to. If I get another 17.5 percent raise, that means somebody else has shortchanged me.'

"I'm not sure where I got the strength to believe I could do something proactive to change my circumstances. Being that way, of course, has pluses and minuses. But for better or worse, I think it comes from my idealism. I believe honesty is the right thing. I have a quote in my office from Dr. King: 'It's always the right time to do what's right.' To me that's so fitting for who I am and how I behave. It doesn't always work, but that's where I start. Fortunately I got promoted out of that office. Somebody actually pulled me right out."

It took real moral courage for a young southern black woman to go over her boss's head twenty-five years ago, and Robinson did not take the decision lightly or precipitously. In the face of overt racial and gender provocation, she studied her situation carefully and tried everything within her own power to explain it away and to find a remedy. Neither her religion nor the gentle but firm persuasion she had perfected in her relationship with her father helped her. She could not influence her boss, as least on this issue. When she knew she was stumped and knew she had no career if she could not get past this obstacle, she reached out to a former manager, a white woman with whom Robinson had actively maintained contact. Together they devised a very specific and aggressive plan.

Robinson's plan carried great risk. Her influential supporter was far away. When she met in Texas with the New York executive, she had to decide very quickly—on the fly—whether or not to trust him. In addition, she had only a short time to convince him of her value. Then he would be gone, and she would be out there alone, with little or no cover and a humiliated boss. If her plan had failed, she could have lost everything when he retaliated. She prepared her data carefully, practiced her presentation, trusted her mentor, and took the leap.

Robinson used Martin Luther King's words to inspire her. Without the attribution, **Frank Fountain** holds to a similar philosophy: "There are certain things you don't accept, and it doesn't matter what motivated the person." **Ira Hall**, a seasoned civil rights activist, relies on his own experiences to give him the same courage: "Ultimately justice will prevail, so be on the side of justice. And I have found standing up for justice seldom brings the negative consequences most people fear." It was certainly true in Robinson's case.

Jerri DeVard's lesson in managing her boss was more straightforward. After a four-year run in marketing at Pillsbury starting in the mid-1980s, with stellar performance and regular promotions, she found herself with a boss who challenged everything she did. This challenge came at a time when the pyramid was beginning to narrow; there were not as many promotions to go around. It was no longer enough for her simply to focus on an excellent work product. She had to become more politically sophisticated. For someone as outspoken and independent as DeVard, this was a problem initially. Fortunately she found a mentor. "I had to enter the political realm, and an angel helped me navigate. My angel had just arrived as the first African-American director for Pillsbury, a very strong woman and very bright, not only about business but about the world. I learned so much from her, beginning with how to manage my boss. She said, 'Well, okay, I know something about this individual and how he thinks. Let me tell you a little bit about how you can handle that.' I started thinking from a different perspective, and it was very useful.

"Up until then everything had been just great. I spent all of my time running the business, head down, saying, 'Okay, my results will speak for themselves.' I never, ever put any energy into managing my boss. I just hopped on the bike and rode it. I didn't stop and say, 'Maybe this is a mountain bike. Maybe this has four wheels.' I never managed up, or was even just a little bit deferential, like saying, 'That's a good point. I hadn't thought about that.' My whole thing was, 'Why would we do that? I mean, what more hoops can I jump through?' 'Well, these, now that you mention it.' That was difficult for me. I had to understand how my boss made decisions and recommendations and change my old way of doing things. I had to learn to work with him on his terms in order to accomplish what I needed to accomplish.

"Although part of me asked, 'Why do I have to prove this to you?' most of me said, 'I'm going to be promoted, and I'm going to do whatever it takes. I'm going to be relentless about proving to you I deserve this.' I refused to quit because in my mind that would have been out and out failure. I don't know if race and gender were factors, but I don't think so. I think it was truly that I had not demonstrated to him I was ready. Then he left the company. I got a new boss, and I was happy until it was time for the next promotion, and the same thing started again. I've seen this movie before. I turned myself inside out to get that promotion, too."

DeVard's honesty and bravado allowed her to move quickly beyond race and gender as obstacles. As a "second-generation" African-American manager, she was able to turn to a black mentor for advice, and a woman, too. She is under no illusion that all her mentors must be black, but it was a great solace to have one, especially for this instance. Her description of why she valued this mentor is instructive for another reason. In reverse, it explains why blacks are cautious in reaching out to whites. "I didn't have to filter. I didn't have to second-guess. She helped me by telling me things that no one else would or could, because there was a trust. I could accept anything she said at face value. There was no ulterior motive. And it was great."

Cultivating Support

If you learn to manage your relationships with different bosses and then a number of other people, you can build the more complex and effective network to support your rise in an organization. Here is how **Al Little** used supporters to turn around a disappointment at work.

"Generally in life I've been able to turn my anger or disappointment at something at work into a positive strategy. On a few occasions, I have thought that missing out on a promotion was unfair treatment. I even thought race might have played a part in some decisions. As angry as I sometimes felt, each time I said to myself, 'I have choices. I can challenge the decision, I can look for another job, or I can think it through and decide how to overcome it.' The first time was when I was hired as assistant manager for industrial relations at a plant, and they told me I'd be manager in a year or two. Eighteen months into the job, my boss was promoted to corporate, but they didn't make me the manager. They appointed an older white man at the plant and made him my boss.

"Fortunately for me, I had been working at building relationships, so I went to some people I trusted to find out what they thought was really going on. Frequently you need to be able to get perspectives from several different sources and piece them together, like a puzzle, because one person's story is rarely the whole story. I was told, 'Many people thought you were the guy for the job, but they didn't think you were quite ready. The guy they put in is probably not going to last, because he showed weaknesses in a similar job in the past. Stay calm, continue doing a good job, and give it eighteen months.' Sure enough, a year later, I was promoted to the manager's position."

Getting passed over for a promotion you think you deserve can be difficult to handle, and Little went through an intellectual process that allowed him to channel the emotional hurt into positive action. Information from supporters he had developed was the starting point of his process. Without their input, he would not have had an accurate picture of the decision-making process, and his planned behavior would never have been as effective. While he thought race might have been a factor in the decision, he was able to put this impression aside and focus on bringing about the result he wanted. A short time later he succeeded. His response is particularly important for young managers to understand. You are frequently judged by supporters on how you handle disappointment. It is an opportunity for you to demonstrate to them maturity and balance, as well as your ability to be a good team player.

Don Brown had a cool, knowledgeable, and unbiased built-in supporter at Kraft. His older brother was in human resources at Kraft and had convinced Brown to apply there in the first place. That's who he turned to when he had to face losing a promotion he thought he deserved. "My brother was a few years ahead of me and had a broader perspective on how a company evaluates people, since he was in human resources. He's my go-to guy, when all else fails. The first time I got passed over for a promotion where I felt I was the best candidate and the best prepared, I was real disappointed. Everybody was even coming up to me and saying, 'Man, you should have had that job. You're head and shoulders above that guy.' It was a significant promotion, and it was in the days where every additional dollar meant something to the family. And the guy who got it was good friends with the guy who made the decision.

"Lucky for me I had my brother, and lucky for me I knew to call him. I said, 'Hey, look, I'm thinking about quitting.' And right away he said, 'Hey, cool that. First of all, the way you handle this disappointment means a lot to your image in the company. So don't go out pouting and don't allow yourself to rant and rave. First thing tomorrow morning when you get to work, you shake that guy's hand and congratulate him. Tell him how happy you are he got the job and how you'll support him. The next thing you do is talk to your boss about what you need to work on in order to be ready for the next promotion.' I never asked him how he knew all that. I know it had happened to him, but I never talked to him about it. I took it at face value. It felt right, and I did what he said. Two months later I got a promotion."

The advice from his brother was the kind every young manager needs, and Brown was lucky enough to have access to it and to see the wisdom in it. It was a lesson in managing his disappointment, but it was also a lesson in managing the relationship with his boss. Just as his brother predicted, Brown's request for his boss's advice won him respect and positioned him for the next opportunity. It signaled to his boss, in a nonthreatening manner, he was a team player, but one who expected to be considered for the next promotion.

Brown would relive this promotional drama many times, but more often than not he would be the one receiving the congratulations and the promises of support. "When I became vice president of the eastern region, the Welsh guy who gave me my first break, the one who'd been teaching me and probably expecting to move up himself, was now working for me. I didn't go out and make any apologies for the promotion, but I called him and said, 'I just wanted to let you know I got promoted to vice president, so we're going to be working together.' That's how I told him. And he said, 'Absolutely wonderful. I'm proud of you. I'm happy for you. Anything you need to know, you'll get, and everything I taught you, you'd better use.'" Sometimes you work for key supporters who promote you, and other times they are happy to work for you.

David Hinds, like most people and certainly most African Americans, had to build his own network at Bankers Trust, now Deutsche Bank. "Along the way you find people who provide a level of insight which allows you to get rid of blockage. Some of them are only temporary in nature, some are much more long standing. When I think about role models, I don't think about someone who is in a particular position I aspired to or someone I tried to copy. It's about recognizing we all need assistance, and along the way you find people who are able to provide the guidance and analysis you need.

"A series of advisors helped me sort out problems along the way. I have a good friend, a consultant. I met him early in my career, and he has remained an advisor. I've been able to sit down with him a number of times and say, 'I don't understand.' We have known each other a long time, and I know he can read situations better than I. Other people can provide insight and perspective. I remember one boss I had when I was just an assistant VP, I told him I was going to leave the bank, and he spent the whole day with me talking about how to make decisions about life choices. He was one of the good managers, who took the time to bring perspective. Another friend, an African American, was the first person to show me how to use force field analysis to deal with problems, to dissect the situation, to identify those things that are creating resistance and those things that are enabling."

When Hinds was assigned to run an international profit center, a position he had fought for and won, he sought advice from someone internal and discovered another supporter. "That job was very significant for me because it meant moving from the cost side of the business equation to the revenue side, and revenue was where all the hotshots were. I started seeing myself with a revenue future, but I was also concerned. I never saw myself as a guy who was going to be on a plane going to visit clients and trying to influence the business from that end, and here I was pushing for that job.

"I knew I could deal with the strategy piece. I knew I could get the operations turned around. The question in my mind that I wasn't sharing with anyone was whether I could convince clients to do business with us as opposed to someone else. Within the banking community, African Americans never had good representation. Banks were no different than any other industry. When I first started to travel to Asia, Europe, and Latin America, I think only once I ran into someone African American in the front of the plane.

"I called someone in the bank I knew had been in the international community for a long time and said, 'Why don't we have lunch?' We sat down at a table and, before I could say a word, he said, 'Before you say anything, let me share some thoughts with you. You probably are nervous about the client contact, but I will tell you right now I have worked with you a lot, I have seen you in different situations. This will not be a problem for you.' I was shocked. He knew I might be concerned about that and took it upon himself to lay it on the table. He was a very good guy.

"At the same time we had a stream of clients coming in to visit their New York correspondent banker. Where I might have had three months to get organized before seeing clients, clients started coming to see me right away. I found that I was comfortable with that kind of environment. The issue went away almost overnight on two fronts. One was my lunch partner, someone I had a lot of respect for, saying, 'You're not going to have a problem,' and two was being forced to deal with it. For the next six years I got people focused on what the issues were, but now it was global. We had salespeople and service people in every single principal country coming together to drive the business. Every year we raised more and more revenue. I was having a ball, a great time."

Along the way Hinds acquired yet another supporter. Vernon Jordan is a Washington insider, an African American, who sat on Bankers Trust's board. "Vernon called me one day many years ago and said he was coming for a board meeting and could we have lunch. I appreciated that. I guess he knew my name as a high-potential individual, because he participated on the human resources committee. I found we could meet once or twice a year and talk about a variety of things. He has the reputation of advancing both the image and the careers of African Americans, and he was always very open with me. He is obviously a skilled business person as well. I could see how respected he was every time I made a board presentation or observed him interacting with the other members of the management committee. I have said to him on several occasions that I would love to be in his hip pocket, because I can only think about most of the things he really knows."

You can also gain supporters by performing well in an unplanned, spur-of-the-moment situation. In the early 1980s, **Frank Fountain** was assigned to write a speech for a new controller. "One of the times I was working outside of headquarters, I got notified I needed to come back to get some direct exposure to a new controller. When you get to a certain level, your name comes up on the short list, and people advise you, they let you know what's happening. Developing a relationship with him was not something I wanted to do, but I knew from the messages I had to. Early on he had to make a speech to some business students at the University of

Michigan, and I was asked to write the speech and then accompany him to the school.

"Afterwards in a bar or pizza place, the students really cornered him on the concept of the government bail-out for Chrysler. 'How could you think it was a good thing, when you're supposed to depend on the free market and free enterprise?' They were just hammering him, and he wasn't doing too well, because he was still relatively new with the company. So I stepped in and took the questions. And from that day on I was golden with him. It had nothing to do with financial analysis or that kind of thing. He grew to be a very powerful guy, and so then I eventually got the opportunity to have a job I had been wanting." Any new boss could have resented the loss of face at being rescued by a subordinate, and a black one at that. Fountain's instincts on when and how to step in were impeccable.

One supporter has appeared at different times in **Bruce Gordon**'s career, each time wearing a different hat. He first met this supporter in the late 1960s just because he wanted to express his moral outrage. Martin Luther King, Jr., had recently been assassinated, and Gordon regretted that he was not directly involved in the civil rights movement. His response was to apply to Crozier Seminary, King's alma mater, for a masters in social change. He wanted a night job at Bell, where he was already employed, even as a janitor, to help finance what he thought of as his sabbatical, and he obtained several levels of approval. "So all my momentum was building. I was really excited. I was sure I was going to go. Then the word came down from the VP for human resources, 'Absolutely not. You ain't going.'

"People thought I was really crazy, but I walked into the lobby of the headquarters building, called him, and said, 'My name is Bruce Gordon. I hear you're the guy who made the decision I can't go to Crozier. I'm disappointed, and I'd like to sit and talk to you about it.' He said, 'That's fine, come on up.' So straight to his office I went. He said, 'I didn't hire you to get a masters in social change. I hired you with the expectation that you would become a business manager some day, and you're on course to do that. If you take a year off to get this degree, I don't see what good it does me. It certainly doesn't get you any closer to being a manager. It's up to you what you do, but I'm not going to support that.' That was pretty direct, and I understood it, so I decided to stay at Bell. We sat there for a while and talked about other things. I kind of liked this guy, and I figured we had a relationship. I just bumped into him from time to time over the years, but it turned out I had created a presence with him. He was crucial to my career. He later became COO and then CEO."

The human resources vice president's insistence that Gordon stay on the track for manager signaled he was on the "A" list, expected to go far in the company. Gordon may not have realized that then, but he did recognize he was treated with dignity and his commitment was respected. He also could accept the explanation as supportive and reasonable. Had the human resources officer used a different approach, Gordon might have quit and taken an entirely different path. Instead, he was encouraged to see his mission at Bell Atlantic. This is an example of the cause and effect Gordon believes in.

Over the years the same person influenced his career at critical junctures. With the AT&T divestiture, Gordon was presented with two alternatives. One of his great supporters, a man he had worked for on several different assignments, was moving to AT&T and asked Gordon to join him there. Gordon accepted, only to find that Bell would not approve the transfer. "My supervisor said, 'Gee, what makes you think that's your decision?' I said, 'Why wouldn't it be?' He said, 'Well, the way this works is not the way you think. We decide who goes and who stays, and you aren't going.' I was shocked. I called my old boss back, but he already knew. He said, 'I got a call. And just so you know, this decision is being made at a very high level. The president of the company knows about it. The fact that they want to keep you is a good thing, not a bad thing.' I said, 'They don't control me. I'm in control of my life, and

I want to work with you at AT&T.' He said, 'It's probably not a good idea. I'd love to have you, but my guess is they've got an idea that's much better for you.'

"So I went back and tried to find out what that idea was: 'If I don't go to AT&T, what are you going to do? Are you going to promote me?' 'No.' 'Well, what am I going to do?' 'We don't know.' 'You don't know what job I'm going to get?' Didn't make sense to me. But I respected my old boss's point of view, that there was more to it than I knew, and that they were not going to demand to keep very many people. I believed their keeping me was good.

"Another thing happened just about the same time that sort of cemented the message. I ran into someone senior to me on the street, someone I hardly knew. He said, 'I understand you're not being allowed to go to AT&T.' I was stunned. 'How did you know?' He said, 'I know, and this is a good thing. Let me put it this way. In a divorce, you know how people fight over the knick-knacks? You're not exactly a knickknack, but they're fighting over you. You have to feel good about that. Each side wants to keep you.' The bottom line is that I was in a good position, there were people who wanted me in the business, so I stayed."

Gordon was willing to accept the ambiguous status because he knew whose advice he could trust as genuine. From his vantage point today, he understands the answers he got then. "It started out with all bad answers, but then the plan unfolded. They just knew a lot of things I didn't know. Now that I have been in a similar position with the Bell Atlantic merger, I understand. I can see further than people in my organization. I can see myself saying to someone, 'I care about keeping you with me. I don't know where you're going to be, but you're going to be okay. This will turn out to be a good thing.' I can see now what they could see then.

"They actually had something for me to do back then. They put me in a job I thought I had already done, managing a lot of customers including the city of Philadelphia. Of course I complained again, but it turns out there was a big deal we needed to do with the city, and they wanted me to handle it. I did, and we were very successful.

"Later I learned the former VP of HR, now the COO, had insisted on keeping me. When he became the CEO soon after, he promoted me to vice president of sales. It worked itself out. Sometimes you just have to pay attention to the people talking to you. You reflect on what's happening, you listen to people you trust, and you make a choice."

The same COO intervened again on Gordon's behalf to move him to the upper echelons. "He was presented a slate of moves involving three people. These people had been in their assignments for a couple of years, all talented people, people they wanted to move up. It was a classic Bell Atlantic move. They swap jobs so they each get several new experiences. He said, 'What's the possibility of putting Bruce Gordon into this? Can we make this a four-person slate instead of a three-person slate?' So I played musical chairs, too, and got in the go-ahead group."

Another key supporter was someone he did not even know. "Within the first couple of weeks after I came to work, the man who was the VP of public relations and public affairs held a meeting with several members of the Initial Management Development Program, what we call IMDP. That's the high risk/high reward training program I was part of. I thought nothing of it at the time, and beyond that meeting I had very little interaction with him. In hindsight, however, I realized he had that meeting because he was trying to get my face and my name together. He was a Gettysburg graduate, my alma mater, and a Gettysburg trustee. His son was in my class. Because I was the only black student in my class and played football, he certainly knew who I was. But I didn't know him at all. I found out decades later he had been watching my career since the minute I walked in the door.

"Since we were both Gettysburg trustees for a period of time, I now know how he works. He is a master player. He used his skills for me, and I never even knew. I've seen it on other boards where I sit. A director can ask a question about someone, never talk to the person, and never make a statement, but get a point across. That's the way it works." Gordon earned this support every day. It would have stopped at any time in his career if he had not continued performing at a superior level, and he would never have known.

Gordon understands how crucial internal support is and how challenging it is to seek, earn, or just recognize. Therefore, he is uncomfortable trying to squeeze it into a simple formula, much as many corporations today try to do with formal mentoring programs. "I had the benefit of supporters, the benefit of people whispering in my ear, no question about it. But I never called them mentors. That's a new word. And to try to use one word to describe all the ways people can help your career, or to try to set up a formal process to achieve it, can give a wrong impression. It's talked about so much, but not about what it really is. You have people watching your career, and some of them you know because you've got a very direct relationship and you've got the chemistry, and some of them you don't have a clue they are checking you out. So if you focus on, 'I don't have a mentor,' or 'I don't really get along with my mentor, so I won't get anywhere,' you may miss the real thing.

"Today I do assign 'mentors,' knowing that it may work out, but it probably won't. I call it a mentor, but it's really not. You can't go out shopping for a mentor. The key is your work performance. You don't find a mentor, a mentor finds you. When you and a mentor get together, be glad and take advantage of it, but you don't just go out and ask somebody to be your mentor."

Chuck Chaplin often says he didn't have mentors, but he realizes by saying so he gives the wrong impression. "I think the problems come from trying to come up with a simple definition of mentor. I'm often asked at career events, did you have a mentor? If mentor means someone who really knows the ropes and spends a meaningful amount of time with you teaching you step by step, bringing you along, I didn't have that. But I did have people who cared about me, who stepped in at key moments with key messages. I absolutely had help from people who really knew what was going on. I can identify a few key situations where a person pulled me aside and said, 'Chuck, the right answer is X, and let me tell you why.' And they were people who were close to me, who I simply believed had my best interests at heart, or who crystallized things I had started to observe but hadn't quite articulated. The key was that it came at the right time for me to hear it."

"Here is a really simple example, but it was very important to me at the time. There was an African-American woman just a couple of years ahead of me I knew only casually. She went to Cornell and was one of the people who stormed the administration building, so she knew the value of being bold. I guess she picked up at times I was tentative and timid in my approach, because I wasn't sure if I was right about things or not. She just let me know I had as great an ability to be successful in this place as any of those guys. She said, 'Don't let their comparative polish or self-confidence or bravado intimidate you. Put your hand up and volunteer for stuff. You have to do that. Take it on, figure it out, and thrash at it. You may make some mistakes, but you won't make any more than anybody else.' That was the way she approached things, and it was very good advice. It gave me a greater degree of self-confidence." Sometimes a well-timed word is all that is necessary for the support to be meaningful.

Brenda Lauderback was happy in a relatively small world, the world she had dreamed of since she was in high school. She was at Gimbel's in Pittsburgh, her home town, and she was promoted very quickly to buyer. But all of a sudden she found herself in a category—children's clothes—she did not want. She kept requesting a return to ready-to-wear, because that's where the future executives were trained, but instead she kept getting more responsibilities within the children's department. Being a woman certainly had something to do with their decision to assign her there, but Lauderback didn't see herself in that pigeonhole. She went outside Gimbel's to find a place where she would be seen as an individual rather than a category.

126

"It was clear to me that Gimbel's didn't want to move me to another area because the business was good. I didn't know what else to do, so I kept asking for a transfer. Finally in New York on a buying trip, a friend of mine introduced me to a woman at a cocktail party. She turned out to work for an executive search firm. She said, 'Have you thought of leaving Gimbel's?' 'No, not really.' 'You may want to consider it. There are a lot of great companies out there, a lot of great opportunities. You have obviously done well. You have moved fast, and you may just want to look at a broader landscape.' I thought, 'Well, why not?'

"After months of talking to people, going back and forth, I got final job offers from three, Bamberger's of New Jersey, Macy's Kansas City, and Dayton Hudson in Minneapolis. Both Bamberger's and Macy's would have taken me on as a buyer, but not Dayton Hudson. They said, 'Come in as an assistant buyer, because the buying position we want for you won't be open for six months. We'll pay you as a buyer, you can learn our company, and if you do what we think you're going to do, you'll get the buying job in six months.' It was hard to turn down two buying jobs, even though the pay was basically the same. But I was more comfortable with Minneapolis and the people at Dayton Hudson. I liked them a lot. It felt right." She met the right supporter at the right time, who had just the right suggestion to tap her ambition.

Margaret Jordan came to Kaiser Permanente at the urging of Kaiser's general counsel, a long-time colleague who was influential at Kaiser. She wanted to bring her children back to California, where they had spent most of their youth, and to her the career move was secondary. She therefore did not discuss in depth with anybody her own goals or the real opportunities at Kaiser. Misperceptions on each side would cause problems later. She took the job and moved. Her assignment was a staff position, to clean up their state accreditation issues and then institute a system to monitor those as well as quality issues, a task she completed in short order. Since she had fifteen years of productive positions in public hospitals and senior government administrative work, she expected to be rewarded with senior line positions.

"My forte is running things, and that ability wasn't being used. But when Kaiser started a program in Atlanta, I got assigned as one of four on the management team. The regional manager had difficulty making decisions, so the rest of us made him look good. I had a meeting with the Kaiser CEO when he was in Atlanta. I said, 'After being here, I realize how much experience I really do have. I am underemployed. When can I be a regional manager?' He said, 'Oh, in about ten years. That's how we do it here.' So I said to myself, 'I give this two more years. If I'm not a regional manager by then, I'll go someplace else.'

"When the regional manager's position became available in Dallas, the general counsel stepped in again and really pushed for me to get that job. The regional manager of Southern California, who was very powerful at Kaiser, was advocating for someone else. I believe part of his problem with me was I was black, but he also objected to giving me the job when I had been in the organization such a short time. The CEO had to get on a plane and go deal with him on it. I also found out later from one of my board members in Dallas that a Kaiser executive had quietly called a Dallas director to ask if an African-American woman running a business unit would be accepted in Dallas.

"About six months after I got the regional manager position in Dallas, I realized I needed somebody to do marketing. Kaiser first asks its regional managers, 'Who in your region ought to be considered for the job?' The Southern California regional manager recommended a black female, and I was encouraged. But I realized soon she was bad news, and he knew it. I asked, 'Why in the world would you recommend someone you knew was a problem?' 'Well, we thought she'd do better there.' Wow. 'Here we have the toughest region in the world to deal with, and you send me someone who has to be rehabilitated.' You question whether they're trying to make you fail, especially when they make the problem between two black women."

Jordan had a number of important supporters, beginning with the general counsel who brought her to Kaiser. With his help, she was able to round up enough support to get an excellent position in spite of Kaiser's normal operating procedures. That is an impressive accomplishment. But ultimately she was not able to consolidate her base and win over or neutralize her enemies. Perhaps there was no way to do that. It takes a long time to read your environment accurately, and even longer to build enough relationships to sustain success there.

Development Jobs

A clear signal you are slated to move up is being offered a development assignment, one that allows you to build critical new competencies or the opportunity to interact one-on-one with the most senior executives. **Ed Howard** was offered the position of vice president and director of Investor Relations when he was director of merchandise for the geographic division of J.C. Penney, but he did not immediately recognize it as a development job. "At the time, I was totally unaware of the importance of the offer. I didn't even know the position existed prior to the offer. They called me one day and described an 'opportunity' and what they needed out of it. I told them, 'I'm not your guy, because I don't know the slightest thing about investor relations, dealing with Wall Street and major stockholders.'

"Then they informed me I'd be a vice president. That would make me the first black vice president in the history of the company. And their reasoning for selecting me was good. They wanted someone who'd been in a line position, because everyone on the finance side understood the finances but fell on their faces when they tried to explain what the stores were doing. It was a nightmare. Some of the explanations I heard about why we were doing certain things had no rhyme or reason whatsoever. They needed someone who knew stores, knew the retail side of the business, and they had a finance staff to teach me what I needed to know to get by with the investment community.

"I realized later Vernon Jordan probably had something to do with the offer. He was the head of the board's Personnel Committee. And believe me, it was a tremendous experience. It gave me a perspective I'd never even thought about. Wall Street asked questions mainly about what was going on in the stores, but they could ask you about anything in the company. So you had to stay abreast of everything that was happening. No one was feeding you the information. You just had to keep in communication. You visited, you had lunch with people in different positions, so you knew what was going on. I could go anywhere and meet with anyone, and I did.

"We were going through two years of very tough times then. Regardless of what earnings we were reporting that day, I would focus on twelve to eighteen months out. Anything they asked me, I'd answer, but I'd always wind up talking about twelve to eighteen months out. I always made sure there were no surprises. Wall Street doesn't like to be blindsided. You could see they wanted to be seen as experts, but they weren't experts. They usually didn't have the foggiest idea what was going on, and I realized real fast most of them had egos so big they barely fit into the room. So that was pretty much where my strategy came from. Make them the experts everybody wants them to be. Find out what makes the whole process tick. We hadn't done that before, not to this extent, and we not only kept the stock price up, we increased it during that two-year period.

"The best part about the job was working very closely with the chairman. I'd made a presentation to the board and the chairman, and I'd been at dinners with him every now and then, but I had not had a lot of direct contact with him. Now, we often talked one-on-one about strategies, where we needed to go, and how we needed to guide the investment community. We had a lot in common. We were both very aggressive and didn't hesitate to make decisions. You could sit down with him and talk about the pros and cons, say this is what we're going to do, and then do it. In fact, sitting with him is when I made up my mind I'd like to be a regional president. I remember exactly when I decided that's what I should be. That job was a tremendous experience."

The influential board member subtly pointed out to the executive team someone they might otherwise have overlooked, and they discovered a gem. But it was Howard alone who capitalized on the opportunity, for himself and his company. He quickly rose to the occasion and built the job into a platform to showcase his creativity and commitment to Penney. He did not apologize for winning the slot, nor worry about what he didn't know. He did not pay attention to the inevitable talk that he had won an opportunity he didn't really deserve because he was black. He quickly figured out how to leverage his knowledge of the Penney operation, learned through years of work on the line. That and his lifelong ability to read an environment quickly and accurately spelled great value for the company. He and the chairman found themselves comfortable working together. Because of his experiences in the development job, he knew he was more than ready to become a regional president.

Don Brown knew he had been identified, at least informally, as a high-potential manager, and he was quite sure his next assignment would be as a plant manager or in a corporate development job. It proved to be the development job. "I was called the operations manager, which basically was the assistant to the vice president for all of manufacturing, at that time twenty plants. They brought me in to review the capital spending budgets of all twenty plants, a total of about $180 million, to make sure that every one of the projects was a worthwhile project. That kind of gave me the full finance piece and the business rationale for the investment.

"That business rationale part took me into marketing and sales, and I'd never been exposed to either of those. 'Well, you want a sliced cheese? You've got to have the equipment. You want to put it in a different package? You've got to have different equipment. You want a different color on a promotional item? Talk to marketing. Okay, why do you want to do this? Why do you want to go out and spend $10 million for this kind of equipment to produce this?' You start to get a little sense of how it all fits together."

A development job means you are regarded as a valuable member of the team. It is an opportunity for you to test yourself—and be tested—usually at a significantly higher level. Use it to demonstrate your skills effectively to the decision makers. From another perspective, this may be the first real opportunity you have to demystify those top positions. It is the time you begin to see yourself there as well.

As African-American managers, you have seen supportive relationships and wondered how to find the strategies to make them work for you. Spend some time taking another look at your past. You will probably uncover many examples of relationships with people who stepped in and influenced you to choose a positive path or move further along one. Chances are, you found them—or they found you—in surprising and unexpected places. Hopefully when you think about your past relationships in this new light, you can readily apply the insights to your current organizational experiences. You can tone down feelings of being an outsider whose approaches are likely to be rejected. To help you focus more sharply on the process, here are a few examples our executives remember.

In **Frank Fountain**'s experience growing up in the segregated South of the 1950s, whites, especially young men, constantly stepped over the line to terrorize or otherwise abuse blacks. Even in this rigidly segregated world, there were informal but very definite networks for such situations. "There were certain white folks you could go and talk to. They would deal with it, and that usually worked. Those white leaders would protect the blacks they viewed as okay, if you paid deference to their status. My father's uncle was well connected, so he could sometimes get things taken care of.

132

But if you didn't have that connection, then you were at the mercy of whatever was going on."

When **Don Brown** was in Vietnam he found surprising support from his commanding officer, a white man from North Carolina. Just before he was scheduled to go out on patrol one night, he received a letter from his mother informing him his younger brother had been shot just walking on the campus of the University of Arkansas, where he was the first African-American football player. "A car came by, and they yelled out, 'Hey!' And pow! Shot him in his knee and busted his kneecap. He could never play sports again. And here I was getting ready to go on patrol. I went to see the CO and said, 'I ain't going.' He said, 'Do you know what's going to happen in your life if you refuse a direct order in the military?' I told him I did, and explained why I didn't want to go that night. I don't know why he did this, but we sat there and talked for about two hours. He found a way for me not to go on patrol, and I found a way not to be insubordinate. It helped a lot. I still remember that.

"You think about those times where your life could take a different turn. I could have been in the stockade. Why this white officer did that for me, I have no idea to this day, because we never stayed in contact. But you know there are those points in your life where the road splits. I could have very well gone in a different direction. But he said, 'Hey, you don't need to be out there today. Tell you what you do. We need to get this other thing done. You do this, we'll talk when you get back.' Nothing happened to my buddies on patrol that night, thank God."

Even though it could have ended his military career, Brown's instinct was to approach the commanding officer on a human level. The officer met him halfway. Their compromise maintained military discipline while accommodating the legitimate anger and frustration of a valued soldier. Brown was amazed, but the compromise was probably not as incredible from the officer's perspective. The commanding officer knew about Brown's excellent reputation and contributions to the unit. He made it possible for Brown to avoid the stockade and stay engaged.

Feeling like an outsider at MIT, **Cleve Killingsworth** decided to spend a summer documenting the historical treatment of blacks at MIT. What he found was not complimentary. Out of the blue one day, a very senior physics professor asked the class about their summer plans. When he heard Killingsworth's plans, he invited the young student to his office. "It was a very impressive layout in the business part of the main building. I'm thinking, 'Geez, who is this guy?' So I go in, and he said, 'I've been thinking about that project you're doing.' I showed him the material I had collected, and he said, 'You're not really a historian. You're a scientist. Why don't I get you a summer job at Lincoln Labs instead?'

"I think he liked me and saw something positive in me, but I think he was also protecting the institution. But Lincoln Labs was important. MIT essentially ran it, and it turns out this professor was vice president for research, a very powerful man, not just at MIT, but internationally. He became a kind of mentor to me. I'd go up and see him every now and then, and we'd talk about how things were going. I always felt he was somebody I could turn to. I think I had one of the most powerful mentors you could have." Despite the professor's possible motivations, Killingsworth decided to take advantage of the opportunity. He also understood the opportunity this relationship presented, and he continued to build it. Perhaps he knew then his path would lead him to greater contributions.

7.

Understanding Power

The idea is to get exposure to the individuals who have the power to make change.

—**Lloyd G. Trotter**, President and CEO
GE Industrial Services

Today I understand power and how to leverage it, how to maneuver it. I wish I had understood it earlier. I could have had an even larger impact on the organization and on people's lives if I had learned how to leverage power sooner.

—**Ronald C. Parker**, Senior Vice President
Frito-Lay North America

In management circles you hear about personal power and position power. I think personal power is in part a gift, an aura, a presence you can develop if you've got it. But in complex organizations, you also have position power. The organizational structure gives you this, whether you have the gift of personal power or not. You've got the super power, so use it. Other folks use it, and they expect you to use it. Why wouldn't you?

—**Bruce G. Gordon**, Group President
Verizon

SUCCESS requires an understanding of power. You must understand your relationship to it, both personally and as it works within your organization. Make no mistake, the competition for individual and organizational power—usually discussed in terms of euphemisms such as "responsibility," "influence," "authority," "leadership," or "effectiveness"—is the key dynamic around which all corporate activity swirls. Train yourself to enter the competition, and enter to win. Power is elusive; it is not tangible. If you are given power, and you seldom are, and you do not know what to do with it, you will squander it. If it is there for the taking and you do not recognize it, you will miss the opportunity. You must know what to do with it—how to acquire, use, and maintain it. Here we're stripping away all euphemisms and calling it by its name: power. If you do not grasp the essence of this dynamic, you will never have power, no matter what you call it.

Power defines how a corporation is organized. It puts the heat into the competition for space, budget, and titles. At a deeper level, the same competition exists around ideas, projects, products, business priorities, and the distribution of plum assignments. Power sets the parameters for an organization's system of reward and punishment. The amount of power an individual has, no matter how great or small, is a major determinant of his or her ability to get things done. Power sets the terms of interactions and engagements. It is the major, if hidden, component shaping the behavior of both the power holder and the followers. Whether stated openly or not, every organizational transaction is a statement of who has and who does not have power. The contest for power never ends. Sometimes the struggle is visible and direct, and other times so subtle as to be undetectable to the untrained eye. Competition for power begins at entry level and continues to the highest reaches of every institution, public or private, sacred or secular, for-profit or not-for-profit. Those who understand this dynamic early and those who most effectively incorporate it into their overall strategy will invariably have the greatest impact.

Understanding the dynamics of power and making it a part of your corporate persona is a huge undertaking. But you are ready to synthesize all your skills and leverage them into real power.

What Is Power?

There are many lengthy and complicated treatises on power, but for our purposes we can define it simply. It is the ability to influence behavior, change the course of events, overcome resistance, and get others to do things they might not otherwise do. Put another way, the drive for power is the drive to have more control over one's work environment.

No discussion of power can continue without acknowledging a basic fact: Power will always involve conflict and disagreement. Both are constant realities of organizational life. If everyone in a department or on a team agreed about what to do and how to do it, there would be no need to exercise power in order to influence others. Therefore, for those who aspire to positions of influence, a critical personal attribute is the willingness to engage in conflict with others. You must be willing to invite disturbance. Those who are conflict-averse, those who shy away from discord and disharmony, and those who dislike the jousting for position and advantage are unlikely ever to understand power, let alone acquire it.

Al Little knows how to use power to negotiate the outcome he wants, whether on behalf of his corporation or for his own professional advancement. "I always size up the situation in a conscious and purposeful way to determine how I can achieve the best outcome for my company and for me. As long as it's ethical, I will do whatever it takes, whatever I think will work in that particular situation. I'm a pretty good negotiator, and I've learned to use a number of different techniques. Maybe it's ambition. I know it's confidence that I can persuade people to my point of view."

Witness Little's confident style: "I was the best labor relations guy in the company. I reached contract settlements in cases that resulted in strikes when others led the negotiations, and I did it at lower cost. I really learned how good I was as a result of those experiences. My boss was promoted, and I was a candidate for the corporate director of the department. Instead, they brought someone in from outside the company. I was pretty young to be a corporate director anyway, only thirty-two. This had happened to me once before, and I had waited it out and got the promotion a year later. But this time I decided to look for another job and see what I could leverage in the meantime.

"First I got a raise, because they wanted me to feel okay about bringing in the outsider. That helped, because then I could command a higher salary at a new company. In a few months, my strategy worked, and I was offered a great job at a new company. Then I went to the vice president of HR at my old company as I was leaving and said, 'I did a great job at the last negotiation, and I think I deserve the bonus I would have had if I were not leaving.' It was an unprecedented request at that time, but it worked. That vice president sent me a check at my new company. I almost framed it. The bottom line is, 'Why get angry? Just get even.' I got the money and a better job."

Linda Keene's understanding of power helped her correct a company business decision, and she did it without harming her career or the careers of the people who worked for her. By the time she arrived at Pillsbury, ten years out of business school, she had learned how to influence decisions at all levels. "I was director of marketing for microwave and toaster products. In food parlance, that meant new foods. All these foods prepared in microwaves and toasters were separated out from their food category, and that's the way they appeared on the grocery store shelves. It didn't take long after getting there to realize that it made no sense at all from a business standpoint to separate them that way. Recommending to management that they needed to be reintegrated into their food categories was the first big risk I ever took in my career. It meant eliminating my division and putting the products where they really belonged from a consumer standpoint. Even internally we were competing for resources against departments that should have been compatible, not competitive.

"When I reached this conclusion, I had to get my team to the same point. People had a lot of concerns. They feared they might not have a job. I told them then, and I believe it even more today, that if you do good work, there will be opportunities for you. We are being paid to give them our best thinking and our best judgment. If we know something to be right, that's what we have to recommend. As we talked as a group, we came to the conclusion that this was the only thing we could recommend with any integrity.

"But I didn't just recommend it. I laid a lot of groundwork first. I started talking about it with my boss, preparing him for what was coming, telling him we were thinking about these things. 'Here's where we are. I just want you to understand that directionally this is where we're going.' Then I began marketing my team. I looked personally for opportunities for other people. We were hiring across the marketing department. Reassigning the products did not have to mean most people would lose their jobs. If you worked on pizza in the microwave division, you could work on microwave pizza in the pizza division. I really didn't feel there were a lot of people who would be totally displaced. After we talked through what it might mean, there weren't a lot of people who were terribly frightened, but you can't eliminate all concerns. Finally everyone felt it was the right thing for us to do."

Developing this ability to influence events takes a long time. Early in most careers, people encounter difficulty controlling outcomes. That, too, is not a problem if you learn from your mistakes. **Elynor Williams** learned the hard way how to build the support necessary to sell an idea. "At AT&T, one of my first corporate jobs, I developed a wonderful corporate-wide program. My boss liked it so much, he said, 'I want you to present this to the executive committee.' I knew this was an important opportunity, so I worked hard on my presentation. I did a tremendous amount of research. I was terrified, but I felt ready for my moment. Well, instead it was a painful experience. There was no support for the program around the table. In fact, when I was presenting the research and benchmarking efforts, the senior vice president for human resources boomed, 'What research? What experts? You haven't talked to me. I haven't seen any of this.' I learned about giving people 'ownership' and about getting feedback and support before entering a meeting. Believe me, that will never happen to me again. To make matters even worse, during my next performance review, my boss used this failure against me. In hindsight, I find it strange he didn't tell me along the way that I needed to review the material with certain people, walk me through the process of getting a program approved.

"This turned out to be only one of the lessons I learned at this company. I was only there three years, but I felt I got a PhD in corporate power. You must make your boss look good as much as possible without undermining your values or your own career. Never allow your boss to be blindsided. Give him or her credit for adding new ideas to the process, and keep him or her involved in your projects. At the same time, parlay what you're doing to gain visibility. Hiding your talents will get you nowhere. Seek out and develop several allies and supporters. Never align yourself with only one person, because if and when that person disappears, you disappear, too. In essence, I learned to play the corporate game, because you either play the game or become a victim. You also have to be on the alert for new rules, because the rules of the game can change at any time. But through all this, you must stay true to yourself, your values, and beliefs. Always remember who you are."

Did her boss set her up? Did he assume she knew, because it was obvious to him? Williams had a lot of ground to cover. She started as a home economics teacher, raised in the South, and was in the process of transforming herself into a corporate executive. This incident occurred early in her career, and she continued to increase her ability to play the power game. Each attempt to discard victimhood status and learn the rules leads to an advantage in the next encounter.

Competition for power comes almost naturally to some people. As a child in Oklahoma City in the early 1950s, **Ira Hall** listened to his father, an Assistant Superintendent of Education, talk about his efforts to influence budget allocations for the state's black school system, thus receiving early lessons in power negotiations. "My father had a keen understanding of the structure of society and an ability to identify the leverage points. Because the other superintendents underestimated his intelligence, they did not deny him access to any information. So he analyzed cost per student, revenue per student, and all kinds of expenditures for students, say for books, and then lobbied for the black system. He was fearless in his lobbying. His view was, 'There's nothing good or bad you can do to me that will keep me from being truthful and honorable about the things I believe in.' And I have found there is hardly ever the negative consequence people fear if you take a stand for truth and honor."

Hall learned these lessons well. In high school standing up for what was right helped Hall neutralize the impact of a guidance counselor's hostility and convinced the counselor to write fair college recommendation letters. His strategy was very bold under the circumstances. Hall was one of only a few black students in a newly integrated high school at the beginning of the 1960s. "I had set my mind on becoming an electrical engineer. Who knows why? I was good at math and science, I loved them, and I knew I could do it. With my sister's help—she was the guidance counselor at the black high school—I had narrowed my search to MIT, Harvard, and Stanford. My counselor's view was, 'Who are you to be applying to these schools? Why don't you go to Oklahoma University like everybody else?' I was concerned about a bad recommendation, so I went to him and said, 'I think the Superintendent of Schools would expect you to give me an unbiased recommendation.' Of course he was angry. I said, ' I have his phone number. Should I call and ask him?' I didn't tell him about my father. I doubt he would have believed me, but he must have sensed I was serious. He didn't call my bluff. He sent the letters in, and I was accepted at all three."

African Americans growing up in this society push against restrictions and face feelings of powerlessness every day. **Sy Green** started early testing his ability to influence events around him. "I was fortunate enough to realize you could earn points and get a lot of respect and support from everyone, blacks and whites. Whatever I did, I tried to be the best. In a small town, athletics was the centerpiece for everything, and I excelled in basketball and track. I also excelled in the classroom. I stayed out of trouble, and I worked a lot. I earned a lot of points, and that respect built my self-confidence. I also built important relationships. Those achievements no one can ever take away from me."

Even with the "points" he earned, this young black man knew he walked a thin line between garnering respect and becoming a threat. All African Americans, men especially, walk this line every day. An incident with his white high school basketball coach is all the reminder he needs. "African Americans were only about 5 percent of the population, so our presence didn't usually cause problems. But one night our coach put five black players on the court at the same time. Well, that was just unheard of. This would have been in 1958 or thereabouts. He pretty much lost his job because of that."

A second incident in college tells of similar bias. "Mount Union is out in the country, and there were just a few of us, but only one girl. It was frowned upon for us to mix socially with the white girls. My roommate was a black kid from New York, very bright, who got free board because he was a dorm counselor. But he started dating one of the white girls, and he was always being called in by the president for it. When I applied to be a dorm counselor the next year, I was turned down. They didn't want to take a chance with another black student, even though I only dated my high school sweetheart. Over the summer I appealed to the dean and ended up getting the job. But that was what we had to deal with."

The consequences of crossing the line of acceptable behavior for the black students were very clear, but Green didn't accept the group classification. He felt he had earned enough points and was entitled to be treated as an individual. The issue wasn't just "the money" or even "Sy Green." He needed to influence the dean's decision, and he did. In the future, when other black students faced similar problems, did administrators respond differently? Did Green open their eyes, or was he viewed simply as an exception? However the dean rationalized reversing his decision, Green was able to achieve an outcome in his favor, to wield power in a situation where others might have considered themselves powerless. Look carefully for situations in your own life where you were a successful power broker. If you do not find any, are there situations where you might have changed the outcome with a better understanding of power?

People perceive and use power differently. Power is completely situational, unique to particular individuals and particular sets of circumstances. In every situation, the participants' blend of personality, temperament, character, life experiences, skills, and their relative positions and responses dictates the effectiveness and consequences of their use of power.

Where Does Power Come From?

People who consider themselves outsiders are frequently paralyzed when trying to understand how to achieve power. For a workable knowledge about the sources of power in your organization, concentrate on six basic categories.

Coercive
Coercive power is based on an individual's ability to punish

or frustrate another person. This behavior is no longer generally acceptable, so it is seldom used in modern corporations.

Reward
Power through reward, the opposite of coercive power, is based on an individual's ability to meet or satisfy someone else's need. It is the carrot, the seduction factor, drawing in those who want something from the holder of power.

Legitimate
Legitimate power, sometimes called position power, is based on acceptance of the authority of a given position. This is the most traditional source within an organization. The person assuming the title has authority but also the potential for power. The skill of the person determines whether and how well the potential is realized.

Charismatic
Charismatic power, sometimes called personal power, has everything to do with the individual. It is that unique combination of intelligence and other traits and characteristics, and how the person interacts with the world, which compels and attracts others. Even though others may not know why, they are drawn to this person and want to follow him or her. Charisma can be immediately observable or deeply rooted and only appreciated over time, but it is unmistakable.

Associative
Associative power stems from an individual's close alignment with someone deemed powerful. Thus, a shadow or halo effect is created by the presumption that the person speaks or acts on behalf of someone else.

Expert

Expertise is the most readily attainable source of power in any organization. Power through expertise is conferred on individuals who solve specific problems, and who possess some real or perceived special knowledge others deem useful or necessary. Expertise is independent of title or status but is nonetheless recognized and valued. Young managers can be seen as experts early in their careers, if they are effective in solving problems no one else has tackled.

This list is the first step, the foundation. It is up to you to continue observing, learning, and refining so your understanding can move to a more subtle level. Become comfortable with the language and imagery of power and the ways power is expressed in your organization.

Ira Hall has always been able to use power effectively. He is bolder than most people dare to contemplate, and he lives to tell about it. He has an analytical mind, and he enjoys tackling the most challenging puzzles he can find. "In addition to understanding the conventional wisdom, I like to make my own observations, make sure that things are right from my own point of view rather than just accept the numbers. Just because the numbers are on or above plan doesn't mean everything's okay." Here is one puzzle he solved at IBM.

"As head of corporate business development, I had the opportunity to see the operations and detailed business results of all business units, as well as a wide variety of IBM acquisitions, divestitures, and joint ventures. By most external financial analyses, IBM was doing very well. Although I wasn't responsible for improving the results of existing operations, I concluded that we had room for some substantial improvements. For example, I believed the company could better create shareholder value by more focus on managing cash flow from operations in addition to the focus on profit, and more focus on gaining market share in addition to just revenue growth. Key drivers were the affordability of the asset investments and shareholder dividends relative to the cash flow being generated. We needed to 'right-size' the asset investment and be geared to where the market was headed. These observations were outside the scope of my job responsibilities. One of the biggest challenges I perceived was how to remain a team player and yet exert the leadership required to bring new recommendations to the senior executive management.

"When I was elected a corporate officer after two years with the company, I shared these and other observations and recommendations with the chief financial officer, and he encouraged me to share them with the chairman. The chairman decided I should present the observations and recommendations concurrently to him and the rest of the management committee, the seven most senior company executives. I was acutely aware of the risks of such a presentation and in fact proceeded with some trepidation. It is fair to characterize the session as very intense. I worked hard to ensure that my objectives were increased shareholder value and greater customer satisfaction, rather than just random observations. I also made sure that each point was substantiated with analysis and appropriate benchmarks. I could see the chairman understood with crystal clarity every point I was making. But I questioned silently why I ever voluntarily entered into what I increasingly perceived as a high risk/low reward situation.

"Fortunately the chairman agreed with all of the recommendations and concluded the session by asking that I lead an effort to disseminate this perspective throughout senior management. The management committee embraced these thoughts and invited me to work with their respective senior executive teams. I worked just as hard during each subsequent session to remain a team player working to improve shareholder value and customer satisfaction, rather than just a critic. It was important to remain well-liked and well-trusted in addition to well-respected."

Even if you never have this kind of heady experience, or need or want to, you get the idea. Consider this story a parable about being willing to take risks—to think on your own, document your ideas, and present them with confidence. Test your limits, or you will never know the extent of your ability to contribute, to influence the organization, and ultimately to wield power.

What Do Powerful People Share?

If you watch people in positions of power—in your organization and in your life—you will probably begin to see a pattern, a cluster of traits that work together effectively. You must acquire and refine these traits if you want to be a key player in your organization. The following traits are found in all powerful people, and they all cut across race, gender, and age lines.

Endurance
Endurance over cleverness and brilliance. If you understand the true meaning of endurance, you understand the importance of bringing energy and strength to every endeavor. The tortoise—the one able and willing to work long and grueling hours over an extended period of time—wins the race.

Focus
Focus entails being single-minded in the pursuit of a goal, along with an obsessive attention to the details of the task at hand. Having focus means being able to set priorities and recognize new assets while filtering out any and all diversions.

Ego
Putting yourself first can hamper your ability to achieve a goal. Sometimes making yourself secondary will help you manage people and relationships more effectively.

Tolerance for Conflict

Because disagreements are inherent in any act of acquiring or using power, anyone unwilling or unable to engage in conflict is unlikely to become a serious contender. In a corporate setting, conflicts require focus on the issues at hand and preclude emotional involvement with other participants. A successful manager is able to separate the person from the conflict.

Sensitivity

Effective power players are keenly attuned to the wants and needs of others. This means understanding people, their positions on issues, and how best to communicate with and influence them: what John Gardner calls "social perceptiveness." You must be devoted to observing others' behavior and appraising accurately their readiness or resistance to move toward your goal.

Flexibility

Flexibility requires constant reassessment of all available information in order to recognize when a change of course is necessary. When your values and principles are constant, being flexible is not the same as being wishy-washy or indecisive.

What else do powerful people share? They possess above-average intelligence, ambition, and emotional strength. They work to keep their emotions and their intelligence in alignment, working together, with neither trait dominant. They have a sense of certainty, about themselves, their abilities, and their decisions. They also desire acceptance and are comfortable with conformity; corporate America is not a place for anarchists and rebels. They appreciate and excel at the subtle rather than the grand gesture. They have a high threshold for emotional pain, and know how to act with grace under pressure. And they are constantly deepening their reservoir of good will, among peers, managers, and those who work for them.

Stripped to the basics, power traits and attributes for black Americans are the same as for whites, but you shoulder an additional burden of proof that your white male counterparts do not. Where white men arrive innocent unless or until proven guilty, you arrive with pressure to prove your innocence. Since innocence can never be proved definitively, your struggle will be continuing. You work against a backdrop of conflicting assumptions, more muted than in the past but still a part of many peoples' thinking. Rather than the old stereotypes of dumb and lazy, you may be viewed as too cautious, too sensitive, or too aggressive. In the area in which you have chosen to compete, your emotional skin must be so thick as to be impenetrable. The contemporary nuances of race and gender bias, the pressure of your own and your family's expectations, as well as the harsher consequences of even small mistakes can, as **Westina Matthews Shatteen** said, "wear you down." Yet you must build and maintain self-confidence in the face of the challenges. Take heart in knowing you have been fielding those challenges and overcoming them all your life. You are ready.

Ambivalence About Power

Many people, for a variety of reasons, are ambivalent about power and, as a logical extension, are conflicted about getting, having, or using it. There are as many reasons for ambivalence as there are people. As African Americans, you may enter corporate life with conflicting thoughts and feelings about power. You may think of it in negative terms, as something others have.

Power is in fact morally neutral. Power can be used for good or evil, depending upon the personal value system of the one holding power. Human history is filled with examples of people who abused power—Adolph Hitler, Idi Amin, Pol Pot. At the same time we find Martin Luther King, Jr., Franklin Delano Roosevelt, Nelson Mandela. In a society founded on democratic principles, one can win and hold power only with the consent of others. No one will remain a leader for long without sharing the same core values and sense of morality with those being led.

Look at the impact power had on your younger years. You may not have realized the positive role power played at times. What did power mean to you as a child and what was your relationship to it? Did you exercise any power within your family? Your community? Who did exercise power in your community? What about your parents? In your mind, did they have power? Did you see it as strictly within the realm of "the man"? Did you see it as bad or immoral? Did you simply see it as the way things were? Did you yourself experience positive or negative consequences for trying to influence someone or something else? Did you watch what happened to others in similar situations? What, if anything, did you think about power or the lack of it? What do you see today as you look back on those events? What are your feelings today about power?

If these questions strike chords within you and you do not examine and resolve them, then the competition for power, particularly where whites are involved, will consist of running in place or falling behind. You cannot be successful chasing after something you believe deep down is unwholesome or even illegitimate, at least for you. You will hang back and respond passively, because your heart and soul are not in the contest. If other blacks are involved, does the competition for power take on another set of dynamics? Do you secretly feel power is culturally alien, unnatural, and undeserved?

Unresolved, these issues can lead to a variety of avoidance techniques which will hamper your success. You may deny competition is taking place, play too cautiously, or refuse involvement altogether. Another common mechanism for avoidance is being caught up in one's expertise and working twice as hard. If your view of power is narrow, looking at it only from the bottom up, you will focus too much on the trappings of power: its style rather than its substance. The money, the big office, or simple flattery can easily fake you out of the real competition and the real power. If you do

150

not spring free of this narrow view of power, this victim perspective, you will never get beyond mere survival tactics. You will never identify your own self-interest or set the terms for achieving your goals. If you fear negative consequences, either retaliation or retribution, you will be inhibited in your play, blocked from taking the risks that can make you stand out from your peer group. This does not mean you shouldn't be prudent and thoughtful about power and every aspect of gaining, using, and maintaining it. It does mean you cannot let your analysis keep you out of the action.

Our executives enjoy acquiring and using power, and they are willing to stretch themselves constantly to maintain and expand it. Here is what **Bruce Gordon** says about his own personal relationship with corporate power: "I think sometimes African Americans find themselves struggling between different roles. The first is being a member of the corporate executive team with an exclusive corporate focus, responsive to the shareholders and focused on earnings per share. The other is saying, 'There are issues that are pertinent to African Americans, and I am responsible for addressing them.' Sometimes these roles are in conflict. They shouldn't be, but sometimes they are. Quite honestly, it was never an issue for me. I feel fortunate about that. I never found myself in an internal debate about what to do. I did what I thought was the right thing, and in retrospect I also believe the conflicts were perceived, not real.

"If you are agonizing and struggling at each juncture, you drive yourself nuts. I use a metaphor which makes it easy for me. I look for what's 'clear as a bell': that clean, clear 'ping!' when you ring a bell. Years ago I heard someone talking about meeting Martin Luther King, Jr., at his seminary and being impressed that 'his mind was clear as a bell.' I got that. It's great to be that focused. On the corporate power issue, my mind is very clear. I haven't had to wrestle with it. There's no debate. I saw myself acquiring some of the power I wanted to have. Then I focused on things I wanted to get done in a unique leadership role with folks I thought had developed some expectations of me. I just decided to carry it through. It's not easy to put words around it, it's more of a feeling. It's also not easy to describe, but I know it when I see it. Blacks don't realize how much power we have, period. We're under-appreciated by ourselves and others almost all the time, but we have tremendous power."

When you work hard, with focus and determination, learn the rules and build relationships, bring ideas, creativity, and passion to your efforts, you have earned the right to have power. You deserve it as much as anyone else. You have replaced the last vestige of victimhood with the mindset of entitlement.

David Hinds remembers when the sense of entitlement clicked in for him. "I was at the senior VP level, feeling good about my accomplishments, feeling good about my track record, and then the company went through a significant restructuring. I wound up being part of a new business profit center which was going to change the dynamics of my business unit: commercial cash management and financing domestic and international trade. My initial role in that new structure was to head operations and technology. I remember sitting in one of the early management meetings, and the new head guy flat out declared he wanted one of my peers to be his successor. This guy was going to take me out, and it is only a few weeks into a very difficult mission. I'm saying to myself, 'How can you be so sure? You don't know the rest of us at all.'

"Then a further restructuring created two profit centers, the international and the domestic, and the international was in serious trouble. My former boss was sent to tell me I was to work for the man my new boss had announced as his successor. My response was, 'No way.' A couple of weeks went by, and he came back again. 'Why don't you go in as a co-head with this guy?' My response was the same, 'No. The only way this is going to work is if I run it.' Another week went by, and this time he said, 'Okay, he will work for you.' I said to myself, 'This will be interesting.' Over the next two years, we not only turned the operation around, we tripled its income.

"Something changed in me in the few years right before this incident, when I told him I had to run it or I wouldn't do it at all.

Harvard was one thing, and 'welcome to the club' and my promotions were others. It was probably a convergence of a number of things. The more successful you are, the more successful you think you can become. There is a confidence that comes from succeeding."

Hinds knew what he was capable of and focused on what he deserved. He didn't hesitate to push for it and had the confidence to keep pushing even after rejection. What was going through his head as he waited out those weeks? He could have lost everything. Instead he found he had read his environment accurately. He had the right amount of "juice." Then he delivered the results. Next challenge, please.

Shortly after Chrysler and DaimlerBenz merged in 1998, **Frank Fountain** was in the familiar position of having to win the respect of a whole new leadership. "I was in Africa, and the German guy responsible for sales in that area decided he wanted to meet me. What he really wanted me to do was accompany him to meet with an African head of state, someone who had written to Chrysler, and the letter had been forwarded to Stuttgart. Every day in Africa I followed the same routine. I had meetings all day, came in to change clothes, spent about an hour relaxing, showering or whatever, called back to the states, and then headed out again for all the evening events. He had the hotel operator interrupt my call to my assistant twice, even after I told him I would meet him the next day. So I didn't go. I sent some of my colleagues to meet with him. He didn't like that.

"The next day I had a meeting with the Chrysler Jeep distributor, and the guy from Stuttgart actually showed up at the meeting. I promptly kicked him out. He went back and told Stuttgart I had thrown him out of a meeting. When people asked me about it, I said, 'Yes, I did. He was rude, so he was lucky that was all I did.' I thought, 'Well, there goes my reputation in Stuttgart.' But instead, they asked me to get involved. I was invited to a conference the chairman held in Berlin about southern Africa. And the government affairs guy over there wanted me to go to Nigeria with him."

Fountain has a clear sense of acceptable behavior, and he treats everyone with similar dignity. But if you are disrespectful, he will let you know. Under the circumstances of the merger, the Stuttgart sales representative's behavior was an attempt at dominance, what one executive called "dogs peeing on the fire hydrant," and Fountain called him on it. As many have learned, some earlier than others, if you stand up to power at the right moment, for the right reason, with the right attitude, and with enough accomplishments and good will under your belt, you will not lose.

Race and Gender Issues

The rules of corporate life were made by and for white men. If you are not white or male, when you compete for power you are challenging a basic paradigm. For a black man there is always a delicate balance between competing effectively and being labeled as having "a chip on his shoulder." Women have different issues with power. To begin with, many women—and men—perceive power as the male domain. Even if power itself has no gender, then the imagery of pursuing it is decidedly male. Women are not expected to be aggressive or even assertive, and the label "bitch" is applied all too quickly, tainting their participation, often irreparably. Black women, even more than black men, are still relatively new in the corridors of real power, from the men's perspective as well as in their own heads. With growing savvy, determination, and skill, women are beginning to succeed.

Paula Banks was subtly cast in the "teacher" role when she began the Sears management training program. The coordinator of the training program, an ex-military man, confessed to her he did not understand race and gender, and asked her to help him. She readily complied. She responded to this special attention and was certainly interested in the subject. "There were three women and three blacks in my training group of 33, more than they'd ever had.

The coordinator said to me, 'I don't have much experience working with women and no experience with blacks, so I need you to help me.' Without missing a beat, I told him, 'I'm going to bring some books in for you tomorrow, and I need you to read those. After you've read those books, then we'll talk about the issues.' And we still communicate to this day." In a corporate setting, for a woman to break out of the female roles, in this case, teacher, can be difficult.

Why did he choose to approach her on this topic? There were other blacks in her group. Right away she had a hint of how hard it was to be considered a real business partner. She easily slid into the pigeonhole of teacher, on a side topic, and in essence gave away some of her ability to compete fully.

"I was a good trouper, a good team player for twenty years, handling some of the most sensitive labor and public relations problems Sears faced. Then I was pushed aside for five years in a job I didn't want. Suddenly I recognized I had allowed others to guide my path. I always said Sears had broken promises to me, but maybe there never were any real promises. Maybe I was operating from a place that said they were going to take care of me. Then it hits you: God takes care of those who take care of themselves. I had been so thrilled every time I got promoted. I never asked myself, 'Is this what I should do?' That never crossed my mind. It was just, 'They recognized me, somebody thinks I'm worthy, so I'll take this assignment.' It's only been in the last four to five years that I stepped back and said, 'What do I want? What am I going to do to get it? And what is the least I will take?' Because I had so much HR background, I knew how to leverage what I had. I knew what was possible, because I knew what they had done for others. So I got ready.

"Everyone sensed the change in me. During the last restructuring, my boss at Sears actually allowed me to develop my own job. And six months later I was gone. I wasn't planning on moving, but I was psychologically ready. When I got the third call from Amoco, I said yes. And from there it was just a fait accompli. At lunch that first meeting, I was asked, 'What would it take to get you?' I gave my list. Two days later, I spent eight hours talking to almost every senior officer in the company. Three weeks later, I was sitting in my new office. My new boss said, 'You entered like an Olympic diver, with very little splash.'

"And from there it has been just one thing after another. It's been learning a whole new industry: petrochemicals. It's been the Harvard Advanced Management Program. It's been the merger of BP and Amoco. You come to work one day, and the world is totally different. What doesn't kill you, just makes you stronger. I have continued to get stronger."

Banks, like many women—and probably many men as well—was a slow learner when it came to competing for power. A master negotiator on behalf of Sears, she had never stepped back and read the Sears environment on her own behalf. Now she began to play the game successful managers were already playing. She stopped waiting to be called. With her new attitude, she made demands and got what she asked for.

Kim Green's insurance brokerage firm overlooked her as a serious player to its great detriment. Inspired by the eight-week training course in London to learn Britain's entrepreneurial insurance underwriting system, she moved up by ten years her own schedule to become an entrepreneur. She returned to New York with a first draft of a business plan for a minority-owned brokerage firm. She ran the plan by several of her top clients, and they said they would support her endeavor. How could she take clients with her? Because her firm had never asked her to sign a non-compete agreement.

"I was the only person in my department that had not been forced to sign a non-compete. I was the only woman, and I guess they just didn't see me as a competitor. I had one of the largest, most profitable units in terms of book of business, and I had great relationships with all the key players within those Fortune 500 clients. When I told my boss I was resigning, he really tried to persuade me to stay. He offered me more money, a better title, a bigger office. Then the managing director of the division and the president of the New York office proposed even bigger increases in grade level and the competitive compensation package.

"Everything was money, title, office. I explained again and again that this was not about money. It was just something I wanted to pursue, and I felt the timing was right. They worked hard to change my mind. The message was communicated to higher management, and the situation continued to escalate into pure craziness. That's when they said they wanted me to sign a non-compete agreement. Of course I was not going to do that. If they dismissed me as real competition in the beginning—too young, too female, too black—I wasn't going to help them now. My work at that firm was meaningful. I was given great experiences, and I was able to develop great skills, but I was happy to leave. I left with my dignity and their respect."

Green took an insult and turned it into an advantage. Of course, she had to withstand enormous pressure to do it. She had to cope with the anxiety of going out on her own, the possibility of very public failure, and she also had to wonder what level of retaliation her former firm might be able to engineer. Given the consolidation in the insurance industry already underway, she also knew she could expect to cross paths with those very executives who had tried to convince her not to compete against them. No other employer will ever make this kind of mistake about her again. Green has only one shot at this apple.

As a corporate manager you are competing for power, whether you know it or not, whether you like it or not. Power is the name of the game. You must understand it and then focus your energy and intellect on acquiring it. How you do that must become a part of your overall career strategy. You alone can decide if you want to be in the arena rather than in the stands or on the sidelines. Those managers who can't, won't, or don't formulate a strategy for acquiring power will be bested by those who have done the necessary preparation.

8.

Acquiring Power

My group of seven peers met each month for dinner. We traded information. We talked about openings in our departments. We talked about whatever the politics were. We leveraged each other, and it continued to work for all of us.

—**W. Frank Fountain**, Senior Vice President
DaimlerChrysler Corporation

Everything we do here is hard. There's no other way to say it. It's even hard to define where my responsibility begins and ends and where anyone else's begins and ends.

—**C. Edward "Chuck" Chaplin**, Senior Vice President and Treasurer
Prudential Financial, Inc.

ONCE you have determined that power is your goal, how do you go about achieving it? Coordinate everything you have learned from the words of our executives in earlier chapters. What exactly do you do? How do you transform yourself from a mid-level manager into an executive? Start by recognizing that acquiring power is an on-going process which begins the moment you arrive and continues until the moment you depart, even at your going-away party.

This is the way complex organizations work. Each success—or setback—only sets the stage for the next round of competition. The challenges and the exhilaration of success never end.

Mapping a Strategy

Ask yourself, "What exactly is my business reason for wanting power?" You have to know where you're going in order to plan the route. Focus on that goal, the decision you want taken or changed. Ask yourself, "What benefit will my power bring to my organization? Will it improve the bottom line? How will it help me execute my job better?"

That last question may seem out of place, but it's not. It will always be true that excellent performance is vital to your quest for organizational power. What will change is how excellent performance is measured. Leave nothing to chance. From the earliest opportunity, publicize, in the most subtle and skillful way, who you are and what you do. Demonstrate your intellect, skills, and performance. See where you fit into the hot areas, the new processes and products. Determine for yourself the organization's critical problems where, with the right plan, you can be the one to solve them.

The first step in your plan is to perform what **Lloyd Trotter** calls "the mirror test." Take an inventory of your skills. Be brutally honest about your shortcomings and don't let your head get too swelled about your good points. If you cannot be objective at this task, execution of any of your strategies will be flawed.

Now look beyond yourself. Who are your allies? What favors have you done for people, those who work for you, your peers, and your managers? What obligations and dependencies have been built up between you and others? Favors are wasted if you don't keep track of them and collect on them in the service of your goals. This is not selfish or evil manipulation. These are the rules of the corporate game. Either play to win, or admit you don't want to play. There's nothing wrong with opting out. It's your choice.

Make a study of the "politics" of every situation. Diagnose the power and power bases of all the players around you. Don't stop at potential allies. Study those with different agendas and even those you expect to be neutral. Identify the people in various alliances and cliques, and follow the patterns of who is loyal to whom and why. Who seems more dedicated to ideas and who to cronies? Think through who is affected by your plans and try to anticipate their responses and reactions. What can you do to shape those? Who should get what information? How should your information be disseminated? What form should your communications take? At every step, be judicious in how you share information. Never show all your cards. Never go off duty.

Access to the organization's communication network is always critical. For those who begin as outsiders, it is even more so. The earlier you receive information, the more opportunity you have to leverage it. Information is power. If you are outside the information loop or the last to know something, you are behind. Everyone else has already had time to react, readjust, and respond. To be a permanent participant in the loop, you also need to have a reputation as someone who keeps confidences, or no one will share information with you.

Be acutely aware of the organizational climate in which you are operating. Who is up? Who is down? What are the organizational priorities? Have there been recent changes in personnel or structure? What is the mood of your department? Is it reflective, optimistic, or frantic? These factors affect the timing of your actions. Should your plans be executed quickly? Should you take more time for study and deliberation? Should a planned course of action be abandoned temporarily? Keep on reserve fallback positions and alternative strategies. Your plan should be specific, and you should refer to it constantly. But at the same time be flexible. Be prepared to revise your plan as events unfold.

Always remember, power is most effective when it is unobtrusive. This is even more true for African-American men and women who aspire to success. Don't flaunt your power. You will only make enemies, even if they wait patiently for a chance to put you in what they perceive as your place. Make fairness a part of your behavior and the opinions of others a part of your considerations. Above all, make sure your positions and actions are seen as the result of rational and logical procedures and processes.

Finally, never be apologetic. You are entitled to have and use power. This belief must be at the core of your being.

Whatever your reasons for wanting power—to prove the world wrong, to pave the way for other African Americans, to gain personal wealth and security, to have more control over your life, to be recognized for your contributions, to be a leader in your company— you must first acquire power. The following specific suggestions may help you to begin.

- Position yourself to receive early information about decisions, policies, and organizational shifts.

- Gain regular and frequent access to decision makers.

- Fight to win additional resources, whether above-average salary increases for your department or more money, staff, equipment, or space for projects.

162

- Strive for desirable assignments—for yourself and your subordinates—particularly those at or near the center of organizational priorities.

- Work to get your ideas on the agenda at key meetings.

- Rescue a colleague or a project in trouble.

- Protect your boss or the company's image by solving a delicate problem.

- Participate on problem-solving task forces and other high-visibility activities.

- Know when to back off.

Some of these steps are obvious, others will turn on lightbulbs in your head: "Why didn't I think of that?" The stories throughout this book contain insights into acquiring power that should spur your own ideas. Think back on **Mannie Jackson** and the five-member committee at Honeywell. **Frank Fountain** stepping in for the new Chrysler controller with the business school students. **Chuck Chaplin** and the Macy's deal. **Milt Irvin** and the Argentine bond deal. **Alana Robinson** neutralizing her boss with the help of a headquarters executive. **Ed Howard** handling J.C. Penney's investor relations. Or **Kim Green** going out on her own. Create your own stories. There is truly no limit. What can your imagination devise? What do your circumstances suggest to you? Your ability to read your own situation, see what no one else has seen, think from a new perspective, is your unique advantage. You're now doing what every successful executive and manager does. You know the drill. Kick it up a notch.

As you map your strategy, never neglect subordinates and peers as a part of your support base. As we have seen with both **Linda**

Keene and **Alana Robinson**, subordinates often have critical information. Their willingness to share with you depends on how you regard them, how you treat them. Given the sensitivity of many African Americans at being seen as a representative of a group rather than as an individual, it is no surprise our executives said treating everyone with respect was the cornerstone of their management style.

Managing relationships among your peers is a delicate process. You begin as colleagues, on the same team, learning to swim in the same water. At early stages of a career, healthy competition is a part of the equation, but at that stage there are enough rewards and promotions to go around. Then, as you work your way up the pyramid, the competition assumes a more significant role. Although trust earned through shared experiences remains an important factor, very quickly you learn to distinguish what you can take at face value. Because there are no formal lines of authority and no one of you has the ability to reward or punish the others, you must learn to convince and influence. That means finding those places where your self-interest intersects with the self-interest of your team members.

Frank Fountain developed a simple but brilliant strategy for building supportive peer relationships in his early years at Chrysler. When he saw a relatively young man appointed CEO, Fountain began asking veterans, "How did he achieve his lofty status so quickly?" The answers, of course, were complex, but everyone cited close association with an important company executive. Fountain doubted he would ever duplicate that kind of personal support, so he created his own support network.

"I got together six or seven of us, all basically on the same level but in different finance departments. I had gotten to know them through work assignments, and I had confidence in them. I was the only black one. I thought by getting together and communicating, developing a tight-knit group of pretty smart people—I thought they were smart—we could leverage each other in a very informal but deft way. The key was having people you felt had potential and were ambitious and yet whose egos would allow them to share. One was someone I'd worked with in an assignment in the president's office, another had been my manager in the parts division. But, of course, we were all still at a level where we didn't have a lot to lose.

"We didn't have a name, but once a month we went to a very good restaurant, probably a little upscale from what we would ordinarily be able to afford. We got together just to get together. It wasn't over golf, it wasn't at a bar. It was a formal dinner. We traded information, and we talked about other issues, like each other's dress, if we didn't think it was appropriate. We talked about openings in our departments. We talked about whatever the politics were. So when the new controller from Ford put together the team to run his reconstituted group, almost all of us ended up there.

"It continued to work for all of us. People in finance are always constantly moving. So when guys started looking for a replacement, well, guess what? The list is created, and we got our friend on the list. Then we talked about what talent this person has: 'And at the very least, you should talk to him.' We leveraged each other. And we must have stayed together maybe three years. Beyond that we didn't. We were now competing with each other in a different kind of way, and we didn't hold the group together, even though today, we will occasionally get together. If a group like that forms, and you're strategically placed, and if you operate not secretly but just informally, it can be extremely powerful."

Indeed. Sharing information and pushing each other enhanced the performance of all members. They learned about successful operating ideas in other departments and got credit for introducing them in their own. They identified opportunities for coordinating activities between and among their departments. They turned to each other for advice. They gave advance notice about job opportunities in their respective divisions, then promoted a group member to their bosses and prepared him for the job interview. You score better in an interview when you get a heads-up and can tailor your strengths to the needs of the department. It was not surprising, therefore, that so many of them were selected.

None of this thinking was new to Fountain. He began in high school figuring out ways to influence his peers. Because he was one of the students from the "feeder" schools, those in the rural areas for the farm kids, he was looked down upon by the sons and daughters of the black town elite, primarily teachers. "No feeder people had ever held any of the school offices, so I set out to change that. I also thought I could succeed, because I considered myself a student of politics at the time. I listened to people talk on the radio, and I read. I got a sense of how politicians did things. I viewed everybody the same, and my relationships were genuine with all of the people. I wasn't identified with the elite group or the regular folks. I was me, not that the elite would ever have considered me one of theirs. I wrote my own speeches, I didn't have the teachers help me the way some of my opponents did. I was the junior and senior class president and then student council president."

Avoiding Race and Gender Sidetracks

All of **Don Brown**'s experience was as a line manager, and he was highly regarded for his results. In addition, he was in a high profile development job as assistant to the manufacturing vice president, overseeing capital budgets for many plants. However, he still had to fight pressure to switch to human resources. This "soft" side of the business is where many minorities and women find themselves: well compensated but off the track to the highest line positions.

"One day my boss called me and said, 'The vice president of human resources would like to know if you're interested in a job in human resources.' I said, 'Is this developmental?' He said, 'Well, it is, but it could also be a change in career.' I said no. He said, 'That's pretty quick. Why did you say that?' I said, 'Well, first of all, I really want to be part of the organization that gets things done.

I like the sense of being involved in how we operate to supply the trade with product, and I just can't see the same kind of excitement, the same sense of challenge every day, that makes every day on the line a new world.' I had talked to HR, worked with them, and I had my HR brother, my mole in corporate America, telling me about the work. So through my own personal observations and listening to him, I knew it wasn't what I wanted to do. I found out almost ten years later that this happened to most minorities, but I just said no because I didn't think I would be happy doing that."

Virgis Colbert disposed of a similar request, to work in community relations, also with dispatch. "When I was still a plant manager, the VP of human resources asked me to go into community relations. When I told him no, he asked, 'Why not?' I said, 'I like what I'm doing. I do community relations as a part of my line job, while I'm doing what I like doing.'" As in Brown's case, the simple refusal worked.

Sometimes refusal doesn't work, which is what happened to **Paula Banks**. She began as a management trainee at Sears and did well as a line manager. Then she accepted several extremely delicate labor relations assignments, with the promise that she would be able to return to line management. "One day I got called in and was asked if I would like to become a part of the employee and labor relations team. That was the group that negotiated all union contracts and handled all union grievances in our various facilities. I was the only person of color, and just the second woman ever in this job in the company. The first woman had a nervous breakdown. Very high stress. I found out about six months into the job that all the guys on the staff en masse told my new boss he had made a terrible mistake. They begged him to pull me off. Instead—and I give this guy lots of credit—he gave me the responsibility for those states where we had the biggest contracts to negotiate. I had Illinois, Michigan, and Wisconsin, the largest automotive service centers. And I was only twenty-seven years old."

Even though she was always promised these assignments would

keep her only temporarily off the line, there was one delicate situation after another to divert her. At first the attention and the challenge of the assignments were enough, but eventually she realized she had no alternative but to stay in human resources. What had been promised as her last special assignment was a plant closing. "Right before the actual closing, the guy who talked me into taking that assignment was getting ready to move from Sears to AllState. He called me in, we sat down, and he said to me, 'I made a commitment to you that this would be your last HR assignment, and you have done it like no one else could have done it. I knew you could. So now, this is what we'll do. We'll fast track you, put you on a six-month training program, in and out of small stores so you can get operating, merchandising, hard lines, and soft lines experience. Then you'll get a B store manager assignment, and in another year and a half you'll manage an A store.' I'd be only thirty-two then, so that sounded good to me.

"I was sitting in my office a couple of weeks later, still working my way through the closing, and I got a call. 'We need to talk to you.' Now my guy has moved on, and the new head of HR is someone I had not gotten along well with in one of my earliest assignments. He told me the new plan. There was no fast track, and I would not be an A store manager for at least eight years. Or I could become the head of HR for all of Midwest catalog distribution. I looked at him and said, 'You know I don't want HR.' He said, 'Then you can take the eight-year path to becoming an A store manager.' I said, 'That's not what I was promised.' He said, 'Well, this is the offer now.' I talked to the president, and he said, 'This is the way we have to do it.' So I took the HR job."

There is nothing wrong with positions on the "soft" side, if that is what you choose. But if you aspire to line positions, "soft" assignments are sidetracks, no matter how attractive the package, and each one makes it harder to return to your original career path. Sometimes you can bide your time and find a way back, but other times you have to rethink your path, which is what Banks had to do.

168

The sidetrack offers come to men and women, and some can be easily avoided, as Brown and Colbert found. But there are deeper questions for ambitious women to ponder. Is it easier to sidetrack women? Why was Banks's refusal not accepted? Is it because corporate men assume women will bend to their will? If that is so, are the men even aware of the assumption? If women don't develop strategies to overcome or at least neutralize this and other limiting perceptions, they will never be in the game. There are no parallel tracks. As our women executives have learned, being accommodating does not work. In corporate America for the near future, nice girls—and boys—will probably finish last.

Women must understand in their gut the rules of the game and take them seriously enough to play to win. But even if they believe they know the rules and are playing to win, do men take them seriously in the competition? For too many women, the answer is no. Yet if women do not find a way to be serious players, as corporate men define serious players, they are not only eliminating themselves from the competition, they are also buying in to the corporate male view of them as non-players. Women have made progress, so these questions point the way to the next steps. And the path for African-American women is undoubtedly longer and more difficult. The stories here prove there are strategies that work. These women are slowly but surely bringing clarity to the murky area where the unresolved issues of race and gender intertwine.

Consider **Margaret Jordan**'s achievements in light of these questions. Was she rewarded for turning around Kaiser's Dallas region? No. "Kaiser got a new CEO, someone I had come in with. I considered him a good friend, and I supported him when his name came up for CEO. But after he got it, he talked to me twice about taking what I call 'totin' and fetchin' jobs.' He said, 'We are getting ready to go into health reform, and we need someone with your national connections.' Another time he said, 'I'm thinking of putting human resources and information technology together, and I'd like you to be over all of it.' Well, no way. The power of the organizations is in the line, and I am a seasoned executive. I was so disappointed, especially when I found he didn't even want to make the position a senior VP. It was just going to be a VP.

"Then something else happened that really made me receptive to leaving. First he raised his salary. I can honestly say the prior CEO had an artificially depressed salary, so everybody else's salary was depressed. The new one went the opposite way, and that prompted a look at all the other officers' salaries. I found I wasn't even on the first step of my salary range, which means I was not where I should have been before either. I was furious. When you are feeling this way, when these things happen, you start listening to the headhunters when they call. One of those calls got me the best job of my life."

Competing for Power

Acquiring power and becoming a successful executive requires the use of all your skills in combination, at different times, and in different ways. For example, you are unlikely to receive key assignments unless you already have key supporters, have worked hard, and have proved yourself technically and politically capable. Power acquisition is a complex chess game that never ends, and you have to work hard to keep up with the competition.

Here is what **Frank Fountain** did when he, as an assistant controller at Chrysler, found himself caught between the operations people and a new and difficult controller who wanted to keep them in line. He called it "delicate surgery," a perilous assignment for someone in contention for top finance jobs. "After the downturn of the early 1990s, my boss, the controller, was named the VP of personnel. The new controller had a different style; people say he was heavy-handed. The operating people had their sights set on bringing him down, because he made their lives miserable. Finance and operations can be serious adversaries, but I had always worked well with both. It helped that I'd had so many finance assignments throughout the company over the years, but also my history and political science background gave me a broader perspective than many others in finance.

"But now I was the one assigned to manufacture bumps for operations people, to put together the tough analysis, the bad news, in a way that would cause them concern. This was the controller's way of trying to keep their spending in line. Delivering the bad news is as dangerous as creating it, sometimes more so. All of this was against my better judgment, but loyalty is a very important part of the corporate environment, and it's even more important to some than others. All through that year it was very tough for me to survive. On the one hand, I had to figure out how to be loyal to the controller. On the other hand, I had to show the operating officers I was separate from him. If the operations people succeeded in bringing the controller down, I could go down with him just because I was close to or at the scene.

"I managed it through a combination of things. One, I low-profiled it, stayed as far in the background as I could. And the other was having lunch with some of the operations officers, not to talk about finance or any issues per se, but just to get acquainted. In the process I could let them know some of my philosophy on things. I never had to talk about my boss or say anything negative about what he was doing. Finally, we had two quarters of profitability, and the crisis was over for then. I got through a pretty intense environment in good shape, and I was implicitly in the queue for one of the top finance slots."

When **Chuck Chaplin** made his decision to compete for the treasurer position, he had done everything right. He knew where he stood: He had the commitment of top executives at Prudential; he had the full support and confidence of his long-time supporters at the top of its mortgage company. He thought he understood the new challenge he had accepted, but as if to mock his thorough analysis, most of the elements he relied on when he took the leap disappeared. The property and casualty subsidiary was destroyed by Hurricane Andrew, and within a year and a half the board had replaced the entire top management team. He was left with only his own experience and the confidence to adapt and grow. That was enough.

"The part of my job that was supposed to be easy was reporting to the rating agencies. Our reserves were in order, the risks were minimal, and it was a nice way for a new guy to get involved with all that was going on in the company. Andrew changed all that. My first meeting I'm telling them, 'We're going to lose $300 million.' A week later I'm in there saying, 'No, it's going to be $1.5 billion.' So I started out under stress, and it just got worse. The CEO who looked so favorably on positioning me was replaced. Within a year and a half of my start, everyone who had signed off on my development plan was gone, promoted, changed jobs, took early retirement, left the company, downsized, fired, whatever. They were all gone. 1993 was worse than '92, and '94 seemed like the end of the world.

"Then the new management team said, 'Nobody moves.' So they're doing their triage, but what they're really doing is keeping everybody in place while aiming at them. It's easy to hit targets if they don't move. Now I had to prove myself all over again to a new group of people. I just continued to work, to do what I had been doing. The problems we had were business problems as opposed to treasury problems. It was a trial by fire for me because I was the one who had to go up and explain why we had these business problems. I guess I did that in a fairly credible way.

"Within a year my then boss, the treasurer, and I had our fondest wishes granted. We were both promoted. He became the CFO of one of our major businesses, and I became the treasurer. See how easy? Anybody could do it. So I become part of the new chairman's team, and you could say it was a completely new team. All but one of the 200 top executives of the firm were new to their

172

roles. About half of them were from the outside. The other half were retreads like me, people who were inside Prudential and either promoted into their roles or transferred from other places."

Recognizing the constant shifts in terrain and adjusting to them is your only choice if you aspire to top positions in a large organization. Even for CEOs there are no guarantees. Learning to function effectively anyway is what mastery is all about.

Sometimes your best efforts, even after years of successes, are not enough. You cannot figure out why certain things are happening to you, and you therefore cannot devise a strategy to remedy them. That happened to **David Hinds** after more than twenty years of excellent reputation, excellent performance, and many promotions. Even though he was a partner, he was passed over for a job he believed he deserved and had been promised.

"I was in Italy on a client call when one of my peers called and told me. I was completely unprepared and more than slightly annoyed it happened when I was out of the country. So I called the person I was working for, the most senior person in the equation and the one who had promised me the job. He told me he was moving on and that other decisions had been made. What could I do, especially in Italy? When I returned, they started offering me staff positions, saying they wanted to test my strategic skills. Of course, those had already been tested, and I'd scored well.

"The next three years were probably the most difficult of my career because I was not in challenging or frontline positions. It was tough to walk into an environment every day knowing full well people think you're a player, but you know you're not. You say to yourself, 'Do I really want to put up with that kind of pressure?' I came to the conclusion I didn't. This was just not the way I wanted to end my career, doing some also-ran stuff. Here I was feeling I had accomplished, had produced, had added value. There was a major disconnect between my view of myself and the company's view of me. So why bang my head against the wall? I wasn't going to starve.

"I decided to break the connection on my own terms. I was planning a trip back to Barbados with some friends to celebrate turning fifty. It would be my first visit since my family left when I was six, and that seemed an appropriate transition. I told my boss, 'Listen, it's been a great run. I have been able to contribute.' I had lunch with Vernon Jordan just to let him know. I felt very good.

"When I came back from vacation they offered me the job I didn't get when I was in Italy, and the rest is history. I think what happened was that a couple of things came together. We had a change of management at that time, and my old area was a big problem. The chairman wanted to restructure the group and bring more management into it. That's when Vernon Jordan said to the chairman, 'You ought to have a conversation with the guy, and then sort out what you want to do.' The chairman called when I returned, and I sat down with him. I think our conversation made him aware of my past performance, so they basically put two and two together: 'Here's a guy who knows the business we're having issues with and who has contributed to that business in the past.' I said, 'This could be fun.' When I took over the group, within a year we turned it into a winning proposition and one of the most profitable businesses around."

When BP and Amoco merged, **Paula Banks** received an assignment she didn't want, the BP Amoco Foundation. "I had to accept, because they offered it to me in a kind of public platform, with other people around. But I immediately went into my boss and said, 'You know I won't do this. I will not run another foundation, not under any circumstances. I don't even care how much money you pay me. I've been there. I've done that. And I am bored beyond belief.' He said, 'The only other job would require you to move to London, and I didn't think you would want to do that.' I said, 'And why not? I can decide my own priorities. You don't need to decide them for me.' So I moved to London.

"Then the adventure became restaffing and refocusing my whole area on a global stage. It was by far the most challenging, the most professionally lonely, and at the same time the most rewarding experience of my life. I was a trailblazer. There was absolutely no blueprint for what I was doing. Global businesses can no longer stay successful unless the markets in which they do business actually support the very existence of the businesses. We had to learn how to be an effective partner in those markets and those communities. I was turning something soft, something never well regarded or respected by the line people, into something they must respect and, 'Oh, by the way, part of your performance contract, Mr. Line Manager.' It was no longer enough for a business unit leader to produce net profits without viewing the work in a broader context. The business has to be sustainable. That's the part that was exciting, but it was also mentally exhausting.

"My unit was designated an appropriate development job, and I got talented line people for a year and a half as part of their succession planning. Those years were the most freeing. I finally came into my own. I recognized my capacity. I was at the point where I knew what I could do and could choose what I did. I was prepared to say, 'I can walk away from this,' and that makes everything I do meaningful."

One can only imagine what a struggle Banks went through to get her department recognized as a true business initiative. And she accomplished this in the oil industry, which has traditionally been inhospitable to women and minorities.

Power acquisition requires orchestrating events and people in the right place and at the right time. Position yourself in the organization so you are dealing with strategically important problems. Marshal the resources necessary to achieve your objective—people support, information, equipment, personal assets, rewards and punishments. Now your job is to bring about the results you want in your specific environment. Your ability to get results will expand every time you test your limits and learn from a mistake, and every time you test your limits and succeed.

9.

Using Power for Leadership

A person who goes into a room with all the answers, who thinks he can give orders for everyone else to follow, tends not to do well over the long term. If you look at the senior VPs who report to the CEO of any major corporation, they are not sheep. They're not going to roll over and follow your orders. You have to influence them and win them over as followers.

—**Gerald Adolph**, Senior Partner
Booz, Allen, Hamilton

It's a very rarified political environment in which we operate here, where one can suffer loss of cabin pressure any time. But having influence over financial policy in an organization of our size and scope is so exhilarating. That's the trade-off for dealing with the hard part.

—**C. Edward "Chuck" Chaplin**, Senior Vice President and Treasurer
Prudential Financial, Inc.

POWER used effectively is leadership. Throughout this book we have talked about the building blocks of power and, ultimately, corporate leadership, especially as they apply to you, African-American men and women. You have learned not only to understand the ambiguous nature of corporate life but also to make it your personal friend, a motivating factor. You have learned strategies to understand and then to manage race and gender issues as well as the disappointment, frustration and even rage that flare up on those occasions. You have learned the step-by-step process of building your own self-confidence in your business ability and then marketing skills and ideas throughout the corporation. You have cultivated the kinds of relationships with subordinates, peers, and managers that should propel your upward progress. You have learned to take risks and to build on successes and learn from failures. You understand the value of power and influence, and you are comfortable competing for it. You have set your goals, and you are using your power to allow you to accomplish them for your company and for yourself. Now keep your leadership position polished.

- Constantly stroke and massage your relationships. If networks are not tended to, people will find new power sources. Give time and information to the people you value, so they know they are aligned with the right person.

- Be ever vigilant to the reality of changed circumstances—different alliances, new people, changing facts, data, and priorities—and be prepared to adjust your strategies accordingly.

- Keep your antennae tuned to power shifts: all people who have influence over you, your job assignment, your ability to carry out your tasks, and your performance appraisals. With every shift there is a need to establish or reestablish relationships with all relevant players.

- Remain acutely sensitive to the consequences of your decisions and actions. Be willing to back step to make certain you keep the right people informed.

- Don't squander your power on needless fights. Set priorities so you can identify the issues and situations you must influence, and say no to issues that are unimportant to—or can divert you from—your goals.

- Make certain every exercise of power is focused on benefiting the interests of the organization. If others perceive your use of power as only self-serving, the organization will turn against you.

You have a formidable task ahead of you. But rest assured, if you have taken to heart the words of our successful executives and held a truthful mirror to your own experiences and capabilities, you can and will make progress. The more you practice their mindset and incorporate their actions and strategies—and your own—into your daily work life, the more natural and automatic the behaviors become. These are the skills that build and maintain corporate leadership. Now it is time to coordinate everything, add more insights, and put it all to work, for you and your company.

Models of Leadership

Gerald Adolph, a management consultant, has made a study of leadership in many corporations. His job is to help corporate leaders understand where they should go, where they can go, and then how to get there. "The leader is the person who can make something happen. Can you get people to rally around and move in the direction you want them to move? Can you come up with something that is going to inspire them? You have to try to figure out where this crowd would like to go and then how to tease that out of them. How do you make it explicit, so they can all go there together?

"Many people think those in the corporate environment come up with ideas and then lead everyone in that direction. There aren't very many great leaders who lead that way. It is a flawed model of leadership that says, 'I have the answer.' That's not listening and figuring out, 'Where does this group, whether it's a client corporation or a group of senior executives, want to go? How can I get them to the intersection of where they want to go and where my analysis says they ought to go, taking into account their politics and all the other things they're trying to manage?' So it's *getting* them somewhere rather than trying to *put* them there. A person who goes in a room with all the answers and thinks he can give orders for everyone else to follow tends not to do well over the long term.

"Leadership over the long term is figuring out, 'What is it that the people I'm leading are naturally inclined to do? How do I make the best of the talents and the resources around me? I can't force them, even though I can give them some orders and maybe hold up a paycheck or two.' There is the illusion of authority, but it's just an illusion. If you look at the senior VPs of major corporations, they are not sheep. They're not going to roll over and follow the CEO's orders. You have to influence them."

You will be able to influence the behavior of others by using your power effectively. This analysis applies to any leader, black or white, male or female, at any level of the corporation. But when you are black and/or female, there are more layers to consider. For blacks in leadership positions, there is still more resistance and more scrutiny, and evaluations can be less than fair. The testing is often subtle, and you must work relentlessly to neutralize any lingering resentment. Sometimes that resentment takes the form of what **Lloyd Trotter** calls "malicious obedience," following the letter of your instruction in such a way that the process is damaged or destroyed. Trotter used humor to surmount one of the many "managerial hurdles" put in the path of early black managers on GE lines. "I had assigned some work to an individual who was a very good tool maker, but a piece of equipment had gone down. He came back to me and said, 'I can't finish because I can't use the tool to put the threads into this part.' I said, 'It'll take longer, but why don't you set it up on the lathe and do it manually?' He said, 'I don't know how to do that, and no one else in this shop can either.' I didn't believe him, but I said, 'Go get the lathe ready, and I'll show you how to do it.' He never expected that. I called the whole shop, stopped all work so everyone could watch. I said, 'It's just come to my attention that some folks don't understand how to chase a left-handed thread, so we might as well all learn together. This is the on button.' And we went on through it like that.

"There was a lot of back and forth, and it got hilarious. At the end of it, everybody was laughing, and it began to be more of a joke than real tense. The guy who started it all said to me, 'Why didn't you tell me that you knew how to do it?' Of course, everybody knew how to do it. But I knew I had to solve this right there and then and not let it fester. There have been a lot of challenges like that."

A test **Paula Banks** faced on one new assignment was a political hot potato. The one black service technician in a service center had an alcohol problem but had been kept on and on. All eyes were on Banks as the new human resources manager. "I forced our service center manager to fire his only black service technician, and they never thought I'd do that. Young guy, very talented, but he was an alcoholic. He and I put together a contract that both of us had signed. He lasted for six months, but when he fell off in the seventh month, I called him and said, 'You just severed your employment.' All the managers said, 'You can't do that, he tried so hard.' I said, 'We can't do this to him. We can't be enablers.'

"I went on to get five more African Americans promoted into jobs, but they were quality people. I took the opportunity to put people into positions to succeed rather than positions to fail. None of them would ever have been allowed to be there because they kept pointing to this one guy who had an issue. He became the standard by which they judged everybody." Banks's ability to see the bigger picture allowed her to clean up a situation that had stymied diversity in that department. Her strength won the respect of the other managers and workers.

David Hinds is realistic about African-American men in corporate leadership roles. "I don't think you can sit down and write a formula, but for us there are many more skills to acquire before you can lead. For example, certain people can be autocratic and get away with it. No African American I know would ever be successful with a dogmatic style, irrespective of how brilliant you are, how right you are. It ain't gonna happen. That kind of behavior would conjure up all sorts of terrible images in peoples' minds, and you would get resistance immediately."

He sees a distinct advantage for African Americans in the delicate balance of the emerging global economy. "There is a unique skill set, especially in the leadership arena, we bring to the table. Clients come from all over the world, and that will be increasingly true. Being able to appreciate their differences and deal with them across language and cultural barriers is important. We know about that, because we have been on the other side. I believe the path for us to cross that bridge is clearer than for others who have not had that experience. We have an intellectual, as well as an emotional, understanding of managing complex personnel issues in complex organizations. It emanates from having navigated many systems that were not necessarily hospitable. We recognize this as an opportunity where we can add value. We know the need to create an environment that is broader and more responsive to and appreciative of human differences."

Being a leader is never easy. There are endless tests, even if you see yourself, as Hinds does, with more finely honed insights about people. Leaders are constantly striving for the delicate balance between stressful work and the thrill of success. Here is how

Chuck Chaplin describes life at the top. "It's taken longer to get happy here. Everything's hard. There's no other way to say it. In the field, your responsibilities are so clear. You don't waste any time figuring out what they are, or negotiating with anybody about them. My responsibilities were to generate profits for the company and manage the loan portfolio. Those are easy to measure. What we do here is not. It's even hard to define where my responsibility as treasurer begins and ends and where the controller's begins and ends. It's the same with every other position.

"It's a very rarified political environment in which we operate, where one can suffer loss of cabin pressure any time. There's just so much political infighting. All the executives are trying to coalesce as a team and at the same time make enormous change in the company. Anything you do, you have to coordinate across a wide variety of business and corporate centers. It's very stressful. Everything we do is hard.

"But having influence over financial policy in an organization of our size and scope is just so exhilarating. The ability to help take our company from private to public ownership, to help make that happen is enormously motivating. And that's the trade-off for dealing with the hard part. You have to balance the stressful part with the great satisfaction you take from the accomplishments. It's taken me longer to figure out how all this is fun, but I'm getting there."

Do you have to mask who you are as a person in order to lead? Many blacks outside corporate America, and even many inside, believe becoming or at least acting a different person is part of the bargain. Do you have to become "white," whatever that means, to be successful? Are you selling out? There are many perspectives from which to view events, and you have to find the one that works for you, that allows you to be yourself and continue to achieve.

Linda Keene, a very successful marketing executive, found no such requirements. "About ten years ago, our division president sent all of his leadership team through an executive development program. When we talked about the characteristics of successful leaders, one of the things that kept coming up was that they are comfortable with who they are and generally present themselves in a consistent manner. People tend to be much more comfortable following when 'what you see is what you get.' This concept of authenticity has really stayed with me over the years. It's being who you are in all phases of your life.

"I feel I am able to be myself, be authentic, in a corporate setting or in the community. Of course, I modify how I communicate depending on the audience, but it's never really all that different. And that's one of the reasons I think I've been able to build successful working relationships. People feel they can trust me to be honest and direct with them, and they know I won't change my position on an issue depending on the audience. If I have a genuine concern about something, they will know I have that concern wherever I am. I think my company benefits from that.

"Sometimes when I talk to young black people, I get the sense they feel that being in corporate life will force them to choose between being themselves and being successful. While there are places that might be true, I've found you can seek out environments where your personality and the organizational culture are compatible. I have tried to avoid placing myself in situations where I feel I have to be something alien to who I am. Even when a particular work environment wasn't necessarily the most familiar to me, I always felt there was at least the potential for someone like me to be accepted. Since there weren't many black or female executives in the companies I joined early in my career, I'd look for clues like whether the white men all seemed cut from the same mold. If they were, I concluded the organization's tolerance for differences was probably limited, and I moved on."

Leadership involves seeing beyond what others can see and then enlisting their help to bring about your vision. You need a clear vision of where your organization should go and the ability to articulate that vision clearly. Those who work for you must

184

understand not only your vision but also their roles in bringing it about. **Lloyd Trotter** describes that ability as one of his key strengths as a leader. "I understand how to take complex problems, distill them to issues, and then put very simple, clear directions around them. Then everyone is involved in the movement to resolve or at least improve the situation." He increases his power by empowering others.

The same ability helped **Alana Robinson** as she integrated her local high school, and it guides her today. "I was always in awe of the influence my dad had on other people, and I always tried to model myself after him. He was very practical, very simple. So I always broke complex things down into some simple things first, so that I was not overwhelmed with how big or hard some things were. I'd pick out the pieces I could do something about and make baby steps at progress instead of trying to conquer the world. Then when I was a programmer at IBM and had to train customers, I found the same principles made me an effective teacher. It's no different from what I do today, design and implement company-wide technology systems. People are able to adapt to very big changes when they understand what you want and how it will improve their own results."

Mergers Are Opportunities

A merger or acquisition is an increasingly common event in the corporate world. Familiar landscapes change radically and immediately. As **Paula Banks** said, "You go to work one morning, and it's a whole new world." It's a world where everything is unknown and uncertain, even for the CEO. It is said that power abhors a vacuum, so mergers present an opportunity for the leader who is ready to seize it to make the uncertain certain, to bring clarity and new vision to a situation in flux. Being in the middle of a transition can bring out the worst in people; their very livelihood is threatened.

But it is also an opportunity to use power to show leadership. Within two years of **David Hinds**'s promotion to the Bankers Trust job that had eluded him for three years, the bank to which he had devoted his entire career disappeared. It merged with its main global competitor, Deutsche Bank.

"I had been around this company a long time, and I saw it grow from a localized commercial bank to a well-respected global financial organization. Having been a part of that progress and then to be acquired by someone else is tough emotionally. As a member of that company, I had put a lot of my own energy and time, blood, sweat, and tears into a particular image, that branded product. For that product to virtually disappear from the face of the earth as an entity was tough. Mergers are very traumatic experiences for everyone, even if the other company is just down the block. But contemplating a merger from across the Atlantic, with a different language and culture, makes it that much more complicated. If you had asked me in the beginning how successful I thought we could be at the new company, bringing the heritage of Bankers Trust together with the heritage of Deutsche Bank, I probably would have said, 'This is going to be a very difficult proposition, without a high degree of probability for early-on success.' Being in the more vulnerable position because we were bought out, we had to work hard to focus on our strengths.

"But people are people, whether they are sitting in Germany or Sri Lanka. People can get focused on common goals and common objectives. The trick is always having enough patience to spend the time understanding what drives the other person. You really have to understand the past, because sometimes the same terminology does not mean the same thing. If you are not willing to take that time, you create a whole lot of other problems. I've been pleasantly surprised at how people can come together.

"Not that things were simple. There are certain areas where you can make quick decisions, where people agree, and other areas that are more complex. Typically, the complexity comes from the human factor in that equation, and you really have to figure out a way to get around it. When people get focused on the mission and the objectives, that is when people begin to forget about the heritage of Bankers Trust, of Deutsche Bank. People become driven more by the prospect of being successful now and in the future than they are by the past.

"In our particular case we had unique strengths to bring in the area of global payments. The U.S. banks, and certainly Bankers Trust, had been running these products and services as businesses for about the last fifteen years, much longer than the European banks. Our technologies turned out to be complementary. There was overlap on some clients, and they had a much greater market share, but because of our dominance in the dollar, our products were also complementary. When we found we didn't have many people overlaps—the synergies came from the revenue side of the equation and not from reducing bodies—the rationale became relatively straightforward: 'Here is a well-established business model. Let's integrate DB into this business model, and then take to the market something that is better than old BT, old DB.' When we moved from the emotion of the merger to the value proposition for the client, when we really got people focused on that side of the equation, we made a lot of progress. I think for the most part, that is how you get over the rocks in the road. Of course from the client perspective, this is great stuff."

Hinds's ability to influence people, even across language and culture, made him a respected leader within his corporation and played a large role in his ability to bring in and maintain clients. "I have never been a person who even attempts the hard sell. What you are really trying to do is establish a confidence level with the specific person you are helping. They need to believe that you, as a senior individual, understand their issues and are driving the organization to help them be more competitive. At the end of the day, clients really want to feel good about who you are as an individual, the company you work for, and then how you help them be more successful, almost in that order. If you focus on establishing a personal rapport, on making sure clients feel you're operating in their best interest, and on getting some economic value for them, they will want to continue doing business with you.

"Clients have to know you will be there if and when something goes wrong. There have been a number of situations where I've flown twenty hours to see a client who was concerned about something. You could be the greatest organization, but if you have lousy client coverage, you're not going to do business. The consistency of your dealings—and the economics of the transaction itself—instills confidence and gives you history and integrity. That's the cutting edge. That's what makes a client want to work with your organization versus another."

Once the difficult trans-Atlantic transition had been essentially completed, Hinds retired at the top of his game. Listening to him talk about respect for his colleagues and clients, and knowing all he accomplished for his corporation despite a few years of being pushed aside, one realizes what a terrible loss it would have been for Bankers Trust, Deutsche Bank, and their clients if Hinds had been excluded because of his race. As **Bob Johnson** concluded, "All considerations that don't contribute to the business of the corporation, including race, are just distractions."

Sometimes in a merger, however, there is no chance for your leadership skills to influence the situation. Here is how **Brenda Lauderback** handled the acquisition of her company, U.S. Shoe, by Nine West. "My CEO at U.S. Shoe used to work at Nine West, and I knew the company as a customer from my Dayton Hudson years, so we knew there were going to be challenges. The Nine West chairman was one of the brightest men I've ever been around, but he had a dark side: He liked to belittle people, stir things up. He could be very negative. I don't like that style. I don't treat people that way, and I don't like to be treated that way. But we went with the new management team. We decided to give it a try.

"The deal was marketed to us as a merger. U.S. Shoe would no longer exist, but we believed we could transform the Nine West culture. That chairman was supposed to leave after a one-year transition period, his CEO, who I admired greatly, would become chairman, and my U.S. Shoe CEO, who was the Nine West president, my long-time colleague, would become the CEO. I would then be next in line for president. But when we got to Nine West, most of them called it an acquisition. They had acquired us, and that was the way it was going to be. A few of them thought they should have had my job, and they were very difficult for me to deal with.

"I had plenty to do. I had to transition all my businesses to the East Coast, build a whole new infrastructure. So even with the resentment surrounding the merger, the first two years went by very quickly. But then the chairman was still there, and it was very clear he had no intention of going anywhere. We found out the chairman had never wanted to buy U.S. Shoe. It was the CEO's idea, and now the two were barely speaking. They wouldn't even come to the same meeting. So you had to do one meeting for the chairman and one meeting for the CEO. Well, you'd get to a point where one says, 'Go right,' and the other says, 'Go left.' Okay, where do you go? And the president was always caught in the middle.

"Nine West overpaid for U.S. Shoe. Because of this, decisions were made to pay off the debt, not necessarily the right ones for the business. These two companies were the best in the shoe business, and if they had focused on that, they could have formed a phenomenal new company. But we all paid the price for their mistakes and their bad relationship. Then the government investigations started, something we had not expected. For the first time in my life I was disappointed in my work. I didn't have the passion. I didn't have the joy. I didn't have the fulfillment of going in to work every-day and running my business. I didn't see things getting better anytime soon.

"At the end of the third year, the change of control clause in my U.S. Shoe contract was expiring, so I told the CEO I wanted to leave. He and the president talked me out of it. They really had me believing we were over the hump, that the two companies were coming together, that the worst was behind us. I got a new contract with Nine West, and it was a long one.

"But things did not get better, and a year later the president, my old U.S. Shoe CEO, decided to leave. He knew the two companies weren't ever going to come together the way we wanted, and I knew I never wanted to be there without him. There was no money, no title, no responsibility that would make me stay in that environment. But then there was the question of my long-term contract. The president and the CEO went to bat for me. Nine West bought out my whole contract, bonuses and all. It was pretty shaky and nerve-wracking there for a period of time, especially after the chairman got involved. They could have done it differently, because I was so anxious at that point to go. I probably would have settled for something less. I just wanted to get out of there and out of the chairman's energy field.

"Having a buyout on my contract was phenomenal from my standpoint. My husband and I had always been able to save throughout the years, and we were able to invest all my contract buyout. Quite honestly, it gave us financial independence. I decided to take some time off and spend some time with my family, get to know my kids.

"Less than a year later they had to sell the company to Jones New York. The company was in total disarray. Both the chairman and CEO were gone. Of course they did very well for themselves. Maybe I should have waited another year. But I made my decision based on what I knew, and I was so glad to be gone, I could've cared less. But this whole thing is something I never would have believed could happen in a five-year period. No one who was there at the acquisition is involved anymore. It's a sad story. It should be a case study of what not to do with a company."

Once you have reached a level of leadership where you have confidence, skill, a track record, and a measure of financial security, you have more options, including choosing a different environment.

Leading at Smaller Companies

Leadership opportunities at smaller companies are no less exhilarating and challenging. After almost twenty-three years at Kraft, **Don Brown** was assigned to run the operations group for Kraft-General Foods Canada, and there he got a taste of what it was like to be the leader.

"The operations office was independent, in a different city than our corporate office. They didn't pay a great deal of attention to us, not unless we screwed up. But we made our operations very successful. We turned around a high cost, low quality, low morale company, with terrible internal problems. I went out and made sure we had a good, strong staff, and then we worked, we played, we agonized, we did a lot of stuff together that made us forever friends and forever connected. Almost every one of us went on to something more significant in our careers. People who were in my organization are now running operations at other companies. Most of those guys were taken away by other companies to do the same kind of turnaround.

"I wanted the opportunity to use my Canadian experience to turn another company 180 degrees. That's all I was down for, and it wasn't going to happen at Kraft. Kraft was not only large, it was also very siloed. In other words, sales did its thing, marketing did its thing, and operations did its thing.

"Coors was in much the same position as the Kraft Canadian operations, but the problems were both inside and outside the company. I believe we had pissed off every group in the world. I bet you even today if you go out and start talking about Coors, you'll get negative reactions from the gay community, the Hispanic community, and especially the African-American community. It was the charge of the current CEO, the Coors patriarch and son of the founder, to change the image. Now I had already researched some and knew it was going to be a challenge within my community. But for me it was an organization much like the one in Canada.

"Coors beer was so popular in other parts of the market, it could basically get away with a bad image and bad service for a while. But Coors was a group of people who never changed. They resisted everything that ever came along. But times change, and they couldn't maintain that. They went out and got a whole new team, marketing, sales, HR. But they could never find the operations person.

"They said to me, 'You're the missing operations piece. We knew you were the man for it ten minutes after you sat down, so you've got to come with us.' I couldn't walk away from that kind of money, but the biggest hook was, this was a great chance to apply what I thought I could do. And we did it. Our organization deserves and gets a lot of credit for doing things to control costs, improve morale, and get people more concentrated on service. We became seen as providing the best service in our industry, one of the best places to work of any brewery because of the diversity we had and the atmosphere we built, and I was a big part of increasing the diversity. Coors is just about one-tenth the size of Kraft, but I had greater influence and a higher degree of satisfaction.

"You could say I had a lot less work, because I had fewer plants and the same size staff. I had the ego and image thing working at Kraft, but I had just the operations group. The real power brokers there were not in operations; it was marketing and the COO. At Coors I had a greater influence on the company. I was part of a group of ten people who ran everything. We made all the cans and bottles, designed all the products, made the beer, shipped it, and marketed it. So if marketing wanted something done, we had to talk. The head of sales and marketing and I were always talking about what's selling, what's not, how do we get product, what are we going to do next year, next century.

"Had I maybe had less ambition, I'd probably have stayed at Kraft. I will always cherish the learning opportunity I got there, and I still have a lot of respect for the folks there, but I'm just so happy I left. Somebody was watching over me out there."

Al Little's move from Sunoco to Newport News Shipbuilding in 1996 was prompted by similar considerations, and the outcome was the same. NNS was being spun off by Tenneco, and the new CEO was recruiting key executives to take the company public. Little became one of five members of the company's management committee, a real seat at the table. "I was quite content at Sunoco. It was big and safe, and I had been very successful. NNS was really a start-up and much smaller than any other place I'd worked. I had to think hard about giving up the big corporate label. As I think back on my decision, I feel strongly that we as African Americans often put too much emphasis on the prestige and perceived security of the 'big corporation.' I'm so glad I moved. My influence, my freedom to act, my personal satisfaction, and my financial rewards grew immensely. I now know bigger is not always better."

Early in her career, **Kim Green** decided to leave a large insurance brokerage firm, where she was doing very well but sensed she would be limited as a black and a woman. She opened her own firm and soon discovered she had found a strategy to overcome these very limitations. She had become a valuable commodity. Thanks to the absence of the non-compete agreement, she had a roster of major corporations for clients, and before long, a number of brokerage firms approached her with joint venture and co-broker opportunities. She was in a position to pick and choose. " 'Kim, come and have lunch. We'll talk about doing some joint ventures on some of your large accounts where you probably need help.' We talked, and right before I left, a very senior individual said, 'Whenever you get tired of this, we'll hire you. We'll make life easy for you, so call me.' I was insulted. Moved on.

"The next was a private company, very conservative, the 'blue blood' club. After many social occasions with the most senior people, I had a meeting with the woman who ran the New York office. She was not happy I had been meeting with the senior people, meetings she knew nothing about. She said, 'Senior management doesn't run the day to day,' telling me indirectly she was going to make my life difficult. This whole political situation was not anything that interested me.

"Aon, where I did accept, was another offer. My boss from the beginning of my brokering days had become Aon's vice chair, and he invited me to lunch with one of his colleagues. I remember thinking, 'It would be nice to reconnect,' but I wasn't sure about his agenda for the lunch. We discussed our industry and the challenge that consolidation presented to all of us, minority or majority. We discussed some of my opportunities with Fortune 500 companies, and the problems a small firm like mine faced on the global resource side, the 'back office' operation. They offered support in a co-broker arrangement, and gave me an open offer, whenever I was ready for a change. They didn't say business was too difficult for me, or that I would fail without help. They were not patronizing; they saw mutual opportunity. I had clients, business solutions, and expertise to bring to their firm, and they offered me the back office resources that would deepen my service. This approach, plus their entrepreneurial spirit, vision and global resources, sold me. I went in as a senior vice president."

Board Membership

The clearest message that you have been accepted in the leadership ranks of corporate America is to be asked to serve on a board of directors. Until very recently boards were what **Elynor Williams** describes as 'a thick layer of white men' that minorities and women could not penetrate. A deliberate strategy by black organizations and executives, and a number of supportive corporations, have begun to chip away at that barrier.

Jim Kaiser got his first opportunity from his own company. Corning put him on the board of one of its subsidiaries, Dow Corning. "Even though it is an internal board, it gives you some level of promise and credibility. You've got one. Then in moving me from a Corning division to a Corning subsidiary, they gave me the title of CEO. That, plus the Dow Corning board, made me acceptable to other boards." An Executive Leadership Council member who served on the board of Stanley Tools, what Kaiser calls his first "real board," recommended him to fill a vacancy. "Now you have an independent Fortune 500 board, and you have the CEO title. That leads you to other boards."

Kaiser's next board was Sunoco. This invitation came because of his connection to a particularly influential board member. The head of the nominating committee, a former Dean of MIT's Sloan School, recommended him for the board. "That's how the second one happened." Then he was in the pipeline, and executive search firms started calling.

Board membership can be more than a reward for demonstrated leadership. It can make you a better leader by affording you a broader perspective. When **Brenda Lauderback** found herself in the negative environment of the new Nine West Group, it was outside board membership that saved her sanity and eventually gave her the courage to leave. Once again, it was the company's failure to see her as real competition that gave her that option. "I wasn't thinking about joining boards, but my attorney insisted I put a board membership clause in my employment contract. No one objected; they probably never even thought it was possible for me.

"Then a family-run financial services company came after me to join the board. They were looking for someone with a retail background because they were beginning to concentrate on marketing strategies, and they were looking for diversity. The CEO was the third or fourth generation of his family to head this company, and he had vision and compassion. The company was about core values. It was like a breath of fresh air. You would see how the team worked there and how they felt about the company and their CEO. You could see how they were growing and putting long-term strategies in place, as opposed to doing whatever is necessary for the short-term hit. Their ethical values had been entrenched in the company for generations. So it helped me to see the problems at Nine West for what they were. I used to go home some days and look in the mirror and say, 'Is it me?' Now I knew it wasn't. I've been able to expand the boards I'm on. They keep me up-to-date in the business world, but I don't have to be totally immersed."

Bob Johnson now has the opportunity to show leadership on macroeconomic policy, networking at the highest level. After retiring from Sears, he based his own company in Memphis, and he came to the attention of the Federal Reserve Branch president there. After several meetings with her, he was asked to take a seat on the Federal Reserve Board for the St. Louis district, one of twelve districts nationwide. "Now I understand very literally what it means to cool down the economy by raising the interest rate. We're sitting there tweaking those numbers, trying to keep this thing in balance.

"In every situation you get two kinds of compensation. You get money, and you get experience. If you just work for money, you're leaving half your compensation on the table. Everything I've done in retail, everything I've done at the Housing Authority, everything I've done in the packaging business, everything I've done on the boards of colleges, of nonprofit organizations, of small businesses and the Federal Reserve, everything has contributed to my knowledge and my ability to generate business ideas and business solutions. I've done enough to be able to offer a service in a number of different areas."

For those executives who attribute their corporate opportunities to the successful battles of the civil rights movement, leadership means leveraging your power for some good purpose. This is an issue **Bruce Gordon** takes very seriously. "Dr. King couldn't have worked for a Fortune 500 company. He had the talent—maybe not the desire—but he wasn't going to get a shot at that. But people like him got me in the door. I have an obligation, and I mean that

196

word literally, to use the power he put in my hand. That's just very clear to me. Some folks find their way to that conclusion easily and clearly, and I'm glad I'm one of those. I've got the obligation to use my position power and any personal power I have.

"In management circles you hear about personal power and position power. I think personal power is in part a gift, an aura, a presence you can develop if you've got it. But in complex organizations, you also have position power. The organizational structure gives you this, whether you have the gift of personal power or not. You've got the super power, so use it. Other folks use it, and they expect you to use it. Why wouldn't you?"

The rewards of power and leadership are great for you, your company, and your community.

10.

From Big Business to My Business

More business in dollar amount is done in small companies than in the major corporations. Small businesses generate most of the personal wealth in America, and they pass it on to the next generation.

—**Robert L. Johnson**, Vice President (ret.)
Sears Roebuck and Co.
Owner, Chair and CEO, Johnson Bryce, Inc.

Life is not about home runs. It's about singles. All those singles carry you a long, long way. I look back on my career and say, WOW!

—**Mannie L. Jackson**, Senior Vice President (ret.)
Honeywell International, Inc.
Owner, Chair and CEO, Harlem Globetrotters

O NCE they cracked the corporate code, our executives began to see opportunities in a broader context. You might say they were cracking the capitalist code, with a new vision of themselves in the broader economy. The new frontier for these black executives is ownership—leading their own businesses. Ownership allows them to create family wealth and, at the same time, prove the business value of diversity. In the process, they are providing jobs and critical business training opportunities for other minorities. For these executives, who planned well, it was a small step from the leadership roles they played in their corporations. They reinvested their business expertise and their connections into successful new businesses.

How do you get in a position to start your own business? There are of course many considerations, but one thing is clear. You need capital, or you cannot even begin. The best place to start, therefore, is building some capital of your own. Who better to believe in you than yourself?

Bob Johnson's father always tried to inspire him by saying, "'If you really want to help poor people, don't become one of them.' He was right, in the sense that you can help a lot more with assets than you can with just attitude. Now I have an attitude about wealth: it's essential. The opportunity to create wealth is the energy America runs on. I don't have any argument with what America is, I just want everybody to get a fair chance. I want to see everybody involved in the game, on a level playing field, and no cheating during the game. I think it's unfair we've been held back so long, but now we're in the game, and it's important we play it."

The first step is saving—literally. Since her marriage right out of Grambling, **Alana Robinson** has been part of a two-income family. "My husband and I always worked, but we always saved half and lived as if we had one income. Now, after more than 25 years, those old savings have really panned out." **Mannie Jackson** has always been a saver as well. "I always saw not just a rainy day but a thunderstorm out there. I can't remember a year when I didn't save close to one fourth of my income, even when I was a bartender at the country club in high school. I have every piece of stock I ever got from Honeywell. I didn't cash them in to buy things the way other people did. Today I'm actually in the Globetrotter's 401(k) plan."

An entrepreneurial spirit has also served him well in this regard. Thanks to his vision, discipline, and a temperament that expected a "thunderstorm," he had the opportunity to start building a nest egg, and he did not squander it. He learned early how to leverage his capital. "When I was a young athlete, I was given a paid-up $10,000 life insurance policy. I had no appreciation for what $10,000 was worth back in those days, but I never cashed it. I used it to give me borrowing power. I bought homes at a very early age and financed them through the equity I had in that policy. That was how I was always able to have a great home, which seemed beyond what my corporate salary would allow. It was a small amount by today's terms, but it ends up being a big deal. Even today I haven't used it. It's still there. It still accumulates. It's worth a lot right now. You can always make enough of a living to pay your bills, but the trick is to have some left over and let it grow. Then you can get involved in things that build wealth. That's what that small policy has done for me."

At General Motors, where he worked for a few years before moving to Honeywell, "I scored what was for me a huge hit. Among the programs I handled was an apprentice training program. After months of research and analysis, I struck gold. Students from General Motors going to college in Dearborn had been charged the full tuition, but because General Motors was paying it, they should have been charged resident tuition. So General Motors collected the difference—millions of dollars—retroactively, and I was paid a piece of the savings for discovering the mistake. That was, at that time, the largest payment ever in their employee program for identifying money-saving procedures. It took me into a different league."

What do you do with your capital? For **Bob Johnson**, once he reached financial security, it was finding opportunities to serve others. "For me there is a responsibility that goes with what I've earned. You can use your wealth to buy trinkets for yourself, or you can use it to invest, to help other people achieve their goals."

Johnson chose to become involved in small businesses. When you consider that the last company on the Fortune 1000 list grosses more than $1 billion, "small" can cut a wide swath. "More business in dollar amount is done in small companies than in the major corporations. But even then, what's known as corporate America really gives a distorted view of business. When General Motors counts its sales, they are counting the retail value of the finished product. But all General Motors did was assemble many small products they bought from an army of small businesses. That's where the action is.

"These small, closely held or privately owned businesses generate most of the personal wealth in America, and they pass it on to the next generation, much of it tax free. Yet there is hardly any African-American representation. I think a lot of it is a question of exposure. In other communities, it's a topic of conversation, but not in our community yet. When we think of business and what business we'd like to be associated with, we think of the big companies, the names we recognize. But there are fewer and fewer people who are going to spend all their careers at one company. More people today must open their sights beyond those affiliations.

"We have little appreciation for small businesses. We walk right past the little buildings. But somebody's sitting there every day grossing $25–30 million a year, netting 5–6 percent and dividing it up between two or three people, every year. You go in, he's just sitting there puffing a cigar, got a flannel shirt on, sleeves rolled up, talking on the telephone. Doesn't run around. Gets in a two-year-old car, goes to a reasonably nice house, and chills out. He belongs to the country club. He lives pretty comfortably. He takes a vacation to the Bahamas every year. He's way beyond the American dream. He is part and parcel of the central core of America. This is America, and it's starting to penetrate our community."

202

Corporate America is an excellent training ground for entrepreneurs. You can build on the experience and contacts gained working inside large corporations to start and run your own business. **Bob Johnson** thinks that is the best starting point for another reason. "Just moving from corporation to corporation means you can investigate alternatives, scout out new business opportunities. Downsizing and outsourcing is providing plenty of fuel. When a large corporation starts discussing outsourcing and divesting, that's your cue to start investigating a possible investment. You're in a situation that is fluid, and before it recasts itself and hardens, there are opportunities. Get into the loop, ask questions. Not so much, 'Why are we going to get rid of it?' but, 'Where is it going? How much do we want for it? How valuable will it be? Will we continue to do business with it? If the company doesn't want it, do I want it?' Get in a place where you can study the opportunity and assess its value and the risk involved."

Of course it is easy to say, 'Assess the value and the risk involved.' But what do you do? How do you know if you're on target? How do you get comfortable? Again, Johnson shares his insight and experience, taking much of the mystery out of the process. "What is seen as risk is frequently just lack of knowledge. What may look extremely risky to one person on the basis of what he knows, to another person may be not risky at all. To evaluate an opportunity, you have to look at all its circumstances. You can't look at any one thing and say, 'That's not good.' Take for example regional shopping centers. Retail sales in large and small stores aren't that good, too much competition, and customers are showing decided preference for other alternatives. So on the face of it, if somebody said, 'I'm getting ready to sell a shopping mall,' you might say, 'I'm definitely not interested in that.' What you really ought to say is, 'How much and under what conditions?' There is always a price and a set of conditions that make it a good deal for somebody, regardless of what the business activity is. It is a good deal for somebody.

"On the other hand, if someone said, 'I'm selling a software company,' you can't just say, 'Wow, that's exactly where I want to be.' They may owe too much. They may have all old equipment. They may be located in a market where they can't find qualified people. They may have a bad reputation. You have to know yourself and look at all the facts and circumstances."

What did Johnson do with his insight and experience? In 1985, he was "close to the top" at Sears and only five years from the 55-year-old retirement option. He knew he would not be going any higher at Sears but expected to work at least until 2000, so he began looking around for a new career. He did not yet think of himself as a small business owner. He was just feeling his way along, so he did not look at Sears's downsizing and outsourcing plans. "There could have been some excellent investments I overlooked at Sears, but my response then was sort of emotional: I've been doing this for twenty-five years, I want to do something different. Today I might do it differently." Johnson's opportunity came from another network, the board of Rymer Foods, a small New York Stock Exchange company that no longer exists. Most of his fellow board members spent their time investing in small businesses, and one was looking to divest the Atlanta plant of the Bag Craft Corp. Frito-Lay was its largest customer.

For Johnson, owning his own business was not a great leap from his Sears experience, but he took the time to plan carefully. In 1988 he bought 51 percent of the Bag Craft Atlanta plant and brought his daughter, a recent Wellesley graduate who was a young manager at New England Bell, back to be "my CEO in training." Next was to buy the Bag Craft roll stock business, including the Frito-Lay contract. That business would be refinanced in a new joint venture with Johnson as the majority owner. It wasn't quick or easy, but Johnson had "great support from the ARTRA board members, Bag Craft, and Frito-Lay."

He stayed at Sears one year past the twenty-five-year mark, until 1991, and thus was able to negotiate a substantially better retirement package, enough for the equity contribution for the new joint venture. Through Frito-Lay he found a partner, Bryce, a large packaging company in Memphis; a bank loan secured by his massive new equipment; and a plant to lease. That same year the newly formed Johnson Bryce, printer and laminator of plastic packaging, premiered. He grossed $15 million in the first year. Johnson has more than doubled the plant size and increased his employees by 50 percent. He now grosses in excess of $30 million. Already he's looking for his next challenge. "I'm no longer interested in operating a business. An equity stake, I'd be interested in that."

Mannie Jackson tried a more traditional route but ended up following his heart back to basketball. He spent 25 years at Honeywell, attaining senior vice president and executive committee status. Once he realized he would never be CEO, he set a new goal. "I started to prepare by taking Honeywell assignments that would teach me how to lead a company. I got the job in the new venture business section. I wanted that job really bad, and I worked at it like nobody's ever worked at it. I wanted to learn how to buy and sell companies, how to evaluate new business opportunities, and how to run businesses that were in distress, in start-up, or recently sold. I wanted to learn all of it. I did that for almost a decade with twenty or so companies. I felt comfortable. I was just looking for the right vehicle to leave on.

"My first idea was a joint venture I'd put together between Honeywell and Ericsson in Sweden. Honeywell was getting the technology from Ericsson, but we weren't putting enough capital into the business to make it pay off. It was a situation where you couldn't play small, but that's what we were trying to do. Then there was talk of divesting the company, and I wanted to buy it. This was in the mid- to late-1980s, and the overseer of the company told me he could not in good conscience take a recommendation to his board or go public with a deal for me to buy the company I had built. He saw it as a conflict and unethical. At the time I said I could understand his position, but now I wish I had fought harder. The business eventually did come apart, and we ended up selling bits and pieces of it. I still think it could have become a great growth business.

"Then in the late 1980s I tried to buy an NBA franchise. At that time you could buy an expansion team for about $25 million, and I had enough cash and personal assets that I knew I could leverage the rest of it. But I didn't have the right partner, and the location was wrong. It didn't happen, although I spent two years and a lot of money. I came out of that a little frustrated but no less determined that I would stay in the entertainment business. It was just a couple of years later the Globetrotter opportunity came up, because of the bankruptcy of its holding company."

In 1993 he and a long-time friend put together the syndicate that bought the Globetrotters, and Jackson was installed as principal owner, chair, and CEO. He modernized the Globetrotter's theme and mascot as well as its financial base, with corporate sponsorships, licensing, and merchandising relationships, and he was able to pay off all but two of the original investors in five years. It was a textbook turnaround. The Globetrotter business is more than basketball; it is classic brand management on a global basis. Jackson is right in his element, still building his sports, entertainment, and communications empire.

"In retrospect I realized the most valuable thing you have in life is time, and I probably expended some valuable time waiting on perfection at Honeywell. I probably could have left Honeywell in 1988 or 1989 instead of waiting until 1994, and it wouldn't have made a big difference. But the Globetrotter buy was perfect for me. It could not be better financially. It could not be a better lifestyle. I got lucky. It's the best thing that ever happened to me. There's no comparison."

After thirty years at Corning, **Jim Kaiser** also wanted to do something different. After looking at opportunities to serve in government, in higher education, as an association executive, and as a large city school superintendent, he settled on continuing his career in business, but as an entrepreneur. "At first I was looking to buy a manufacturing company so I could run it. But I soon realized that I didn't have the capital to have a significant equity interest. That meant I'd be working for a venture capitalist instead of myself. So I started looking for a smaller business to own. The dream was to make money and not have to work so hard. How do you do that? You have to find a partner to run the business who really cares about it. That means you have to give the partner significant equity, and the business has to be big enough so the two of you can make money. I ended up deciding to buy a franchise with a brand name, a Lexus dealership in Memphis, and I took the general manager of the dealership as my partner. He runs the business day to day, and I spend about one week a month in the store looking for ways to improve the business and focusing on the big picture. I put my money in, trust my partner, and draw a salary plus the equity. I'm at peace with that."

Joe Anderson came late to corporate America. He was a thirteen-year career Army officer, much decorated and on the track to becoming a general. While serving as a White House Fellow with Secretary of Commerce Juanita Kreps in 1985, he resigned to become a plant manager at General Motors. He clearly has a different formula for planning and measuring risk. He had to fight through some obvious ambushes, but as an Army veteran, he was not troubled. He has a healthy appetite for the unknown and for making his way on his own. That process ultimately works well for him, but it is not for everyone.

Anderson was completing his first decade at General Motors in the early 1990s as a business unit director, with 7000 people working for him, when the auto industry began a cyclical slide. The continuing reorganizations that followed prompted him to take a call from a headhunter. "I was bored. I was not challenged. So when the headhunter said, 'I got this guy in New York. He's putting together a venture capital fund, he's going to start buying companies, and he needs somebody to run them,' I listened. My first response was, 'I don't know anything about that.' And he said, 'Just meet him.' So I met him, a Harvard guy who had done a lot of great things. Very smooth. And we talked, and finally we agreed. I resigned my position with General Motors and went to work for him. I became the president and CEO of an automotive parts company, the one company he already owned."

When Anderson's boss was ready to start buying other companies, he realized the venture capitalist had a very different understanding of their partnership. "We were looking at some businesses General Motors was selling off, and this was the industry I knew very well. So I said, 'Let's have some discussion about my piece in all this. What is going to be my level of ownership?' He said, 'We don't need to be talking about that, it's going to be OK, don't worry about it.' I said, 'Wait a minute.' Naively, I had not understood and appreciated that venture capital guys were not about their team members owning significant pieces of the deal. And that's exactly the conversation. I said, 'I didn't resign General Motors to work for you. I wanted to become a part-owner.' It didn't have to be a minority-owned business, but I wanted to be a part-owner and have a piece of the rock. When we concluded we were on different wavelengths, he bought out the rest of my two-year contract, and we went our separate ways.

"But now what do I do? I've left General Motors, and I don't have the company to run. I thought, why not try to buy a company myself? Rockwell Automotive was selling its plastics division, so I partnered with half a dozen guys I knew from my General Motors days, all of us interested in owning our own company. A couple of them were already entrepreneurs, small restaurant franchise owners, and a couple of the others were auto executives, but not line. We were always talking about doing something, so they said, 'Joe, you're free because of your transition. You take the lead and do the due diligence. Let's look at this $200 million division Rockwell wants to sell.' Among other things, I talked to a colleague who was very senior at Rockwell about what we were trying to do. I came back to the group with a proposal, but it was bigger than they'd appreciated or had the appetite for and more risk than they were prepared to take on. The division had a number of plants around the country, and it meant borrowing $50 million. And there were no minority businesses of that size, period. They said, 'Joe, we're just not ready.' I said, 'Fine, I'll do it by myself.'

"I partnered with another colleague who had left his company about the same time I resigned from General Motors, and I knew he was looking at acquisitions for himself. We went to the banks and got soft letters of support and credit. When we took those to Rockwell and said, 'Okay, we'd like to have an exclusivity agreement so we can firm up our support,' Rockwell said, 'We are not quite prepared to give you exclusivity.' The bottom line is they had somebody else. The deal with me and my minority partners was their fallback position. They were confronting the other player with our offer, so the other player upped its price a little bit above where we were prepared to go, and Rockwell took the deal. Lesson number one in business: 'Black is beautiful, but green is better.' Ironically, I joined the board of that former Rockwell automotive division. It changed its name to ArvinMeritor, Inc., and it became a $7.5 billion company.

"And so now what do I do? I've still got a year to go on my contract buyout, so not to worry. I started to look at a variety of other businesses, and then, around Easter of 1994, an investment banker contacted me about a car parts manufacturer who was trying to sell his company, Chivas Products, another automotive parts company. They knew about me from the Rockwell deal, and they liked my automotive track record. Would I be interested in talking about it? This was the time the Big Three auto makers were beginning to focus on minority business development, and I was an entity they knew. In my search for financing, one of the banks said to me, 'Joe, what do we have to do to make this deal work?' I said, 'You have to finance all the debt, the senior debt, the mezzanine debt, and the revolving debt around receivables, inventory, and equipment.' They said, 'Fine, we accept.' So I was a 70 percent stockholder, and they were my bank.

"In five months we closed the deal. I borrowed all the money from Comerica Bank, and now I understand why nobody wants to do these leveraged acquisitions. I was so naive. I had no clue about the reality of debt service. Probably wouldn't have taken it on if I had. If I had to do it over again, I'd never do it without more equity. But I was lucky. I had to take it through Chapter 11 to restructure the debt, but it worked out. Soon I had a beautiful balance sheet. Sales went up to about $35 million a year, and I had wonderful cash flow. I enjoyed sleeping nights."

Obviously, flying without a net does not bother Anderson the way it bothers many corporate executives who go on to own their own businesses. Perhaps it is just his temperament; perhaps it is his extensive combat experience. Business risk is relatively tame by comparison.

Carolyn Byrd's experience is a textbook case of how to start your own business. She did not spend more than twenty years in finance at The Coca-Cola Company for nothing. She capitalized on her experience and information to secure an exclusive contract with Coca-Cola when it outsourced part of the work of her department, Coca-Cola Financial Corporation, where she served as president. In 2000, she opened the doors of her new company, GlobalTech Financial, essentially a spin-off of the lease and loan processing services she had in her Coke department. It is a multi-million dollar business, which was profitable in the first year. While more and more men are taking advantage of large-scale opportunities triggered by outsourcing, divesting, and downsizing, very few African-American women have succeeded on Byrd's scale in these high stakes and highly profitable maneuvers.

How did Byrd pull it off? At the beginning of 2000, Coca-Cola announced a layoff of 6,000 people. After confirming that she qualified for the early retirement option, with barely a month to spare, she began thinking about the rest of her life. "I had no intention of sitting around and twiddling my thumbs." When Coke also announced in January that it planned to outsource ten departments, including part of hers, Byrd knew exactly what her future held. She bid for the contract.

She bid against several other major firms, and for several months she was fielding additional questions and waiting on tenterhooks. Just before the April deadline for exercising the early retirement option, her bid was formally accepted. Although the bidding process was arm's length, and Byrd was unable to communicate with the decision makers, they were people she knew, and they were making the decision in an environment she knew intimately. She was able to gear her proposal to what she knew were Coke priorities.

A key advantage was that Byrd tailored her proposal to meet Coca-Cola's technology needs. The cornerstone of her proposal was specialized hardware and software which upgraded dramatically the back office operation of Coca-Cola Financial. In addition, the Coke leaders were her peer group, and she already handled the loans and leases with all the bottlers and commercial customers. "Coke has service from the same people they've depended on for years, and there is a seamless transition for the bottlers and commercial customers. This is the win-win proposition I always look for." Byrd's successful bid can be attributed to her targeted and knowledgeable proposal, her excellent relationships with bottlers and distributors, and a variety of other Coke considerations at the time. Among those considerations was Coke's commitment to invest $1 billion over the next five years in minority and women-owned businesses.

Byrd's new business is not capital intensive, except for the new high-tech equipment, both hardware and software. She easily obtained bank financing with Coke's exclusive contract with GlobalTech and her own personal equity contribution. GlobalTech, not limited to Coke business, also serves banks, credit leasing companies, and other appropriate entities. Byrd also originates loans and leases and handles workouts, just as her internal department did. "I am realizing my lifelong dream of owning my own company, and I am grateful to The Coca-Cola Company for giving me the opportunity."

In cracking the corporate code, you are preparing yourself for the next step. As you can see from the experiences of our executives who have taken that next step, there are many paths to success in your own business. Knowledge of their experiences will allow you to work smarter and travel farther.

11.

The Diversity Legacy I: Inside the Corporation

Once I realized diversity was a business issue, I knew how to add value to it, and it became a leadership issue for me.

—**Lloyd G. Trotter**, President and CEO
GE Industrial Systems

As the only black line manager at Pepsi Cola and then the only black vice president, I was in a position to protect all the corporate people trying to promote diversity. I had the power—the line results, the budget—so nobody could discredit me.

—**Lawrence V. Jackson**, Senior Vice President
Safeway Stores

Today, companies want you to do well. They will give you the chance. You just have to step up and prove yourself.

—**Westina Matthews Shatteen**, First Vice President
Merrill Lynch & Co., Inc.

A S these black corporate executives have earned positions of leadership, they have used their success to create a diversity legacy. In addition to their own groundbreaking achievements, they are determined to see that new generations of African-American managers and executives will never be as alone as they were. They are working to keep the pipeline open and to increase the flow of young managers through that pipeline. They have moved their corporations and made them models for the rest of American business, as the country moves toward a level playing field that will endure.

The first wave of leaders labored alone to disprove the stereotypes for much of their careers. Growing up in an America that was largely segregated, in housing, school, and work, they may have in fact come to their corporations better prepared for the racial issues they would have to confront. Special skills were necessary if they were to obtain what they needed from the dominant culture, whether it was clerks in the grocery store, bus drivers, teachers, or eventually, guards at the factory gate. They had to read unspoken messages from whites, spot the danger signals, and learn to get beyond them. Early on they developed the capacity to separate their own view of themselves from society's view of them and, as a result, they were able to build and sustain healthy self-images. Although they did not analyze their youthful coping strategies, they were already honing many of the skills that would bring them success in corporate America. They were committed to succeeding, no matter the cost, no matter the setbacks, no matter the time, and they were committed to bringing others along with them.

Today's younger African-American managers and executives have grown up with greater opportunity, although many barriers remain. They have a different attitude about how race impacts their lives, and they have less patience with the more subtle forms of discrimination that linger. They also have less experience maintaining a healthy self-image in the face of discrimination, precisely because they have faced less. It is both a testament to the progress we as a society have made and a burden younger generations of blacks still shoulder. Corporate America needs to understand this circumstance, so there can be a true level playing field where the contributions of all are expected, developed, and valued.

The generation of African-American managers who entered corporations in the 1960s were well prepared for the hard work of being "the first" and "the only." They also expected their sacrifices and successes as representatives of their race to pave the way for other blacks. They believed their arrival in corporate America signaled that the battle was won, but the initial exhilaration faded quickly. In fact, each small step had to be taken over and over, and every lesson had to be explained or taught again and again. They, and those who followed, struggled to keep the door open for more blacks behind them, in the process inspiring all other outsiders. The miracle is that in less than forty years, their efforts have facilitated a sea change in corporate culture. Today there are few large American corporations not espousing diversity as a business imperative. In many, women and all minorities have begun to break through the so-called glass ceiling—**Elynor Williams**'s "thick layer of white men"—even at the board level. This is a powerful and enduring personal legacy.

What was it possible to accomplish when you were "the only"? **Bob Johnson**'s experience speaks to that particular burden. In his thirty-year career at Sears, which ended in 1991, he became the first African-American vice president. He still believes he did not accomplish enough.

"I won some battles, but I didn't make as much progress as I thought I would. I was able to get some people into positions in my department where they had a real opportunity. I was able to bring a number of blacks to the attention of the upper echelon, people who might have been forgotten or denied those opportunities had I not been there. But if the managers don't support them, they can't win, and I can't monitor the situations that closely. You have to tell the manager, 'I want this guy to be successful, and if he's not successful, you're not going to be successful either,' and be able to enforce it. I probably had a great impact on the people I placed and maybe a big impact on the department. But did I really change the balance of things? No, not significantly. Even from a powerful position like a Sears VP, you can't do it by yourself.

"If I had to do it all over again, I would have spent my energy convincing the chairman he needed to pay attention to diversity. I would have been closer to him. I would have attempted to exercise more influence on the major decisions being made by the corporation. I would have looked at it from the CEO's point of view and tried to persuade him to lay his prestige on the line. Of course I might not have survived, but I would have taken that risk. And I think now I would have been more effective. The advice I'd give to anyone in a similar situation today is, use your access to the top. You can't go against the flow of the company by yourself. You're going to have to change the flow, and you're going to need help."

Johnson sees clearly why discrimination is bad for business. "In business, the racial consideration is largely a distraction. If the purpose of the enterprise is to perform for the benefit of the customer and the shareholder, then any side issues are distractions. If a company spends energy denying opportunity on the basis of race or gender, it's wasting assets. If you're inside a company, you want the best people, and you want your evaluation to be as objective as possible. If you look for black or white as a characteristic, either one is a negative from the standpoint of a contribution to the business.

"Obviously we're nowhere close to being that color-blind. The primary difference is how the company is led. Racism is woven into the cloth of America. It's not stamped on. It's part of it. It's in the distribution of wealth, in the institutions. So if people are allowed to express the personal values about race they grew up with, then they will make a sizable number of racist decisions and racist evaluations. The leader sets the tone. It is his responsibility to say, 'No, not here. Here we make the evaluations on the basis of objective criteria, and we try to make them as objective as possible.' The companies with leaders like that will look quite different from those that don't.

"When I joined the executive team, I found everyone was very sensitive to the tone set by the leadership, on every issue, no matter how small. People were influenced by what they perceived as the message from the top. And so my movement onto the executive team—I was the first black vice president ever, and vice president was a big job at Sears—signaled to a lot of people that there is opportunity here for everyone. But the company really didn't follow through on that. It sent out the signal, but it was isolated. In part it was the beginning of a backlash, the complaints about reverse discrimination—okay, we have opened it up, but how far do we have to go with this? Second, at that time retail began experiencing dramatic changes, and Sears was beginning to lose its dominance. If leadership is weak under these challenges, it's going to crack."

David Hinds also regrets not accomplishing enough, but the tools at his disposal were different. Because most of his bank's employees were housed in one building in New York City, he also had the ability to touch more people. A line manager, he became involved in advocating for diversity in support of another black employee he believed had been treated unfairly. When the current affirmative action officer moved on, he gave in to that man's urgings to play the role for a brief period of time.

"I am not a staff person; I don't operate well as a staff person. But I saw becoming affirmative action officer for a year or two as a real chance to do something positive at the corporate level. Now I could try to influence change there, focus the recruiting and evaluation process, and change the numbers.

"I got exposure to the top executives when I was in that position, and I gained a new measure of comfort around them. I'm sure both of those things helped me in my career. I solved some specific problems, but the organization never became truly open, where people operate purely and simply on the basis of merit. When an

African American contributes, demonstrates a level of competency, you hope and expect it will jump-start the notion that others can also. But what majority folk typically do is zero it down to that one person. The trick is getting people to understand it's not about one individual person they view as lucky. It's about organizational constraints that prevent an open hiring mindset. The open mindset was there when I began, but we did not build it into our structure, and ten years later it was gone. I never found how to do that, and I must say, even after thirty years in the company, I considered that to be a major failure. I also consider it a major loss for our company.

"One of my greatest work experiences was managing the international group. When we sat around our table, you saw such a mixture. Both the CFO and controller and head of product marketing were female, the person in charge of Asia and the senior operations person were both African American, others were Jewish and Italian. What was fascinating to me even then was that everyone understood this group was different, though no one said it. Everyone knew this was a high-performance group, and each was there to make something happen. We had our tensions, we had our issues, but at the end of the day, performance was driving everyone. It was dynamic, it was exciting, it was productive. Every time we had a meeting, I said to myself, 'This is the way it ought to be, the absolute best at the table making it happen.'"

Bruce Gordon's first opportunity to promote diversity was a human resources assignment, but he came to that assignment unwillingly. "I started out wanting to be in HR, EEO, community relations, or public affairs, because that's what the few black folks in business did. I figured if that's what they did, then that was my goal.

"But after a few management assignments, I concluded I didn't want a personnel job. I said, 'I've got more power as any kind of line manager than I would even at a higher level in HR.' They just set the policy; I actually hire people. But as fate would have it, my first upper level job was in HR. That level is a prize, so I wasn't about to turn it down, but I was disappointed. It turned out to be a

218

great job. I hired the people for the special training program I was a part of, so I had the opportunity to change the race and gender profile of that program. I also hired specialists, CPAs, engineers, and others, so I had the opportunity to get more diversity reflected among the professionals. As I have learned again and again, there is no bad job."

As Gordon continued his rise, he realized part of his job was inspiring other African Americans at Bell Atlantic. "I don't know in hindsight whether I think this is good or bad, but it is what it is. I reached a point where I was the highest ranking African American by far, and people below me looked to me to change the way the company looked at African Americans. In addition to doing my job, I was the one organizing the African-American employees into associations, and I was the one who was taking issue with policy. I did it in a fairly visible way, so I was a pain in the butt in terms of advancing our cause. And I did it across a broad base of employees: Technicians in the garages, people throughout the business, knew me. To a certain extent I was almost their hope. In me they could see a future for themselves. I really felt that responsibility. Unfortunately, there just aren't enough of us. It's one of the continuing struggles." There's been progress, but there is also much more work to be done.

Lawrence Jackson and **Ron Parker** worked together at Pepsi to convince senior management of the value of diversity. Jackson provided the "juice"; he was a valued and outspoken line manager. Parker was an HR manager with an inclusive style. They were an effective team. Jackson captured the attention of key executives, and Parker kept them interested.

Said Jackson: "There's a point in life where you're going to get run over unless you stand up and say, 'Look, things have to change.' Part of that is the role you are willing to play. I'm more willing to be outspoken than most. If you really want to be king, you have to be careful, because it can come back at you. But once I settled in my own head I would not be king at Pepsi, I pushed even harder.

None of the initiatives Pepsi has would be going down today if we hadn't worked there. As the only black line manager and then the only vice president, I was in a position to protect all the corporate people trying to promote diversity. I had the power—the line results, the budget—so nobody could discredit me.

"If we wanted fifty people to meet, and just the idea of that kind of meeting made the upper executives go nuts, I could walk over and say, 'You got a problem, man?' Because of what I built, I was able to call them out. We were partners in crime for years and really did some great stuff. We accomplished things other companies would never have even attempted, partly because my style was good for some things, and Ron's style was good for other things. As you grow older, you understand people get pissed off by certain antics, and some of the things I did, I can't believe. I might do things differently with what I know today, but I'm not convinced I wasn't right."

Parker developed programs to begin a concerted diversity effort at Pepsi. "We worked with a consultant to start the Black Professional Association at Pepsi and got an audience with the president. We all thought we were going to be fired when we went to see him. We were not so much worried about the president per se, but we expected problems with his middle management team. When you try to change a large organization, you are not necessarily thought of as courageous.

"I recall a session with our consultants. We had black/white teams do role playing around race dynamics for managers. The president joined us for the morning and was so intrigued he canceled all his appointments for the afternoon. The simulation involved a black manager who had been passed over several times for promotion, and a white manager letting him know, once again, someone else had been chosen. Lawrence volunteered to be the black manager, and one of the group presidents volunteered to be the white manager. We had a blast. Talk about making people uneasy. The president was sitting in the audience, and we were showing an ill-equipped, ill-prepared manager, trying to communicate a bad decision to someone talented and bright who just wouldn't buy it.

"In the end, the white manager backed down. He said, 'I can't justify the decision you have given us as part of this role-play. If the information is factual, I think we made a bad decision.' The people applauded the reaction. We were able to convince the president to acknowledge the diverse talent within Pepsi and then to support programs to identify and develop them. We met frequently with the president after that, and he became a champion of diversity. None of us was punished. We all got the chance to prove we were capable, and the rest is history.

"Today I actually understand power and how to leverage it, how to maneuver it. I was introduced to it earlier, but I didn't truly understand it. I wish I had. I could have had an even larger impact on the organization and people sooner if I had learned to leverage power. There are times when I probably could have gotten to the end result a lot sooner if I had used a little bit more of the Lawrence Jackson demeanor, been a little bit more direct with some of my responses to some of the unspoken cues. Unless we put women and people of color in positions of power, where they have more freedom to act, where they are not checked and counter-checked so quickly, all we're doing is pacifying. We will never be accepted as full players. They know it, and we know it. And each time we celebrate cracking one elite circle, we find there is a smaller circle that has just been born. There are circles within circles within circles. Once you enter one circle, you immediately start on the next."

When **Ira Hall** went to IBM after a number of years in corporate finance on Wall Street, he had a lot of experience working closely with very senior corporate executives. He had been a principal architect of many of their IPOs, so he was comfortable interacting with them. He took advantage of this experience to gain access to IBM decision makers and to begin to change their views about managing IBM minority and women professionals. Many of the senior executives welcomed Hall's perspective on executive leadership and the challenges facing IBM. He was frequently invited to address senior customer executives and IBM internal meetings of executives and employees. In 1987 the IBM board of directors elected him a corporate officer, the first ever African American elected to this level at IBM. From this position, he actively championed diversity on many fronts: personal example, mentoring, and stimulating the company to do more.

"In the mid-1990s the CEO and the head of human resources established eight task forces to look at diversity across the company. I was one of the leaders of the Black Executive Task Force. There were about twenty-four black executives then, and for many of us that was the first time we had seen each other. We examined internal employment issues, from the top down as well as from the bottom up. We also examined external relationships, such as with vendors and charitable organizations. We recommended improvements in each area.

"Although senior management was perhaps surprised at our conclusions, they have since then implemented most of our significant recommendations. Today there are more senior African-American executives than ever before, and there are a number of African-American affinity groups—a major change from prior years, when such groups would have been strongly discouraged.

"I believe as long as people are looking at things that are positive for the company—how can we improve skill levels, how can we improve communication—they should be encouraged. Most companies have gotten much better."

Lloyd Trotter and **Jim Kaiser** both had long careers at one company, at GE and Corning, respectively. They each took a page from union organizers and arranged bargaining sessions, layering in their own management techniques and access. Trotter had the advantage of a visionary CEO who made diversity a part of the people development strategies for which he is known. His beliefs, strongly, simply, and repeatedly articulated and acted upon, have begun to change GE and the way minorities and women are managed there, and are beginning to filter up. It was Trotter and other blacks who led the way.

"The climate of any organization, its soul, is the tone set by the leader. You can't push water up a rope, so any agenda that is out of step with that tone doesn't go very far. The tone at GE has allowed us to bring about a lot of systemic changes, and I'm most proud of those. Our CEO was already a driver on this issue, from a comment he made to the senior executive band in 1989. Every year he meets with his top 450–500 executives from around the world in Boca Raton, and that year was my first year. He looked out at the group and said, 'This audience is too white and too male.' I was the only African American, so I felt in the spotlight, although I think most people were trying not to look at me. Now it was our job to figure out how to accelerate the process.

"GE has what we call 'workouts.' They are town meetings, reflection periods. Someone is the sponsor, and everyone touched by a particular problem or issue comes together to discuss it. We try to come out of it with actions that might lead to solutions. In the early 1990s, we got our CEO to sponsor a workout on the issue of diversity. I was the most senior African American in the company then, the first vice president, and I was in manufacturing. I got a consultant to meet with us before the workout.

"Now if you know our CEO, he pushes back as much as he gets pushed. That's the culture he lives in, and that's great. So in the meeting when I said, 'Just as you've shown incredible leadership around globalization, around delayering, around productivity, that's what's going to have to happen around diversity.' And his push back was, 'Lloyd, how many African Americans have you hired? You hire more people than I do.' And we went back and forth.

"At the end I did a mirror test and admitted, 'I haven't done anything systemic for diversity.' My CEO was right. I wasn't a business leader then, but I was at a high enough level to have a bigger impact. Very little hiring was done at the Fairfield headquarters.

223

Leadership came from there, but change came from how we ran our businesses. And that was a big realization for me. I've always had an open door, mentored, provided support, and so on. What I didn't do was think about it as a process touching many people. I hadn't used the same level of energy and skills I use in managing GE's assets, and I had to do better. If you really want to move the bar on diversity, you have to make systemic change in the way we work, the way we hire, the way we view people and allow them to exercise their skills. And I will never, ever go to a meeting again where somebody can ask, 'What have you done?' and I have nothing good to say.

"Once I realized it was a business issue, I could add value to it, and it became a leadership issue for me. We got a small group of African Americans together. I said, 'Let's go out and use the tools we use running our businesses. Let's do some studies on best diversity practices at other corporations.' Most of them had started as an off-site group that wound its way up to meeting with the CEOs much later. We decided to start at the top. We put together our proposal, what was in it for the corporation and what was in it for us, and scheduled talks with the CEOs of the business units. We've been off and running ever since.

"We did not want our group to exist just for having fun and making new friends, so we started with the issue of self-help. We took the career cycle and broke it into five or six different modules, beginning with orientation and exposure and continuing on to the other elements you really need to further your career. We put a lot of energy into developing these training modules and used them at regional meetings for over two years before we held our first national meeting.

"Some of the issues were simple, like, wouldn't it be nice if you were going to interview for a job in lighting in Cleveland, and you could call another African American there and be better prepared. Winning an interview is not luck, it's preparation. It's not that you're going to be an expert, but you can learn to slant your skills and your strengths to answer their needs.

224

"Other issues involved creating a critical mass. GE is so large and dispersed, most African Americans were alone or one of two or three in any one location, and that wasn't much of a network. How could we ever help each other if we didn't really know each other? We have been able to count on most of the board of directors attending our annual meeting, and people do get discovered there. They get promoted. And there is an ongoing agenda that keeps everybody engaged.

"The African-American Forum was the trailblazer. We convinced GE that groups working on diversity issues make the company better, and soon there were forums for Hispanics, women, and others. I often say that in business you have to practice 'aggressive patience.' I have a little sign in my office from some of the guys who work for me: 'God grant me patience. And I want it right now.' I always thought I attacked problems fairly quickly, but as I look back, I think I wasn't nearly fast enough. Change happens at such an accelerated pace, you really have to move the organization to a higher speed. If anyone asks me again, 'What are you doing?' I have the answer. I'm now doing the things I should be doing."

Kaiser's experience with organizing black professionals at Corning contrasts with Trotter's at GE. Although senior executives were supportive, initially they were not as comfortable as a group with what the black professionals really wanted to accomplish.

"When the Society of Black Professionals first organized in the early 1970s, I was the most senior black. Our first step was to meet with HR. We said, 'The company says it supports affirmative action and is an equal opportunity employer. We want to help you be successful.' At first they were very upset, saying, 'You're challenging our integrity.' We said, 'No, we're just saying if you want to have equal opportunity, we can help. You won't have to guess about our needs and problems; we'll tell you.' This was a very delicate process, because it was a conflict of power. So at first there was mistrust.

"Over time, we developed a relationship of trust, but not without casualties. The meetings were often very intense, and people got upset. One of us jumped up and said, 'There are a bunch of bigots on your team.' After the meeting I spoke to the key manager involved and said, 'He was very upset. Please don't hold it against him.' But he was gone a short time later. The discussions continued, and eventually we got to the chairman.

"Another strategy we used was a scorecard as feedback on company performance in diversity. We measured the company on its performance against stated goals. We gave the chairman a written evaluation each year of our view of the progress we were or were not making. This made some managers uncomfortable. In addition, we had a dinner every year where we recognized the most diversity-friendly manager. The chairman used this opportunity to make commitments for progress. It became an important event in our diversity effort. We helped the company move to a different level.

"We went from a company refusing to talk about diversity issues to being open about problems, putting letters of reprimand in people's records, and then ultimately removing managers. That's how much influence we had in moving up the scale to managing diversity. To move that far was a big tribute to Corning as a company, and in particular to the key managers leading the diversity effort. We used to have a meeting at least once a month with the VP of HR to discuss problems, and they would share their data openly. They took that risk and never had a moment's problem with anybody trying to sue them. We raised issues, and when they said, 'You're right, we ought to do something about that,' they did. And we developed that kind of working relationship with them. Eventually the company set up a quality improvement team to deal with women and minorities. We moved the needle, but there were casualties along the way."

At Merrill Lynch, senior executives pushed for the diversity program, partly in response to a lawsuit, but also as part of its business strategy. **Westina Matthews Shatteen** was enlisted to develop and implement the diversity plan. "I was invited to a meeting with some senior executives and lawyers. It turned out they wanted to talk about diversity. I don't know what I had to do with diversity, so I just walked in there and said what I thought. It was as if my great uncle and mentor from Chicago, Bill Berry, had walked into the room. 'Well, do we agree the emperor has no clothes? Now you've got to find somebody who really is known out in the community, someone with a reputation and a vision.' They listened attentively and said, 'Whom would you suggest?' I replied, 'I have no idea.' They said, 'What about you?' I said, 'I have a job. I'm not interested.' And I went off to host a lunch uptown. As I walked into the restaurant, I received a call summoning me back for a meeting with the president and the vice chairman.

"After about fifteen minutes of conversation, the then-president slammed his hand on the table and said, 'I'm ready to take this on. Write up the plan.' I went into my boss's office and said, 'We have a problem. I think I've been asked to write a plan for a job I don't want.' He said, 'You don't have a choice. The president asked you to do it.' I wrote a strong plan and said to myself, 'They're not going to do this.' After about three months, people started congratulating me for being named the new head of diversity. It was news to me. Finally the head of HR told me about my new assignment.

"I actually had more discretionary authority in that position, more opportunity to have influence. I was in the room where decisions were being made. And because I was now on the human resources side, I had access to so much information. I knew what policies they were thinking about, so I knew where I could add value. I could introduce policies right at the level where things really happen.

"One of the policies I'm proudest of is our reporting on diversity. We created diversity scorecards that kept track of the work force three times a year for every business group around the world. 'What were your opportunities? How many hires and promotions did you have at this level? How many of them were women, how many blacks, Asians, Hispanics?' When they had to turn in those qualitative and quantitative reports, you started seeing a difference.

"Right now we have the *will* to hire and the *will* to promote. They want a reason for you to do well. However, what we hear from the women is that men are cats with nine lives. They can fail and get more chances. But women are so visible, so vulnerable, they often are removed at the first mistake, or they might get a second chance. I think people of color often just get one chance. That's our parents' old warning, 'Be twice as good.' But today, companies will give you the chance. You just have to step up and prove yourself."

Even though corporations have moved beyond overt discrimination, have become more comfortable with organized employee networks, and have begun to understand the kinds of pressures minority employees endure, there are still unresolved issues. **Frank Fountain** describes one such issue: "There is a certain amount of what I call institutional racism. That's where the collective thinking can really make the difference between whether or not African Americans, women, or other minorities get the opportunity to show what they know. There can be various reasons why a person isn't considered the right person, usually not related to the performance score. When I was an assistant controller, quite often we would all sit around the table trying to make sure that everybody got a fair share of the talent, that somebody wasn't hogging it all. I think we had one of the most sophisticated development programs to move people along, yet at the end of the day the names left on the table are invariably minorities. No one expressed or even felt any discrimination. They simply chose others first." Unless white managers must look beyond white males in spotting talent, the managerial ranks are likely to continue being white and male.

This push is what allowed **Chuck Chaplin** to get in the

Prudential door, and he readily acknowledges he would not be there but for affirmative action. This is no 'preference,' as it is commonly labeled in the media and popular culture, but merely the opportunity for one formerly excluded to join the game. His achievements within the company are his own, proof of the value of that push to end the exclusion. Chaplin firmly believes that diversity benefits a company. He calls it 'good management,' and some of the most admired CEOs share his views. Many others will probably arrive at the same place.

"If we had good people-centered management already, we wouldn't need affirmative action or even diversity programs. When I look at successful African-American executives, the things that have enabled them to be successful are fairly ordinary. Either the company or the people they work with and for utilize modern human resources management techniques, like honest performance assessments. Employees are told what it is they have to do to get to the next level, making the rules of the game clear and apparent for all. Companies can go a long way toward creating the level playing field by simply insisting on training their managers this way.

"I see myself as bicultural. I have the ability to move smoothly from one set of rules and circumstances to another. It comes from hopping from one school to another, one clique to another, one profession to another, but most of all it comes from being black in America. That kind of cultural flexibility is a great asset in today's business, and it's something other folks don't necessarily have. It's an asset more and more companies are recognizing. As more learn to value those kinds of assets, diversity will necessarily occur."

12.

The Diversity Legacy II: In the Community

We carry an additional burden because there are just so few of us. We can't stop when we have no more time available. We can't stop until we feel we have filled the need.

—**Gerald Adolph**, Senior Partner
Booz, Allen, Hamilton

Many of us find ourselves seriously overcommitted, inundated with requests to give speeches, serve on nonprofit boards, chair fund-raising events, and mentor minority youth. Yet no matter how much we do, it's never enough because the need is so great.

—**Linda Baker Keene**, Vice President (ret.)
American Express

If you have a chance to influence, to be heard, then you've got to do that. And that includes giving money.

—**Milton M. Irvin**, Executive Director
UBS Warburg

Giving back is a part of who we are and what we do.

—**Brenda Lauderback**, President (ret.)
Nine West

A S this group of executives who have shared their insights and experiences indicates, successful African Americans accept shared responsibility for other blacks. The responsibility, while willingly accepted, also brings conflict. There is a recurring discomfort at being unable to do and be all things to all people. With many blacks still not making it to the playing field at all, and relatively few at the level of our executives, the burden can seem heavy. As more and more white Americans—and their elected officials—tire of government programs and corporate initiatives designed to reach minorities, the burden on black Americans is becoming crushing.

These executives, like most black Americans, recognize the need in their communities. To their credit, they accept, articulate, and respond to that need. Said **Gerald Adolph**: "I think we carry an additional burden because there are just so few of us. For example, when people say they want a senior black from consulting, the list is very short. So we are constantly called on, over and over again. Perhaps the difference for many of my white peers is that when they feel they're at their limit, they stop. We can't stop, even when we have no more time available. We can't stop until we have filled the need. I don't think my motivation is any different from my white colleagues. It's just a function of greater need."

Linda Keene gives a similar analysis: "African-American executives at this level feel compelled to do more. That's why I always find it interesting to hear us criticized, even by some younger blacks, for being removed from community concerns. Many of us find ourselves seriously overcommitted, inundated with requests to give speeches, serve on nonprofit boards, chair fund-raising events, and mentor minority youth. But even then you can never do everything people ask of you. We probably participate in community activities to a higher degree than a lot of our white counterparts, because they don't experience similar pressures to 'give back.' Yet no matter how much we do, it's never enough because the need is so great."

232

Companies often support socially responsible drives. **Gerald Adolph**, for example, says his firm, Booz, Allen, Hamilton in New York, likes its members to be involved. "People at my firm initiate a lot of pro bono projects, work with not-for-profits, from AIDS Walks to home renovations, and our firm supports and encourages that kind of activity. I'm in my second pro bono assignment for the United Negro College Fund, and it's sizable. I don't think my values are any different from those of my white colleagues, but I think I have a different balance because of my different experiences. I don't compare what I do to what whites do. My comparison is to the need."

The ways to give back are infinite, and as your perspective broadens, you will see more opportunities. **Milt Irvin**'s involvement with the Harlem School of the Arts began as a direct request from his Salomon CEO. It became a family passion. "I was walking by my CEO's desk one day, and he asked me, 'What is your wife doing these days?' I told him she wasn't working at that time, so he said, 'Good. I just gave a school $75,000, and I'd like your wife to go on the board. Give this guy a call.' It turned out I joined his board. A number of blacks I ask for money for the school say, 'Black folks singing and dancing? Come on.' But kids that learn to express themselves creatively improve academically. It's an important part of your self-esteem growing up, and maybe this school can influence the lives of a thousand kids. That's an important component to the growth of Harlem. That's why Harlem School of the Arts."

Some have even been lucky enough to make giving back their full-time job. Take **Mannie Jackson**, who now owns the Harlem Globetrotters. "The Globetrotters allow me to give back all the time. That's practically our brand identity: mentoring, teaching, coaching. We convince other businesses to support initiatives that clear ways for more people to come through, and we fight the battles that others below us can't fight. We're ambassadors of good will, and we give and give. We don't do it for a photo op, and you won't find us only supporting one organization or one opportunity. We try to find places, causes, and issues around the world. I really enjoy picking the people, the organizations, and the issues I like and then supporting them. The Globetrotters give the equivalent of 10 percent of net revenues to charity each year, and this year I've established a $1 million trust fund to aid and benefit alumni of the Harlem Globetrotters."

Lloyd Trotter discusses an applicable role model he first observed growing up in a changing Cleveland neighborhood and then again in his more recent charity work. "Jewish folks support each other better than any other race I've ever seen in my life. Helping each other is ingrained in their values: self-help at a very, very high level. That's what the Executive Leadership Council is all about, and that's what the General Electric African-American Forum is all about." Jews and blacks share a similar history of being labeled outsiders, and a history of belief in shared communal responsibility. They also share a history of banding together for political influence. It is logical that they should also share a history of deliberate self-help within their community, now that socio-economic, legal, and political changes have made economic empowerment a real possibility.

All business leaders mentor young people, and black American business leaders are no exception. But with so few black business leaders and now a gap caused by ten to fifteen years of back-pedaling, the need is more compelling. Today the responsibility is much broader than simply training the next generation of leaders. The pipeline must be filled and kept full, and the corporate playing field must be leveled on a permanent basis.

As do their white colleagues, black business leaders support a wide variety of not-for-profit organizations, especially the institutions that have nurtured them. Many, like **Carolyn Byrd**, **Virgis Colbert**, **Frank Fountain**, **Bruce Gordon**, **Kim Green**, **Sy Green**, **Ed Howard**, **Milt Irvin**, **Margaret Jordan**, and **Ron Parker** serve or have served on the boards of their alma maters, with a heavy emphasis on historically black colleges and universities (HBCUs).

234

The difference again is in the small pool of blacks available to provide support for the many institutions that sustain the black community.

Milt Irvin and his wife support her HBCU individually and also a large group of HBCUs through the United Negro College Fund. "We believe in historically black colleges. They play a significant role in the education process. The idea of getting a college education in a predominantly African-American setting has advantages for many students, just as single-sex colleges do for some women. To me, that's what it's really about: making it possible for the next generation to achieve."

Bob Johnson also believes strongly in the mission of HBCUs. "Take an average kid today who has decided McDonalds is not his thing, where is he going to go? Community colleges do not provide much inspiration. He is probably already feeling inadequate, and a large institutional setting only reinforces that. But if he can find his way into an HBCU, he's going to find people there who are very interested in seeing him improve his life. They can save a high percentage of kids, especially if they get them right out of high school. They can bring that kid up—they do it every day—so in four years he can qualify to get into anyone's graduate school. We've got to preserve those institutions, because for many they're the last chance."

Gerald Adolph still participates regularly in the programs of the Archbishop's Leadership Project, the intensive experience he credits with giving him the best preparation for his work as a management consultant. And **Milt Irvin** is still a big supporter of Essex Catholic High School, because "that's where I gained my confidence." This is a loyal group: loyal to the people and places that nurtured them.

Along with the many minority organizations **Sy Green** supports, he always includes his alma mater, even though many black colleagues feel he should be supporting more needy black institutions. He explains his involvement this way: "Mount Union is a Methodist school, and I have the same sense of commitment to it as I have to the church. I find the value-centric institutions, the ones that focus on certain absolute values that never change, help me keep my sanity in a world that is changing so rapidly. It's kind of neat to have a place you can hang your hat and say, 'Well, this is pretty much the same today as it was yesterday.' It keeps me focused, keeps business decisions in perspective, keeps my head small."

As these executives' access to knowledge, influence, capital, and power has increased, so have the strategies they use on behalf of the issues they care about. One example is what **Frank Fountain** and **Milt Irvin** have done at Wharton School of Business. In 1996 they completed their campaign to raise $1.25 million to establish a permanent endowment for the Whitney M. Young Professorship at Wharton. The endowed chair is named for an early civil rights leader who understood the importance of jobs and economic development. A $350,000 pledge from General Mills, obtained by the efforts of **Marc Belton**, was quickly followed by $100,000 contributions from entrepreneur Slivy Edmonds and the Whitney M. Young Foundation. The balance was raised from the 600 African-American Wharton graduates since 1970 and the campus black MBA organization, which runs the Whitney M. Young Conference Irvin began as a student in the early 1970s.

Now both Fountain and Irvin have been appointed to the two Wharton executive boards, graduate and undergraduate. They have a say in curriculum, enrollment policies, and any other issues they deem important. Said Fountain, "I hope African-American alumni at other business schools will want to demonstrate their power and commitment as well." Irvin believes, "These successes come from understanding the process. If you have a chance to influence, then you've got to take it. And if you don't become involved in the process, then I feel you have no right to complain. It all starts with giving money. A lot of African Americans find it very hard to understand why they need to give money to a place like Wharton. But the only way you can sit at the table is to give money. So if we as a group want to say something, we have to give money. We can do it."

Through their work, executives often have the opportunity to have a say in government policies, here and abroad. **Mannie Jackson**, at Honeywell, served on the board of Honeywell's South African subsidiary. From that position he was able to influence the company's response to the demands for divestiture and then to shape its return to the country at the end of apartheid. In the process, he came to know Nelson Mandela and raised significant funds in the U.S. to support the free and open elections that put Mandela in the presidency.

Frank Fountain, as head of the DaimlerChrysler Foundation, has become involved in African politics as well. "I worked with Rev. Leon Sullivan and his African/African-American Summit, and I've supported other groups that focus on Africa. I don't know how that's all going to unfold, but I just happen to have the interest. I hosted a dinner in Detroit for the president and first lady of Mali and they invited me to Mali. Later I met the prime minister, and he invited me as well. So I decided while I was at Rev. Sullivan's summit in Ghana, I would go there. I stayed with the U.S. Ambassador two nights, but right away the prime minister had me come to his place. Television cameras were waiting outside, so I found myself on Malian television. Since it's a French-speaking country, and I don't speak French, I had to have the Ambassador translate for me, so I'm not really sure what the whole conversation was. Then the prime minister made arrangements to fly me to the historic city of Timbuktu, where I spent the day, and that evening I attended a gala in Bamako, Mali's capital, with the prime minister and his whole cabinet.

"The next day I had a private meeting with the president. We talked for an hour about how the U.S. and U.S. business should view the new government of Nigeria. I'm obviously operating on fairly thin ice. I'm trying to carry on the conversation, but I'm thinking, 'What message do I need to leave with him?' I told him U.S. business is willing to take risk for opportunities, but there needs to be some level of stability in the environment, some certainty. That's tremendously important in Nigeria or elsewhere. And I also told him it was important to reduce the level of inappropriate business practices, sometimes referred to as corruption, because they are impediments to free enterprise and open markets. He gave me a ram, a bowl of cola nuts, and two big slabs of salt. I left the ram tied to a tree in the backyard of the Ambassador's residence, so the Peace Corps people could use him for training." Fountain may have already surpassed his youthful dream of becoming an ambassador.

Kim Green speaks for the younger generation of executives. She declares, "I want to make a difference, whether it's for corporate females, or African Americans, or any people who are different. I want to have an impact in the community, and I take my community work very seriously." She brings her business expertise to a number of boards and participates in the activities of many more, but three organizations have been her "real pulse setters": the Partnership for Children, North General Hospital, and her Links chapter. "Those three keep me grounded and don't let me get too far ahead of myself or too way out there with that work thing." And Green has found different ways to use her business and personal skills at each organization.

"The Partnership for Children needed a plan to figure out how they could continue to raise money. I created a very simple business model that anybody could use to keep them in good financial shape for the next ten to twenty years. I introduced them, believe it or not, to the concept of corporate underwriting. To me that was making a difference because of the community they serve, which is at-risk, mentally and physically abused African-American, Hispanic, and Asian kids.

"Something near and dear to my heart is helping transform North General Hospital into a leading health care facility in Harlem. I've been on the board there for six or seven years, and I'm determined to see we get the money we need to make this hospital flourish. It's no secret there is a lack of prevention programs and then acute care within our community. It's also no secret that thousands of Harlem's acute care patients are uninsured and therefore refused treatment at downtown hospitals. Health care in New York State is challenging enough because of the intense regulation, but local politics makes results even more difficult. Harlem is a tough place to conduct business. We are working hard and, I think, getting close to a solution. This one really drives me.

"Some years ago, my Links chapter started a workshop program for young women, 'Linkage to Excellence.' We work with a unique group of teenage girls on Saturdays, and we have been working with them for several years. The workshops are focused on building self-esteem, confidence, literary skills, art and music appreciation, goals, and other everyday survival skills. At the end of each session we sponsor a luncheon to honor their achievements, and we invite their families to applaud some of the talents that have been discovered through the workshops. We try to expose the young women so they will feel inspired to carry on on their own. It takes a couple of years to realize any impact, but then you see them get comfortable with planning a future.

"In the beginning the biggest challenge was establishing trust, even though we were black also. Their facial expressions told us they didn't feel any connection with us, but we worked hard at making a connection by keeping our promises to them and staying with the program for years. Some of those young ladies were caring for dying grandparents, parents, or other relatives while they were going to school. They were raising themselves, asked to carry adult responsibilities when they were still so young. They really deserve a lot of credit, and if we help them believe in a better future for themselves, that's important.

"My parents were passionate community workers, and I think it trickled down to me. They always said, 'You have to give back to the community. If people like you don't, how is our community supposed to grow?" With my own daughter, I take her to some of my projects and we talk about issues: What does homeless mean? Why do I have meetings in a hospital if I'm not a doctor? I hope her exposure to my community work will enlighten her, just as my parents' work enlightened me. I feel it's my responsibility to her. As long as she stays inquisitive and I stay in touch with her, I believe she will understand."

The contributions these black executives have made to institutionalizing diversity and, ultimately, trying to build a level playing field are gifts of incomparable worth. Their creativity, flexibility, determination, patience, and commitment to their personal and communal mission has yielded dramatic progress, benefiting both the corporate environment as well as the rest of America. The direction is clear. The only question is the pace of change. Neither blacks nor whites can allow race fatigue to set in. What will your contribution be?

Appendix A

Biographies of the
Executives Interviewed

Gerald Adolph, b. 1953, New York, NY. BS, Chemical Engineering, MIT, 1975; BS, Management Science-Organizational Behavior, MIT, 1976; MA, Chemical Engineering, MIT, 1981; MBA, Harvard Business School, 1981. Adolph began his career in 1976 as a research and development engineer at Polaroid Corporation. After completing his graduate degrees, he joined Booz, Allen, Hamilton, an international management consulting firm, where he now serves as a senior partner. Adolph serves on the board of the Executive Leadership Council. He chairs the Corporate Advisory Board for the University of Michigan Business School, and he remains deeply involved in the Archbishop's Leadership Project, which shaped his youth beginning in junior high school. Adolph also serves on the board of Helen Keller International. He was a radio disc jockey for 10 years in Boston and has been a pilot for more than 25 years.

Joseph B. Anderson, Jr., b. 1943, Topeka, KS. As a senior in high school, he was selected as one of two Kansas representatives at Boys' Nation. BS, Math and Engineering, United States Military Academy, 1965; MS, Comparative Government, 1972, MS, African Area Studies, 1973, University of California, Los Angeles; Army Command General Staff College, 1977; Advanced Management Program, Harvard Business School, 1984. Anderson had a distinguished 13-year military career. He served two tours of duty with the 1st Cavalry Division in Vietnam. While there he received two Silver stars, five Bronze stars, three Army Commendation Medals, and 11 Air Medals and was the focus of the 1967 Academy Award and Emmy-winning documentary, "The Anderson Platoon." He concluded his military career by service as a White House Fellow, where he served as special assistant to Secretary of Commerce Juanita Kreps during the Carter Administration. Although he had just been promoted to Lieutenant Colonel, Anderson resigned his commission to join General Motors, where in 13 years he headed several business units.

He resigned in 1992 to become President and CEO of CEMS, Inc., an automotive parts manufacturer. In 1994 he acquired controlling interest in Chivas Products Ltd., another manufacturer of automotive parts, soon restructured as Chivas Industries, LLC. Anderson served as the company's chair and CEO. He sold Chivas in 2002 and purchased Vibration Control Technologies, LLC, where he currently serves as chair and CEO.

Paula A. Banks, b. 1950, Chicago, IL. BS, Psychology and Math, Loyola University, 1971; International Advanced Management Program, Harvard Business School, 1999. Banks began her career with Sears, Roebuck and Co. in 1972 as a management trainee and quickly rose through the store-management hierarchy. Then in 1975 she accepted a special sensitive human resources assignment in St. Louis and was never able to return to line positions. She therefore threw her energy into a series of human resources assignments, only to be switched again in 1989, named president of the Sears Foundation. After 24 years, she joined Amoco as the president of its Foundation. When BP and Amoco merged two years later, she parlayed her expertise into a line position at the new company, BP. Now based in London, she is senior vice president, Social Strategy and Policy, and president of The BP Foundation at BP plc. Banks works to advance the integration of business objectives with societal issues on a global scale, partnering with more than 155 BP business unit leaders operating on six continents in more than 100 countries. Banks provides leadership to the company's senior management on strategic direction of social investments resulting in sustainable local development in BP operating locations. Banks is a past chair of the Executive Leadership Council board and serves or has served as a board member of many nonprofits, including Fisk University, the National Urban League, and the National Council of Negro Women. She also serves on the corporate advisory board of The Conference Board.

Y. Marc Belton, b. 1959, West Hempstead, NY. BA, Economics, Dartmouth College, 1981; MBA, Wharton School of Business, 1983. Belton joined General Mills in 1983. After a rocky start, he hit his stride as marketing manager for Pop Secret and went on to win two Chairman's Awards for leadership. Elected a vice president in 1991, he continued to head business units until, in 1995, he was promoted to president of the Snacks Division. After a broadening assignment as president of New Ventures, Belton was named senior vice president of General Mills and president of Big G, General Mills's flagship division, where he was responsible for 50 percent of the company's revenues and profits. His responsibility now covers four business units. Belton serves on the board of the Whitney M. Young Endowed Chair at Wharton, as a trustee of Northwestern Bible College, and as co-chair of the Minneapolis Salvation Army capital campaign. He also served on the Leadership Board for Promise Keepers in 1995 and Rev. Billy Graham's Minnesota Finance Committee for the 1996 crusade. In 2002 he was 36th on *Fortune's* list of "The 50 Most Powerful Black Executives." Belton is a bass guitarist and an expert skier.

L. Don Brown, b. 1945, Horatio, AK. BS, Biology and Math, Arkansas AM&N, 1966; U.S. Army, 1969-71, field-commissioned Sergeant in Vietnam; graduate studies, University of Arkansas, 1971, Southwest Missouri State University, 1972, and Kutztown State University, 1973-74; Advanced Management Program, Harvard Business School, 1986; Manufacturing Strategy Diploma, University of Pennsylvania, 1987. After two years teaching high school and coaching in rural Arkansas and two years in the Army, Brown joined Kraft Foods. In his 25-year career there he handled plant operations throughout the U.S. and Canada and rose to executive vice president of manufacturing and engineering. In 1996, he retired and joined Coors Brewing Company. He retired again in 2002 as Coors's senior vice president of container operations and technology. Brown also served or serves on the board of Alumax,

Inc., the third largest aluminum company in the U.S., Premark International Best Brands, Inc., and Empower.com, a startup technology company. Brown served or serves as a board member for the University of Arkansas at Pine Bluff, Inroads, Inc., Colorado, and the Business in Sub-Saharan Africa Committee for the U.S. Conference of Mayors.

Carolyn H. Byrd, b. 1948, Miami, FL. BA, Economics, Fisk University, 1970; MBA, Finance, University of Chicago, 1972. Set to pursue a PhD in economics at Harvard, Byrd spent an interim semester teaching elementary school in Chicago and was convinced to pursue an MBA instead. She began her finance career with Citibank, NA, in New York in 1972, and joined The Coca-Cola Company as a senior financial analyst in 1977. From 1981-92 she headed the Latin American treasury group and became an expert in foreign exchange, exposure management, cash management, and mergers and acquisitions. She then served as president of Coca-Cola Financial Corporation, an approximately $1 billion captive finance company responsible for loans and leases to bottlers and other customers of The Coca-Cola Company worldwide. When Coke decided to outsource some of the Financial Corporation's functions in early 2000, Byrd bid for and won the contract. She retired from Coca-Cola later that year to become the owner, chair, and CEO of GlobalTech Financial LLC, a multimillion dollar loan and lease servicing business which was profitable in its first year. Byrd serves on the boards of RARE Hospitality International, Inc., a variety of Atlanta-based nonprofits, and Fisk University, her alma mater. She was appointed by the Governor of Georgia as vice chair of both Teachers Retirement System of Georgia and its Investment Committee. She also serves as treasurer of the Executive Leadership Foundation board and is a former treasurer of the Executive Leadership Council board. She is a member of the Finance Committee and chairs the Internal Controls Committee of Cascade United Methodist Church, one of the largest churches in Atlanta.

She is also working to become a more accomplished pianist.

C. Edward "Chuck" Chaplin, b. 1956, Philadelphia, PA. BA, Psychology, Rutgers College, 1978; MCRP, City and Regional Planning, Harvard University, 1980. After working in Roxbury, MA, at a community development corporation and for the State of New Jersey's Division of Planning and its Economic Development Authority, Chaplin joined Prudential Insurance Company in 1983 as an associate investment manager in its realty group. In nine years he attained the position of regional vice president, Prudential Mortgage Capital Group. In 1992, Chaplin transferred to Prudential's treasury office as an assistant treasurer. In 1995, Chaplin was appointed vice president and treasurer, as part of a near-complete turnover of executive management, and in 2000, he became senior vice president and treasurer. When Prudential became publicly owned in December 2001, Chaplin was a key player in the process.

Virgis W. Colbert, b. 1939, Jackson, MS; raised Toledo, OH. BS, Industrial Management, Central Michigan University. Colbert spent twelve years at Chrysler Corporation, where he began as a worker on the line and rose to the position of manufacturing general superintendent. In 1979 Colbert joined Miller Brewing Company as an assistant to the plant manager in North Carolina. After successful plant assignments around the U.S., Colbert settled at Milwaukee headquarters, continuing his rise. In 2002, when Miller was purchased by South African Breweries, Colbert served and continues to serve as executive vice president, responsible for worldwide operations. He serves on Miller's board and executive committee and the boards of Delphi Automotive Systems, Inc., The Manitowac Company, Inc., and Weyco Group, Inc. He also chairs the boards of the Thurgood Marshall Scholarship Fund and Fisk University. In 1997 he was the recipient of the Executive Leadership Council Achievement Award. In 2002 he was 26th on *Fortune*'s list of "The 50 Most Powerful Black Executives."

Jerri DeVard, b. 1959, New York, NY; raised in New York, NY, Jacksonville, FL, Storrs, CT, and Atlanta, GA. BA, Economics, Spelman College, 1979; Spelman/Morehouse Homecoming Queen, 1979; MBA, Marketing, Atlanta University School of Business, 1983. After a year on the commodities market between college and business school, DeVard spent ten years at Pillsbury, rising to group marketing manager. She then served as director of marketing for the Minnesota Vikings and vice president of marketing for Harrah's in New Orleans. When Harrah's closed its doors to improve its bargaining position in a contract dispute with the state of Louisiana, DeVard became vice president of marketing for Revlon. Currently, she serves as chief marketing officer, e-Consumer, at Citibank.

W. Frank Fountain, b. 1944, Brewton, AL. BS, Political Science, Hampton University, 1966; MBA, Finance, Wharton School of Business, 1973. Fountain served as a Peace Corps volunteer in West Bengal, India, and as a consultant for Robert R. Nathan Associates prior to attending business school. He joined Chrysler Corporation's finance department in 1973 as an investment analyst. By 1990 he had risen to assistant controller and was on the short list for controller, one of 25 Chrysler corporate officer positions. Assessing his odds as not good enough, he accepted an assignment in 1993 as executive director of the Washington, DC, government affairs office and, two years later, was elected a corporate officer, but not in finance. He is now senior vice president of government affairs and president of his company's foundation. Fountain is also a former president of the Executive Leadership Foundation and serves on the boards of Detroit's Museum of African-American History, the United Way, Hampton University (chair), and the Wharton Board of Overseers, both his alma maters. He also chairs the Detroit Public Schools Board of Education. Fountain, along with Milton Irvin, headed the successful campaign to establish a permanent Whitney M. Young Endowed Chair at Wharton.

Bruce G. Gordon, b. 1946, Camden, NJ. BA, Sociology, Gettysburg College, 1968; MS, Management, Alfred Sloan Fellow, MIT, 1988. Gordon joined Bell of Pennsylvania in 1968 in a special management training program, IMDP, and advanced quickly through "jet jobs" in operations, personnel, sales, and marketing. In 1985 he was appointed vice president for sales and, following the merger that created Bell Atlantic, president of consumer services and vice president of marketing and sales. In 1997 he was promoted to group president for Enterprise Business, and in 1998, he was named the Black Enterprise Executive of the Year. Today Gordon is president of retail markets at Verizon, the new company formed by Bell Atlantic's acquisition of GTE. Gordon is a member of the board of The Southern Company, Bartech Personnel Services, Gettysburg College, his alma mater, Office Depot, Lincoln Center, and the Alvin Ailey Dance Theater Foundation. Gordon is also national chair of the National Eagle Leadership Institute. In 2002 he was 6th on *Fortune's* list of "The 50 Most Powerful Black Executives." He lives by the philosophy, "If you give, you get, but you have to give first."

Kim Green, b. 1961, Baltimore, MD. BS, Marketing, Hampton University, 1983; London Training Program for International Brokers, 1989. Green began her career in 1983 with Chubb & Son as an insurance underwriter. She moved to the broker side with Alexander & Alexander of New York, where she managed Fortune 500 company accounts until 1990. After attending a training program at the entrepreneurial London insurance syndicate, she founded her own brokerage firm. She was wooed back "inside" in 1995, joining Aon Risk Services as a senior vice president, where every year she has been part of the Excellence Roundtable, recognizing the top producers within the Aon family. In this elite group, she is one of the youngest agents, the only black, and one of very few women. In 1997 Green was featured on the covers of both *Fortune* ("The New Black Power") and *Black Enterprise* ("The Top 20 Corporate

Women"). She has been interviewed on CNN and the "Charlie Rose Show." Green served or serves as a director of North General Hospital, Hampton University, her alma mater, and The Independent College Fund of NY. She is an active Links member, having served in national and regional leadership positions, an avid golfer and skier, and a committed mentor to at risk teenage girls.

Sylvester Green, b. 1940, Anderson, SC; raised Sandusky, OH. BA, History/Education, Mount Union College, 1964; Advanced Management Program, Harvard Business School, 1988. Green began his career with Chubb & Son in 1964 as a management trainee and retired in 2000 as managing director and executive vice president, responsible for all North American operations and one of the seven-member Chubb Executive Committee. He is now chair and CEO of e2Value, Inc., a web-based property valuation company. Green is the national chair of Inroads, Inc., and serves on the boards of Fairfield University and Mount Union College (chair), his alma mater. In 2000 *Black Enterprise* named him one of "The Top 50 Blacks in Corporate America." He is the recipient of numerous community awards. His golf handicap is 10, and he is also an avid skier.

Ira D. Hall, b. 1944, Oklahoma City, OK. BS, Electrical Engineering, Stanford University, 1966; MBA, Marketing, Stanford University Graduate School of Business, 1976. Hall started his career at Hewlett Packard Company. In 1968, following the assassination of Dr. Martin Luther King, Hall helped organize, as founding Executive Director, the Stanford Mid-Peninsula Urban Coalition with William Hewlett and David Packard. At age 26, he became the youngest ever trustee of Stanford University. He began his career as an investment banker in 1976 at Morgan Stanley & Co., Inc. He then served as senior vice president in Corporate Finance at L.F. Rothschild, Unterberg, Towbin, Inc., before joining IBM in 1985 as director of Corporate Business Development. He then held several positions at IBM including treasurer of IBM U.S., director of

International Operations, controller of IBM World Trade Corporation, and chair and CEO of IBM World Trade Insurance Corporation. In 1998, he joined Texaco as general manager of Alliance Management, overseeing Texaco's global joint-ventures; in 2000 he was elected Texaco's corporate treasurer. He retired in 2002 when Texaco merged with Chevron. Previously Hall was a Presidential appointee with U.S. Senate confirmation as a Governor of the United States Postal Service, where he also chaired its Audit Committee. He was subsequently chair of the national advisory board of the Thrift Depositor Protection Oversight Board, which included the Secretary of the Treasury and the Chair of the Federal Reserve. He currently serves on the board of American Express Funds, Imagistics International, Inc., Publishers Clearinghouse, The Reynolds and Reynolds Company, Teco Energy, Inc., The Williams Companies, the Jackie Robinson Foundation, and the African/African-American Summit. He recently completed service on the board of State Farm Financial Services and on the Dean's Advisory Council of the Stanford University Graduate School of Business. He continues to chair the Executive Leadership Council board. He enjoys skiing, sailing, and golf.

Bridgette P. Heller, b. 1961, St. Petersburg, FL. BA, Economics and Computer Studies, Northwestern University, 1982; MM, Marketing, Kellogg School of Management, Northwestern University, 1984. Heller joined Kraft in 1985 as an assistant product manager and managed a variety of brands. In 1993 she took over as vice president and general manger of Gevalia Kaffe, an independent business within Kraft that distributed gourmet coffee by mail. There she introduced new advertising, products, and relationship tools while doubling profitability. She was then recognized as one of "Marketing's Top 100" by *Advertising Age* magazine. In 2000, Heller was promoted to vice president and general manager of a newly created $1.4 billion coffee division. In this position, she restored the Maxwell House brand to growth status with product and packaging innovations as well as customer-specific marketing programs. Heller led the division to the number one sales position in the category. She left Kraft in 2002 to pursue other work and personal interests. Heller serves on the national board of Girls Incorporated and the boards of Family Services for Westchester.

David L. Hinds, b. 1946, Barbados, BWI; raised New York, NY. U.S. Army, Captain, 1966-70; Professional Management Development Program, Harvard Business School, 1981. Hinds joined Bankers Trust in 1970 as a management trainee. In his 30-year career with Bankers Trust, now Deutsche Bank, he was responsible for numerous turnarounds in the operations side of the bank. In 1985 he switched to the revenue side and rose to senior managing director and head of one of Deutsche Bank's four U.S. operating divisions, the position he held when he retired in 2000. Hinds serves on the boards of SBLI Insurance and Carver Federal Savings Bank. He served as president of the Executive Leadership Council board and as a member of a number of other charitable boards.

Edward T. Howard, b. 1942, Huntington, WV. BA, Psychology, Marshall University, 1965. Howard is president of J.C. Penney's West Region, with direct responsibility for annual revenues of more than $6 billion, one-third of Penney revenues. He began his 35-year career with J.C. Penney in 1965 as a management trainee. In addition to his business results, he is responsible for founding and developing the Penney African-American Network and building the company's initial diversity program. He serves on the board of the Marshall University Society of Yeager Scholars. Howard is the 1995 recipient of the BRAG Award, one of the retail industry's highest honors, and the 1998 recipient of the Executive Leadership Council's Achievement Award. In 2001, he was inducted into the Marshall University Hall of Fame, and in 2002 he received an honorary doctorate from that university, his alma mater.

Milton M. Irvin, b. 1949, Orange, NJ. BS, Engineering, United States Merchant Marine Academy, 1971; MBA, Wharton School of Business, 1974. Irvin has had a twenty-five-year career on Wall Street. He is currently executive director for the fixed income department at UBS Warburg. Prior to that he was the president and COO of Blaylock & Partners, LP, and Imbot.com. Earlier, during his 18 years at Salomon Brothers, Irvin was a managing director responsible for the short term, Yankee Bank, and dealer sales units. From 1988 to 1990 he served as a managing director for Paine Webber in its government finance/mortgage sales group. He is a founding member and former board member of the Executive Leadership Council. He was also a co-founder of the Whitney M. Young Conference at Wharton, and headed, along with Frank Fountain, the successful campaign to establish a permanent Whitney M. Young Endowed Chair at Wharton. He now serves as vice chair of the Young Endowed Chair Committee and as a member of the Wharton Undergraduate Executive Board. In 1994, Irvin was appointed by President Clinton to the Pension Benefit Guaranty Corporation (PBGC), where he served as chair. He chaired the first Wall Street Campaign for the United Negro College Fund and its New Jersey Telethon from 1995 to 1997. He also served or serves as vice chair of Harlem School of the Arts and as a trustee of both Kent Place School and Essex Catholic High School, his alma mater.

Lawrence V. Jackson, b. 1953, Washington, DC. BA, Economics, Harvard College, 1975; MBA, Marketing, Harvard Business School (honors), 1979. Jackson worked for Bank of Boston and then McKinsey & Company before joining PepsiCo in 1981. While at Pepsi, Jackson used the power of his line results to promote company-wide diversity. He served as vice president/general manager for Pepsi Cola Company after a series of executive roles in manufacturing, distribution, and sales. Later he became senior vice president of global operations for PepsiCo's

252

food service business. Jackson is now an executive officer and senior vice president of Safeway Inc. In 2002 he was 29th on *Fortune*'s list of "The 50 Most Powerful Black Executives." He serves on two corporate boards and a variety of nonprofit boards and is actively involved in helping many young entrepreneurs start their own businesses.

Mannie L. Jackson, b. 1939, Illmo, MO; raised Edwardsville, IL. BS, Applied Life Science, University of Illinois, 1961; MBA, University of Detroit, 1970. Jackson is the principal owner and chair of the Harlem Globetrotters, the team for which he played from 1962-67. Under his leadership, the Globetrotters have more than tripled revenues and quadrupled in size. They visit 117 countries, playing for more than two million people annually. With their own merchandising and licensing company, they've landed sponsorship and promotion agreements valued at more than $100 million. The Globetrotters garnered Sports Q ratings in 2000 as the most liked and recognized team in the world. In addition, since 1993, their charitable contributions have exceeded $10 million. Prior to leading the ownership group that purchased the Globetrotters, Jackson spent 10 years with General Motors and 26 years with Honeywell, Inc., where he retired as a senior vice president and one of five members of the executive committee. As a board member of Honeywell's South African subsidiary, he became an informal advisor to President Nelson Mandela. The first African-American basketball All-American and Illinois's "Mr. Basketball," Jackson is a charter member of the Illinois Basketball Hall of Fame and serves on its nominating committee. He serves or has served on the boards of five Fortune 500 companies and many not-for-profits, including the American Red Cross. He is the recipient of numerous community and business awards, including NCCJ, Arizona Region, 50th Annual Humanitarian of the Year Award and the Rainbow/PUSH Coalition's Effa Manley Sports Executive of the Year Award, both in 2002. In 1995 *Black Enterprise* named him one of "The 30 Most Valuable Professionals in the Business of Sports," and he was recently named one of "The Top 20 African-American High Net Worth Entrepreneurs" and "The Nation's Top 50 Corporate Strategists." In May 2001, the *Harvard Business Review* published Jackson's first-person account of the Globetrotters' turnaround, "Bringing a Dying Brand Back to Life." Jackson is a founding member and former president of the Executive Leadership Council. He still enjoys practicing with the Globetrotters, and his golf handicap hovers around 5.

Robert L. Johnson, b. 1935, Chicago, IL. BA, Sociology, Roosevelt University, 1958; U.S. Army, 1958-60. After several years as a manager at the Chicago Housing Authority, Johnson joined Sears, Roebuck and Co. as a management trainee in 1965. He became Sears's first black vice president in 1978. Upon his retirement in 1991, he became majority stockholder and board chair of Johnson Bryce, Inc., a printer and laminator of flexible packaging materials for snack food and personal care products. Johnson is a board member of the Federal Reserve Bank of St. Louis, Lemoyne-Owen College, and Mystic Seaport and is a founding member of the Executive Leadership Council. He is a devotee of sailing and adventurous travel and provides extensive advice to young minority entrepreneurs.

Margaret H. Jordan, b. 1943, Washington, DC. BS, Nursing, Georgetown University, 1964; MPH, Health Administration and Planning, University of California, Berkeley, 1972; Kaiser Permanente Executive Program, Stanford University, 1982; Advanced Management Program, Harvard Business School, 1991. Jordan is executive vice president of Texas Health Resources in Dallas. Prior to joining Texas Health Resources, she was president of the Margaret Jordan Group LLC, based in Dallas, president and CEO of Dallas Medical Resource, a vice president of Southern California Edison Company, and a vice president and Dallas regional manager of Kaiser Foundation Health Plan. In addition, Jordan has served in senior executive service positions in the U.S. Department of Health and Human Services. She is a founding director of the National Black Nurses Association and a regent of Georgetown University, her alma mater.

James G. Kaiser, b. 1943, St. Louis, MO; raised Los Angeles, CA. BA, Political Science, University of California, Los Angeles, 1966; U.S. Navy, LTJG, 1966-68; MS, Management, MIT, 1973. Kaiser joined Corning, Inc, in 1968. He became Corning's first black vice president in 1984. Named a senior vice president in 1986, he ran a major operating division, a geographical area, and worldwide businesses until 1992. He then was named president and CEO of Enseco, Inc., a wholly owned Corning subsidiary, which became Quanterra Incorporated, a joint venture between Corning and International Technology. At Corning, he was instrumental in founding and building the Society of Black Professionals as well as Corning's diversity program. He retired from Corning in 1996 and became an owner, board chair, and CEO of Avenir Partners, doing business as Lexus of Memphis, and Kaiser Services, LLC, a private investment company. He serves on two Fortune 500 boards, the board of an internet company, and he is a founding member and former president of the Executive Leadership Council and Executive Leadership Foundation. He has served on numerous business and community boards.

Linda Baker Keene, b. 1951, New York, NY. BS, Business Administration, Boston University, 1973; MBA, Marketing, Harvard Business School, 1977. Keene spent 10 years in marketing at The Gillette Company before moving to Pillsbury in 1987 as that company's first African-American marketing director. She left Pillsbury as vice president of marketing services in 1992 to join American Express, where she retired in 2001 as vice president of market development for the Minneapolis-based financial services business. She serves on the boards of HUFFY Corporation, Scholastic Corporation, and several other nonprofit organizations. She is also a former Executive Leadership Council board member and former chair of its Membership Committee. Keene is an active member of the Links and Delta Sigma Theta Sorority. She is a quilter, an art collector, and the author of a recently published book, *Surviving Senior Year: A Parent's Guide to Successfully Navigating Your Child's Last Year of High School.* She has been recognized as one of corporate America's top African-American women by *Essence, Ebony,* and *Black Enterprise* and profiled in *Working Woman* and *Sales and Marketing Management.* In 2002 she received her professional coaching certification from The Hudson Institute of Santa Barbara, CA.

Cleve L. Killingsworth, Jr., b. 1952, Chicago, IL. BS, Management, MIT, 1974; MPH, Hospital Administration, Yale University, 1976. Currently, Killingsworth serves as executive vice president of insurance and managed care for the Henry Ford Health System and president and CEO of Health Alliance Plan, whose largest customer is Ford Motor Company. He has a long and varied career in health care, beginning at the Hospital of the University of Pennsylvania and the American Hospital Association. He also served as vice president of Group Health Cooperative of Puget Sound and senior vice president of Blue Cross and Blue Shield of Rochester. He then became president of Kaiser Foundation Health Plan of Ohio, Inc., the Mid-Atlantic States, and then its new combined Central East Division. He is a founding member of the Executive Leadership Council and a former president of its Foundation. He also serves on the board of Reynolds & Reynolds Company.

Brenda Lauderback, b. 1950, Pittsburgh, PA. BA, Marketing, Robert Morris College, 1972; University of Pittsburgh Graduate Studies. Lauderback retired in 1998 as president of the wholesale group for Nine West, Inc. Prior to joining Nine West, she spent 18 years at Dayton Hudson Corporation, serving for 13 of those years as Dayton Hudson's first African-American and first female vice president and general merchandise manager. She left Dayton Hudson in 1993 to become president of the wholesale footwear division at U.S. Shoe and stayed in a similar position after that company was purchased by Nine West. Today Lauderback serves on the boards of Irwin Financial Corp., Big Lots Corp., and Louisiana Pacific Corp. as well as the boards of several nonprofit organizations. She is an active Links member, serving as president of its Minneapolis–St. Paul Chapter.

Alfred Little, Jr., b. 1946, Monesser, PA. BS, Business Administration, Howard University, 1968; MBA, Fairleigh Dickinson University, 1980. Little began his career in labor relations at Jones & Laughlin Steel Company in 1968. He later served nine years in senior positions at Inmont Corporation before joining Sunoco, Inc., a $12 billion oil company. There he served 18 years, becoming vice president of human resources in 1992. In 1996 he joined Newport News Shipbuilding as vice president of human resources, environmental, health and safety, and security. He retired in 2001 as a corporate officer and member of the five-person executive committee, and currently consults in the areas of executive compensation, labor relations, diversity, and executive coaching. He is on the board of the Labor Policy Association and in 2000 was elected a fellow in the National Academy of Human Resources, the highest honor available to a human resources professional. Little has been profiled in many periodicals, such as *Black Enterprise* and *Personnel Journal*. He serves on the board of the Executive Leadership Council and a number of other charitable organizations. Little is an avid golfer.

Westina Matthews Shatteen, b. 1948, Chillocothe, OH; raised, Yellow Springs, OH. BS, 1970, and MS, 1974, Education, University of Dayton; first University of Dayton African-American

Homecoming Queen, 1969; PhD, Education, University of Chicago, 1980; post-doctoral fellowships at Northwestern (1981) and University of Wisconsin at Madison (1982), Honorary Doctorate of Humanities, Carlow College, 2000. Matthews has published extensively on the subject of equity in education. Prior to joining Merrill Lynch & Co., Inc., in 1985 to head its foundation, Matthews served as an elementary school teacher in her home town, a secretary at a research institute in Silicon Valley, and, after completing her doctorate and post-doctorate fellowships, a senior program officer at the Chicago Community Trust. During her decade in Chicago, Matthews was the protegee of Bill Berry, her great-uncle and a political and civil rights legend in Chicago. Matthews is currently first vice president, community leadership, global human resources, Merrill Lynch U. S. Private Client Group. She was the first woman and person of color elected as trustee for the Merrill Lynch Foundation and still serves as a trustee of all three of the company foundations. Matthews served as an appointee of Mayor David Dinkins to the New York City Board of Education, from 1990 to 1993, one of the most tumultuous periods in that board's tumultuous history. She also serves as a trustee at Bank Street College of Education and has served on the boards of many other not-for-profits, including the Ms. Foundation, Wilberforce University, the Arthur Ashe Institute, the New York Coalition of 100 Black Women, New York Theological Seminary, and the Executive Leadership Foundation.

Ronald C. Parker, b. 1954, Brenham, TX. BA, Political Science, Texas Christian University, 1976. Parker was drafted by the Chicago Bears but was injured in his rookie year. He then served at American Quasar Petroleum developing joint ventures, as the assistant director of Athletics at his alma mater, and in human resources at the Western Company of America before joining Pepsi-Cola Bottling as a human resources manager in 1982. Since joining PepsiCo, he held human resources positions at several Pepsi divisions before moving to Frito-Lay. He now serves as senior vice president of human resources for Frito-Lay North America and is a member of Frito-Lays's operating committee. Parker is a board member of the Executive Leadership Foundation, the Sickle Cell Disease Association of America, and Texas Christian University, his alma mater.

Alana Ward Robinson, b. 1951, Jennings, LA. BA, Applied Math and Computer Science, Grambling State University, 1972; Grambling Miss Senior, the equivalent of Homecoming Queen, 1972; Advanced Management Program, Harvard Business School, 2001. Robinson currently serves as senior vice president, business process redesign leadership, at R.R. Donnelley & Sons, the nation's leading commercial printer. Prior to that position, she served as vice president, application solutions delivery, in Donnelley's corporate information technology area. She began her professional career at IBM as a systems analyst in Louisiana, one of the earliest women in the technical division. In her 18 years at IBM, she graduated to sales and then served as a branch manager. She went on to serve as a division manager at the Public Service Company of Colorado and then as vice president of information technology at Pace Membership Warehouse, Coors Brewing Company, and Sara Lee Hosiery. In addition, she serves as a board member of the Executive Leadership Foundation and the African-American Experience Fund of the National Parks Foundation, as well as other not-for-profit organizations. Robinson also concentrates on her extensive collection of African-American dolls.

Lloyd G. Trotter, b. 1945, Cleveland, OH. BBA, Cleveland State University, 1972. Trotter began his career with General Electric in 1970 as a field service engineer. Since 1992 Trotter has been president and CEO of a General Electric business unit. Today, as president and CEO of GE Industrial Systems, he heads a $6 billion business. Trotter represents GE on America's Promise, the volunteer organization founded and headed by General Colin Powell before he became President George W. Bush's Secretary of State, and is founder and an active member of GE's African-American Forum. He is a trustee of the GE Philanthropic Fund and a director of the National Action Council for Minorities in Engineering. GE does not permit outside corporate board memberships. In 2002, Trotter was 11th on *Fortune's* list of "The 50 Most Powerful Black Executives."

Elynor A. Williams, b. 1946, Baton Rouge, LA; raised Mobile, AL, and parts of FL. BS, Education, Spelman College, 1965; MS, Communications, Cornell University, 1973. Williams is a speaker and lecturer and founder as well as president and managing director of Chestnut Pearson & Associates, an international management consulting firm specializing in reputation management. Formerly vice president of public responsibility for Sara Lee Corporation, Williams was the company's first African-American corporate officer and was instrumental in defining Sara Lee's reputation as a company that supports women. Williams began her career as a school teacher in Jacksonville, FL, after graduating from college at the age of 18. Her first corporate job was with General Foods Corporation as a publicist and food editor. After completing graduate studies, she held senior communications and public relations positions for Western Electric (now AT&T) and North Carolina A&T State University. In 1981, she ran for the North Carolina House of Representatives, losing by 20 votes. She went on to serve as president of the Guilford County Women's Political Caucus a year later. In 1983, she joined Sara Lee in North Carolina, became a member of its management ranks in 1986, and, after moving to Chicago, was named a vice president in 1991. Williams is the only female founding member of the Executive Leadership Council. In addition, she served or serves on the board of the American Cancer Society, the National Black Arts Festival, and the Chicago Sinfonietta.

Appendix B

Snapshot: Executive Leadership Council Membership

So many young people tell me ELC is unique, that there is no other organization sharing experiences of the business reality, no other place they can learn it. The Executive Leadership Council sustains me and many others.

—**Paula A. Banks**, Senior Vice President
BP

Executive Leadership Council members are willing to extend themselves into the public domain on issues, to reach out and say, "I am here, and I am going to try to leverage who I am to improve the situation for African Americans." In our community, the weight of success means many people look to you to make things happen on their behalf. That is okay. But there is something comforting about fellowship with peers, sharing that responsibility and sharing the pain of knowing that, for all your success, there are limits on what you can accomplish. Everyone here understands, and we can relax. That camaraderie and fellowship makes this a very special organization. And as a group, we can leverage the power we do have.

—**David L. Hinds**, Senior Vice President (ret.)
Deutsche Bank

MOST Americans, of any color, would be surprised to know that there are more than 250 African-American senior executives at Fortune 500 companies. Of African-American corporate executives and managers, they are the top tenth of one percent. Their ranks have increased ten-fold over the last fifteen years, a positive statement about their personal accomplishments as well as the corporations that nurtured their progress. While their representation is still very small in the overall picture, they exert an influence beyond their numbers, especially since banding together as the Executive Leadership Council in 1986.

Who are the men and women of the Council? The average age is 49.5 years, ranging from 37 to 75 with a median of 54. Their average corporate service is 23 years, ranging from 8 to 40 years with a median of 24 years, as befits their very senior status. They worked an average of 5 years before becoming a manager and an additional 7 years, on average, before achieving executive status.

The average budget under their control is $505 million, and an average of 1,650 people report to each of them. More than half of them are line officers as opposed to corporate or staff officers, half of them have seats on their corporations' key decision-making committees, and virtually all of them are within three reports of the CEO, 90 percent of them within two. Half of them have annual compensations of more than $550,000, one-third of them exceeding $1 million. On average, each member sits on one for-profit board. Half of the men and one-fourth of the women list golf as their top recreational activity.

In addition to their membership in the Executive Leadership Council, where they work together to promote a level corporate playing field and to fill the pipeline with younger African-American managers and executives, they use their positions to leverage assistance for their communities in both time and money. Each member sits on 3 or 4 nonprofit boards and devotes many hours per week to community activities. This is approaching a part-time job on top of a corporate job that frequently requires up to 80 hours per week, including travel. And they are generous with their wealth: Two-thirds of them donate between $10,000 and $50,000 to community causes, and 10 percent donate over that amount.

While one-fourth of them grew up in the segregated South, the Northeast and Midwest of the United States have been the most hospitable to their progress. Two-thirds of them were born and raised there, and 70 percent of them live and work there now.

They grew up in stable and hard-working families, to a degree far greater than the American average. They were virtually all born in America and raised by two African-American parents, with more than three-fourths of the parent couples still together, only 12 percent experiencing divorce. Most of them had no more than three siblings, and very few of them were only children. One-third of them were the oldest sibling. All of their fathers worked, 40 percent at white-collar jobs, half of those as educators or government workers, and so did almost two-thirds of their mothers, half of those also as teachers or government workers. More than one-fourth of their parents had college degrees.

Obviously the value of educational excellence and hard work stayed with them as adults, but so did the stability. Two-thirds of them have had only one marriage, and 60 percent have no more than two children. Over three-fourths of them have spouses working as professionals, all of them with at least a college degree. Forty percent of the spouses also have graduate degrees.

Almost half of them began in elementary schools that were more than 80 percent black. By high school the numbers had reversed: Almost half of them graduated from high schools that were over 80 percent white. Virtually all of them have college degrees, more than half of them from public institutions (30 percent), historically black colleges and universities (HBCUs) (20 percent), and the military (5 percent). One-fourth of the men served in the military, most of those with four or more years of service. One-third of the men played varsity football, basketball, and track in high school, and one-fourth of those continued to do so in college. A smaller percentage were elected officers in student government, in high school and college. Most, well over half, did not participate in either sports or student government, finding leadership opportunities in business later.

More than two-thirds of the group have graduate degrees, half of those MBAs. Most moved into mainstream institutions for graduate school, with only 10 percent opting for HBCUs.

The women in general come from smaller families—two-thirds with only one or two siblings—and better educated parents; one-third of their parents had college degrees or better, and one-fourth of their mothers had MAs or PhDs. Two-thirds of their mothers and fathers worked in white-collar jobs, half as teachers or educators.

The women modestly surpass the men in educational credentials, and they were appointed managers more quickly than the men (4.5 vs. 5.3 years) and executives as well (5.3 vs. 7.6 additional years). Their average age is 2.5 years younger than the men (48 vs. 50.5 years), and their average years of corporate service is 2 years less than the men (22 vs. 24 years). More than half of the women are in corporate or staff positions, while less than one-third of the men are. Women's reports average 1,160, and the men's average 1,810, almost 50 percent higher. The men control more than three times the dollar amount of the women's budgets.

Over half of the men receive more than $550,000 in annual compensation, with more than one-third of them receiving more than $1 million. Three-fourths of the women receive less than $550,000 per year and only 12.5 percent more than $1 million.

Certainly none of these executives is complaining. They find great satisfaction in their work and in their financial security. But they know we are nowhere near a level playing field yet. They have joined together in the Executive Leadership Council to leverage their collective power and influence. Their goal is to see that the next generation not only cracks the corporate code but also works in a business world that is ready to value their individual contributions.

Afterword

WHEN the Executive Leadership Council was founded in 1986 with nineteen African-American executives, the executive suites of corporate America were largely white, male-dominated havens, all but closed to black leadership and ingenuity. Time, African-American determination, and professional excellence, however, are changing the corporate landscape.

Today, the membership of the Executive Leadership Council is more than 250 men and women in senior executive positions. Pro-Mosaic, the Council's confidential, internal diversity assessment tool, allows leading corporations to benchmark their diversity status and then draws a roadmap toward future improvements. Through its Foundation, the Council also administers a series of unique programs that allow the members to share their hard-won knowledge with the next generation, for example, the Technology Transfer Project with historically black colleges and universities (HBCUs), the Mid-Level Managers Symposium, the National Business Essay Competition, and Shadow Mentoring. And beyond the Council, more than a quarter of a million African-American men and women hold varying levels of managerial and executive responsibility in corporate careers around the globe. The rising numbers stem from many factors, chief among them societal changes, the opening of higher education, and, of course, a steely determination to succeed against all odds.

Cracking the Corporate Code is a glimpse into the professional worlds of thirty-two Council members, one-third of them women, ranging in age from 40 to 65, across industries and disciplines. Viewed through the insights of Price M. Cobbs, M.D., and Judith L. Turnock, both long-time consultants to the Council, their experiences can inspire rising managers who are trying to find their way through the corporate maze and encourage those who have grown weary on the journey.

Dr. Cobbs is a world-renowned psychiatrist and executive coach with a special relationship to the Council and its members. Ms. Turnock, also an executive coach, is an attorney committed to closing the communication gap between blacks and whites. The results of their partnership, *Cracking the Corporate Code*, illuminates for readers the everyday stories, professional strategies, lessons of self-mastery, and coping mechanisms that have allowed ordinary African-American men and women to achieve extraordinary results in the corporate workplace.

The goal of this book is to offer young African-American managers a resource that many of the people featured in this book lacked in their early career: a network of senior African-American executives committed to corporate diversity and available to guide and build the next generation of African-American business leaders. In highlighting the stories of Council members, the co-authors pass on their knowledge and deftly meet the challenge of presenting and analyzing the lessons in a clear, straightforward narrative that is both compelling and informative. The anecdotes are witty and sad, contemplative and casual, but always insightful and backed by years of thought and experience. All provide powerful examples of the capacity of the human spirit to survive and thrive, even in uncertain and sometimes hostile environments, where much was beyond one's control. As their testimony makes clear, these executives do control their own personal belief system. One's attitude can, indeed, determine one's altitude in career success and in life.

Cracking the Corporate Code records a uniquely African-American perspective, yet its lessons speak to the human experience. This book is relevant for many: students contemplating careers in corporate America; corporate managers and other professionals seeking career success strategies; CEOs and other senior executives, especially human resources vice presidents, as well as diversity managers and executive trainers whose job it is to move managers of color through the complexities of the corporate culture.

Finally, *Cracking the Corporate Code* is an affirmative story, reminding everyone in corporate careers—but especially African Americans—that within each of us resides untapped power for leadership and the determination to drive our success and achievement.

Acknowledgments

THE efforts of many people have made this book a reality. First and foremost, we wish to thank the Board of Directors of both the Executive Leadership Council, Paula A. Banks, Chair, and her successor, Ira D. Hall, and the Executive Leadership Foundation, W. Frank Fountain, Chair, and his successor, Carl Brooks, who later became the Council and Foundation President. They saw the wisdom of the message and supported the project in every possible way, especially financially. Paula Banks has never tired of lending her considerable presence and valuable attention to the success of every aspect of the project. To our Advisory Committee, co-chaired by Dennis Dowdell and Alfred Little, Jr., thanks for your guidance and for taking on one more project in your already busy schedules.

The inspiration for this book came from the annual symposia for corporate mid-level managers sponsored by the Executive Leadership Council and underwritten by the PepsiCo Foundation, Pepsi-Cola Company, Frito-Lay, Inc., and Tropicana Products, Inc. Maurice Cox, Ronald Harrison, Lionel Nowell III, and Ronald C. Parker have led each symposium, and we owe them our thanks for their continued vision.

The thirty-two executives we interviewed gave extensive time and were extraordinarily generous in revelations about their own lives and experiences, in addition to their corporate experiences. They have both our gratitude and our profound respect and admiration.

Thanks to our research assistant Sacha Nelson. We expect to see him as a future corporate leader. To our transcript typists Corrine V. Contrino, Kathryn J. Gonzalez, Carol R. Hagans, thanks for your thoughtful labors, and we do mean labors. Philippa Thompson, our copy editor, and Sharona Berken, our proofreader, provided yeoman service.

Finally, thanks to the many friends and family members who remained supportive through an intensive experience. Special thanks to Clarence L. "Buddy" James, Jr., Frederica Maxwell Cobbs, Renata Cobbs Fletcher, Price Priester Cobbs, computer buddy Eric Merli, Jerry (The King) and Jan Valenzuela, Kellis Parker, Kimberly Parker, Douglas James, W. Eileen Derryck, Carole Hall, Alan Rinzler, Camilla McGhee, Donna Brooks Lucas, Joann Stevens, Matthew Shipman, Byron Yoburn, Elizabeth Turnock, Mary-Thomas Turnock, Susan Mackenzie, Jane H. and Lawrence C. Turnock, and Emily A. Parker. Without the help of all of you, this book would not exist.

Bibliography

America, Richard F. and Bernard E. Anderson. *Soul in Management: How African-American Managers Thrive in the Competitive Corporate Environment*. Secaucus, NJ: Birch Lane Press, 1966.

Bell, Ella L. J. and Stella M. Nkomo. *Our Separate Ways: Black and White Women and the Struggle for Professional Identity*. Boston: Harvard Business School Press, 2001.

Bok, Sissela. *Common Values*. Columbia, MO: University of Missouri Press, 1995.

Catalyst. *Women of Color in Corporate Management: A Statistical Picture*. New York: Catalyst, 1997.

_____. *Women of Color in Corporate Management: Dynamics of Career Advancement*. New York: Catalyst, 1998.

_____. *Women of Color in Corporate Management: Three Years Later*. New York: Catalyst, 2002.

Chideya, Farai. *Don't Believe the Hype: Fighting Cultural Misinformation about African Americans*. New York: Plume/Penguin, 1995.

Cose, Ellis. *The Rage of a Privileged Class: Why Are Middle-Class Blacks Angry? Why Should America Care?* New York: HarperCollins, 1993.

Deal, Terence E. and Allen A. Kennedy. *Corporate Cultures:*

The Rites and Rituals of Corporate Life. Menlo Park:
Addison-Wesley, 1982.

Dickens, Floyd, Jr. and Jacqueline B. Dickens. *The Black
Manager: Making It in the Corporate World.* 2d ed.
New York: AMACOM, 1991.

Drucker, Peter F. *The Effective Executive.* New York:
Harper Business, 1993.

DuBois, W.E.B. *The Souls of Black Folk: Essays and Sketches.*
Originally Published, 1903. Reissued. New York:
A Signet Classic, The New American Library, 1969.

Evans, Gail. *Play Like a Man, Win Like a Woman: What Men
Know about Success That Women Need to Learn.* New York:
Broadway Books, 2000.

Fernandez, John P. *Racism and Sexism in Corporate Life:
Changing Values in American Business.* New York:
Lexington Books, 1981.

French, John R. P. and Bertram Raven. "Bases of Social Power,"
in *Studies in Social Power.* Ed. Dorwin Cartwright.
Ann Arbor: University of Michigan Press, 1959.

Gardner, John W. *On Leadership.* New York: Free Press, 1990.

Greenlee, Sam. *The Spook Who Sat by the Door.* New York:
R.W. Barron, 1969.

Grier, William H. and Price M. Cobbs. *Black Rage.*
New York: Basic Books, 1992.

_____. *The Jesus Bag.* New York: McGraw-Hill, 1971.

Hacker, Andrew. *Two Nations: Black and White, Separate, Hostile, Unequal.* New York: Scribners, 1992.

Halberstam, David. *Playing for Keeps: Michael Jordan & the World He Made.* New York: Random House, 1999.

Howard, Jeff and Ray Hammond. "Rumors of Inferiority: The Hidden Obstacles to Black Success." *The New Republic,* 193, no. 5 (1985): 17.

Kanter, Rosabeth Moss. *Men and Women of the Corporation.* New York: Basic Books, 1977.

Kluger, Richard. *Simple Justice: The History of Brown v. Board of Education and Black America's Struggle for Equality.* New York: Knopf, 1976.

Korn/Ferry International. *Diversity in the Executive Suite: Creating Successful Career Paths and Strategies.* New York: Korn/Ferry International, 1998.

Kotter, John P. *John P. Kotter on What Leaders Really Do.* Boston: Harvard Business Review, 1999.

_____. *Power and Influence: Beyond Formal Authority.* New York: Free Press, 1985.

Morrison, Toni. *Song of Solomon.* New York: Knopf, 1977.

Pfeffer, Jeffrey. *Managing with Power: Politics and Influence in Organizations.* Boston: Harvard Business School Press, 1992.

Pinderhughes, Elaine. *Understanding Race, Ethnicity, and Power.* New York: Free Press, 1989.

Remnick, David. *King of the World: Muhammad Ali and the Rise of an American Hero.* New York: Random House, 1998.

Shipler, David K. *A Country of Strangers: Blacks and Whites in America.* New York: Knopf, 1997.

The Conference Board. *Board Diversity in U. S. Corporations: Best Practices for Broadening the Profile of Corporate Boards.* Research Report 1230-99-RR. New York: The Conference Board, 1999.

Thomas, David A. and John J. Gabarro. *Breaking Through: The Making of Minority Corporate Executives in Corporate America.* Boston: Harvard Business School Press, 1999.

Williams, Patricia J. *The Rooster's Egg: On the Persistence of Prejudice.* Cambridge: Harvard University Press, 1995.

Index

vigilance, 178
visibility, 140
vision, 184–185
vulnerability, 76

Western Electric, 76–78
West Point, 69
Wharton School of Business, 43–44, 236–237
white men, 2–3
white people, 8–10

About the Authors

PRICE M. COBBS, M.D., a Life Fellow of the American Psychiatric Association, is an internationally recognized expert on executive leadership, management development, and corporate diversity. He is the co-author of *Black Rage* and *The Jesus Bag*, books considered classics in the literature about African Americans. He has lectured and published extensively on the dynamics and effects of racism. He lives in San Francisco.

JUDITH L. TURNOCK, an attorney, coach, and talent development expert, has devoted her professional life to the struggle for racial, gender, and economic justice and to closing the communication gap between blacks and whites. For more than a decade, she has also coached managers and executives in private, government, and community organizations. *Cracking the Corporate Code* is her first book. She lives in New York City.